Psychology Revivals

Psychology, Psychotherapy and Evangelicalism

Originally published in 1940, this is a contribution to the better understanding of Evangelical experience and doctrine. It is the author's belief that the application of psychology to religion in general can make little or no further advance except through the study of particular types of religious experience. The various psychotherapeutic techniques provide the means for such a study, and in this volume they are applied to Evangelicalism.

At first the author attempts to justify this application to Evangelical experience and doctrine, and outlines what he believes to be the essence of Evangelicalism. Part 2 of the book begins the contribution proper with an attempt to get a clear view of conscience and proceeds to salvation and its problems: conversion, guilt, sin, forgiveness, atonement. Part 3 deals with Evangelical experience and doctrine and the spiritual life of the Evangelical, and concludes with some general applications of psychology to Church work.

Psychology, Psychotherapy and Evangelicalism

J.G. McKenzie

Routledge
Taylor & Francis Group
LONDON AND NEW YORK

First published in 1940
by George Allen & Unwin Ltd

This edition first published in 2016 by Routledge
2 Park Square, Milton Park, Abingdon, Oxon OX14 4RN

and by Routledge
711 Third Avenue, New York, NY 10017

Routledge is an imprint of the Taylor & Francis Group, an informa business

Publisher's Note
The publisher has gone to great lengths to ensure the quality of this reprint but points out that some imperfections in the original copies may be apparent.

Disclaimer
The publisher has made every effort to trace copyright holders and welcomes correspondence from those they have been unable to contact.

A Library of Congress record exists under LCCN: 41000156

ISBN: 978-1-138-68111-8 (hbk)
ISBN: 978-1-315-56430-2 (ebk)

Psychology Psychotherapy and Evangelicalism

BY

J. G. McKENZIE
M.A., B.D., D.D. (*Aberdeen*)
Jesse Boot Professor
in Social Science
Paton College, Nottingham

LONDON
GEORGE ALLEN AND UNWIN LTD
MUSEUM STREET

FIRST PUBLISHED IN 1940
SECOND IMPRESSION 1941

PRINTED IN GREAT BRITAIN BY
THE ABERDEEN UNIVERSITY PRESS LTD.

TO

GOD'S BEST EARTHLY GIFT TO ME
THE LOVE AND COMPANIONSHIP
OF MY WIFE

PREFACE

THIS volume is meant to be a contribution to the better understanding of Evangelical experience and doctrine. It is my belief that the application of psychology to religion in general can make little or no further advance except through the study of the particular types of religious experience. The various psychotherapeutic techniques provide the means for such a study, and in this volume we have applied them to Evangelicalism.

An editor of one of the religious magazines, Dr. Major, has said, "Today we need a new theology, not a new religion; and that new theology, as Archbishop Frederick Temple foresaw, has got to be presented to the modern man, not logically, but psychologically: 'Our theology has been cast in a scholastic mould, i.e. all based on logic. We are in need of, and we are being gradually forced into, a theology based on psychology. The transition, I fear, will not be without much pain ; but nothing can prevent it.' "

If I needed justification for the examination of Evangelical experience and doctrine, that quotation from the late Archbishop would have given it. I have not, however, tried to give a 'new theology'; I have examined the Evangelical experience and doctrine in the light of psychological and psychotherapeutic principles, but I trust I have given the theologian something to work upon.

The two introductory chapters map out the ground to be covered. The former attempts to justify the application of psychology and psychotherapy to Evangelical experience and doctrine; the latter outlines what I believe to be the essence of Evangelicalism. Both chapters have a critical as well as a descriptive element; that is probably seen at its best in the contrast made between the humanistic and evangelical interpretations of Christ. Naturally this is made from the psychological side.

Part II begins the contribution proper. An attempt has been made to get a clear view of Conscience, for as Karl Heim remarks, Evangelicalism is a 'religion of conscience'. The type of conscience a child acquires colours the later religious experience far more deeply than is sometimes realised. It should be noted that in speaking of 'guilt' it is always the psychological 'sense of guilt' I have in mind; I make no assertion regarding its objectivity. That is a problem for the theologian and moral philosopher. In the chapters dealing with 'Salvation and its Problems' I thought it best to distinguish the experiences which originate the Evangelical quest in different individuals. Too many writers have concentrated on the dramatic Evangelical experience which is analogous to a psycho-neurosis, while the normal Evangelical experience has been largely neglected. A chapter has been given to the elucidation of the dramatic conversion, and here clinical experience has helped me to distinguish it from a psycho-neurosis. The concepts of 'repression' and the 'unconscious', rightly understood, throw great light on the different phases through which this dramatic experience of conversion passes. Unfortunately these concepts are far from being rightly understood, and it seemed best to deal with the misconceptions. For this purpose the misconceptions underlying Professor John Laird's writings on the subject were regarded as typical and subjected to criticism. I should like to point out, however, that although I believe he misconstrues the meaning of the concept of the 'unconscious', as understood in psychotherapy, there is no modern writer on ethics and philosophy to whom I owe more than the regius professor of moral philosophy in Aberdeen University. Many of the constructive pages in this volume owe much to him.

The application of the concepts of the 'unconscious' and 'repression' to St. Paul's experience, both before and after his conversion, is likely to evoke criticism; but whatever modifications enlightened criticism may compel me to make, I believe my study of St. Paul's experience will help to a better understanding of the mind of that truly religious genius.

The chapter dealing with the sense of guilt, sin, forgiveness, atonement is an attempt to approach these profound problems of human experience from the psychological point of view. In a recent article in *The Expository Times*, Dr. Hughes urged that the problem of The Atonement should be approached from the point of view of psychology. Here it is approached from the point of view of both psychology and psychotherapy; I have tried to understand what is involved in Atonement through a deeper analysis of the experience of guilt, sin, repentance and the psychological conditions of forgiveness. This leads, in my view, to the objectivity of The Atonement—something happens in God as well as in man before the experience of forgiveness is possible. Forgiveness can have no meaning as an automatic act on God's part; to use a word of Bushnell's later volume, *Forgiveness and Law*, it always involves 'cost'. Again I remind my readers that I use the term 'guilt' in the purely psychological sense.

The section dealing with Evangelical experience and doctrine roots doctrine in experience. Dr. David S. Cairns, who read the proofs, rightly reminded me that Revelation is also a source of doctrine. Perhaps I have not taken sufficient account of this aspect of the problem. On the other hand, Revelation is an experience; it is our experience of The Word from which originates the concept of Revelation.

In the application of the psychology of personality to the problems of Incarnation and The Holy Spirit I must plead guilty to some degree of speculation; but I trust no one will credit me with the belief that any theological doctrine whatsoever can be based entirely on psychology. Religious experience and doctrine will never, in my opinion, be able to dispense with the need of metaphysics. A short section dealing with psychology and the authority of the Bible owes much to Whitehead's doctrine of "Expression as the one fundamental sacrament". Our problem, as psychologists, is not the problem of the objective authority of the Scriptures, but the experience of the authority they exert over so many of us.

On the spiritual life of the Evangelical I believe psychology and psychotherapy can throw a great deal of light; they can do much to elucidate the experience of Faith, Grace and Sanctification, as well as the life of service which is imperative in a believer.

In the final chapter we have made some applications of principles to evangelism, worship, and pastoral care. No psychologist will demur at my caveat against ministers and clergy attempting to treat severe cases of psycho-neurosis, although none will agree more readily with my contention that doctor, teacher and clergy ought to be equipped with a knowledge of the anatomy of the soul. Twenty years of psychotherapy have taught me how necessary is a training in spiritual direction and moral theology for the wise pastor and preacher; but they have also opened my eyes to the immense dangers to the psychologist himself when he undertakes to treat persons suffering from psycho-neurotic conflict. A book knowledge of abnormal psychology is really the least necessary element in the equipment of the psychotherapist. In addition to such knowledge there must be qualities of insight into mental processes, a capacity to *feel into* the victim of nervous disorder, and, need I say, moral and spiritual qualities of character; the motives and mind must be as clean and antiseptic as the surgeon's instruments. Every analysis is analogous to a major surgical operation. One may know a great deal of psychology and psychotherapy without being either a psychologist or psychotherapist.

Although my own work is the basis of what I have written, I am deeply conscious of what I owe to other workers in psychology, psychotherapy and the psychology of character. They are too numerous to mention. As far as I know every quotation has been acknowledged; and I trust no copyright has been violated.

To Emeritus Principal Dr. A. R. Henderson I owe more than I can here avow. But for his steady encouragement I doubt if the volume would yet have been written. Patiently he read the volume in MS., corrected, where necessary, loose sentences, helped me to make lucid any passage which was not clear, and helped me greatly to avoid over-statement. To all this he added to my debt by making the index and correcting the printed proofs.

I have also to thank Rev. C. S. Duthie, B.D., of Bathgate, for making a second correction of the proofs.

Dr. David S. Cairns, Emeritus Principal of the Church of Scotland Theological College, Aberdeen, did me the great honour of reading the proofs; and his keen and learned critical notes compelled me to modify here and enlarge there. Some of the footnotes are due to his wise criticism. I offer him my sincere thanks.

If the volume inspires some one whose experience of religion is other than Evangelical to apply his psychological knowledge to the elucidation of another type of religious experience, or helps the theologian to a new approach to the problems of our great Evangelical Faith, I shall be more than rewarded for what has been a happy task.

PATON COLLEGE,
NOTTINGHAM

CONTENTS

PART I

CHAPTER I

Introductory

"RELIGION stands at the cross roads. Throughout the world the parties of social progress are, in general, either passively or actively anti-religious."[1] Thus writes Professor John MacMurray. He believes that "organised religion on the defensive, tends to range itself, actively or passively, with the conservatives and the reactionaries"; and that when the progressive forces break through 'the dykes of vested interest', unless religion is found on the side of the progressives, it will 'suffer almost total eclipse'.

He is but one voice among many which cry that religion is in danger unless it does this or that. "Will there be any religion left?" asked Dr. Orchard in a volume on *The Outlook for Religion*. Whether he was afraid of the progressive forces or not, he has taken shelter in the Roman Catholic Church where dogma, at least, brooks no change. But the mark of interrogation is stamped upon the mind of our generation; and even so brilliant a writer as Reinhold Niebuhr has felt it in regard to the function of religion in society, and titles one of his volumes: *Does Civilisation Need Religion?* To be sure, he emphatically believes it does, indeed that it cannot progress without religion; but the fact that he attempts to deal with the mark of interrogation shows that there are many who must be asking the question, or who have become entirely indifferent to the relation between religion and civilisation. Even the enthusiasm with which Karl Barth's affirmations are hailed in many quarters only emphasises the

[1] *The Structure of Religious Experience.*

fear of the mark of interrogation; and beneath that enthusiasm the discerning student senses the degree of uncertainty which underlies the present intellectual attitude to religion.

The fact, however, that religion still lasts, and that at the moment religion still presents itself as a very important element in civilisation should make us careful not to draw the wrong inference from the ubiquitous question mark. The widespread interrogation of religious forms, creeds, and experiences must not be construed as evidence of religious scepticism. On the contrary, much of it is motivated by the religious need itself. The Humanists[1] who believe that "the acids of modernity" have eaten into the old foundations of Biblical religion, nevertheless urge the need for "a religion of the spirit". Likewise, the newspapers, which have exploited the religious unrest, are not altogether inspired by the desire to increase their circulations; one discovers in them a genuine interest in the revival of religious ideals, and, at least, a dim realisation of what every age teaches, namely, that "where religion decays civilisations languish and empires perish". Among serious writers there is no trace of Pilate's sneer when he asked, "What is truth?" On the contrary we find in them the wistfulness of John the Baptist's question, "Art thou He that should come or must we look for another?" Men feel that if ecclesiastical Christianity is not the sure foundation of religious security for the individual and society, then there must be another. The Church may have been wrong in the forms and dogmas on which she has asked us to base our faith, but God's promise stands sure.

That is the new note in religious criticism; and it witnesses to the fact that the mark of interrogation is not a tombstone beneath which we have allowed the 'dead past to bury its dead', but is the result of what Whitehead calls "the self-respect of intellect to pursue every tangle of thought to its final unravelment".

Nevertheless, while appraising this new attitude in our modern critics of religion, we may doubt the correctness of

[1] *A Preface to Morals*, by W. Lippmann (George Allen and Unwin Ltd.).

their punctuation. Is it not possible that the mark of interrogation has been put in the wrong place? May we not enquire as to whether they have asked the right questions? We may believe with Mr. Lippmann,[1] for example, that "the crisis in religious loyalties cannot be resolved . . . by the invention of little devices for the straightening out of the dilemmas of biology and Genesis, history and the Gospels, with which so many churchmen busy themselves", but are men compelled to "choose consciously, clearly, and with full realisation of what the choice implies between religion as a system of cosmic government and religion as insight into a cleansed and matured personality; between God as conceived as the master of fate, creator, providence and king, and God as conceived as the highest good at which they might aim"? Surely there is confused thinking here, and a misconception of the essence of religion. No analysis of religion or the religious sentiment can give us 'religion as a system of cosmic government', or 'religion as insight into a cleansed and matured personality'. Many religious men believe in a system of cosmic government, and many religious people could not tell us what we mean by the phrase; but the psychological fact is that belief is not the basis of the religious sentiment. It cannot be too often insisted upon that beliefs are not the foundations of the religious sentiment, nor do they create religious experience. It is the experience that is creative. All experience involves a cognitive reference; but the experience may be real while the reference is false. The patient suffering from an anxiety neurosis may refer his anxiety to an apprehension that his perfectly healthy wife is on the verge of death. His experience of anxiety is real; but his reference of it to the early demise of his wife is false. In reality his anxiety is caused by the unconscious 'wish' for her death. Religion is fundamentally an experience; beliefs are the cognitive reference of the experience. No amount of belief in 'a cosmic system of government' can be said to be a religion; but religious experience always involves beliefs.

Nor is religion an 'insight' into a 'cleansed and matured

[1] *A Preface to Morals*, p. 325.

personality'. Such an insight may be an effect of religion, but it is not its essence. Professor Taylor, in his *Faith of a Moralist*, has put the relation of religion to a 'cleansed and matured personality' in a definitive way. He reminds us that the great Founders of religions were not primarily concerned with moral or social reform. Often the effect of their lives and teaching was a tremendous advance in moral outlook and achievement; but this was not their primary aim. To quote Taylor: "Each of the great world religions has been for good or evil a potent force in transforming the whole scheme of moral valuations; each has produced a moral reformation—not always a salutary one—on the grand scale. . . . But it is equally true that no great historical religion has aimed first and foremost at a moral reform as its main objective."[1] In other words, the great Founders of religions did their work not by the improved morality they enjoined, but by the new light they threw upon God and His relations to man. To quote again: "No one doubts that Paul improved the morals of his converts. . . . But his immediate concern was not the improvement of manners and morals; it was the preaching of 'Jesus and the resurrection'. The all-important thing with him was that men should accept his message about God and what God had done for them; moral improvement follows, or ought to follow, as a matter of course, *from the consciousness of a new relation to God.*"[2] (The italics are ours.)

It is this *consciousness of a new relation to God* which is vital for religion and, we might add, for morals.

Our contention is that the Humanists have not only made false antitheses but put their question mark in the wrong place. A belief in 'a cosmic system of government' is not inconsistent with a 'cleansed and matured personality'; a matured personality has always some beliefs about ultimate things. There is psychological truth in Chesterton's remark that a lodger should know his landlady's metaphysics! On the other hand, they are right in their insistence that it is not

[1] *The Faith of a Moralist*, pp. 62–3.
[2] *Ibid.*

religion that is standing at the bar of modern judgment, but the *type* of religion. Although their own substitute for the admittedly imposing and majestic system of the older orthodoxy is weak and insipid, they do emphasise, even in their false alternatives, that the fundamental question is not whether religion in general is true, but, *What type of religion is likely to last?* What type of religion does modern civilisation need? What type of religion will produce the 'cleansed and matured personality', and the disinterestedness which the Great Society requires for its practical fulfilment?

Psychology and Religion in General

It is this latter type of question which determines our present study of Psychology, Psychotherapy and Evangelicalism. That psychology has done good work in the study of religion in general even its severest critics would not gainsay. Dr. Edward may be going too far when he regards psychology as 'one of the most powerful instruments of investigation yet devised';[1] but there can be no doubt that it has elucidated what religion means to the religious soul; and it has thrown light on the reasons for the particular beliefs associated with religious experience.

Nevertheless, fruitful as the application of psychology has been in the study of religion, and indeed in the elucidation of the mental processes lying behind all behaviour, it is only at the beginning of its usefulness. Although we are still far away—centuries away, says one writer—from a thorough understanding of human personality, psychology has advanced far enough to move from the study of the general principles of the psychology of personality to the intensive investigation of the particular types of personality. It may be doubted whether psychology has reached general principles; we are told that we have no psychology but only psychologists and schools of psychologists. This is to mistake the present position of psychology as a method of investigation. The different 'schools'

[1] *The Nature and Validity of Religious Experience*, p. 2.

are in reality but representative of different approaches to the study of personality. Freud, the most brilliant of analysts, admits that his interest lies in the mental processes, and not in the constitution of the personality; but he is not slow to admit how much we have still to learn about these processes. It may be found in regard to many of the symptom-formations which he cannot explain now, that their final understanding will come through the deeper knowledge of the personality as a whole, and of its particular type.

Be that as it may, it is our profound belief that the psychology of religion can make little progress until a more exhaustive and intensive study of particular types of religious experience is undertaken. We are apt to forget that 'religion' is a generic term; it includes all kinds 'of behaviour products which are associated with a belief attitude towards some concept of God or Gods'; all experiences of a spiritual kind in which the individual believes that he is in contact with Reality. No study of religion in general can carry us further than general statements; which, however useful, are limited in their applications. Hence the need for an analysis of definite types of religious experience.

Types of Religion already Studied

The psychologist has not been altogether neglectful of the type. Mysticism has come in for a great deal of attention. So far, however, psychology has been attracted only by the peculiar phenomena associated with mysticism rather than the insight into the religious soul which the study should provide. Nor may we forget that James studied the type; but although he gave brilliant descriptions of the 'sick-soul' and the 'healthy-minded' type of religious experience, there was little or no insight into either the morbid or healthy type. It is doubtful whether he actually studied the type; it would be truer to say that he gave us brilliant descriptions of the religious experience of selected individuals. The study of mental conflict and the unconscious as we know it today was only at its very beginnings when James's *Varieties of Religious Experience* was published.

Dr. W. Adams Brown[1] struck out in a new line in his classification of religious types from the socio-psychological point of view. To him the main types of religious attitudes are Imperialistic, Individualistic and Democratic. He sums up his classification thus: "In all historic religions, and through all the different stages in the development of each religion, we discovered the presence of certain persistent parallel types which we called imperialism, individualism and democracy. By imperialism we agreed to understand the type of religion whose representatives believe that they serve God most acceptably when they submit to the control of some existing institution, the supremacy of which in the world they identify with the triumph of God's will. By individualism we agreed to understand a type of religion whose representatives despair of satisfaction through any existing institution and find solace in the immediate communion between the individual soul and God. By democracy we understood a type of religion whose representatives are convinced that they serve God best when they discover His presence in other persons and unite with them in the progressive realisation of the ideal social order which it is God's purpose to establish on earth through the free co-operation of men."

Suggestive as Dr. Brown's study is from the socio-political point of view it carries us no distance, whatsoever, in the understanding of the religious experience of the types. Most men who think at all could be classified by these attitudes. Evangelical types may be just as imperialistic as the most intense sacramentarian; and the imperialistic need not be undemocratic. The social expression of religion and the attitude of religious people to social institutions is a legitimate branch of study; but it is very doubtful whether our socio-political attitudes are created primarily by our individual religious experience. In any case Dr. Brown's contribution does not overlap the present study.

[1] *Imperialistic Religion and the Religion of Democracy.*

A word should be said about the many studies of *conversion*. The psychology of religious experience in its modern form may be said to have had its origin in the intensive study of conversion. Here, however, we have the analysis of a particular religious experience rather than the study of a religious type. It may be that the 'twice-born' experience is due to the psychological type of personality, although Professor Pratt rather thinks that one's religious upbringing has much to do with the phenomenon. Extremely able work has been done in the elucidation of the inner conflicts of the soul which precede decision; and the whole process has been linked up with other aspects of the mental and cultural life. Principal Underwood's volume on *Conversion*[1] convinces us that conversion is not peculiar to any one type of religious experience. The reorganisation of one's personality is not specifically a religious experience; nor is it necessarily sudden. Sudden conversion shows some startling phenomena certainly, but no more startling than many of the 'conversions' seen in the psychologist's consulting rooms.

The Importance of the Evangelical Type

It is not our intention to discuss the classification of the types of religious experience, either from the psychological or sociological point of view. It may be that the strong bias towards an objective or a subjective form of worship has an organic connection with the individual's tendency towards extraversion or introversion. It may be that our religious experience follows our psychological type; certainly our type-psychology must have an influence both upon our experience and our beliefs. Along this line also light could be shed on the rational and mystical types of theologians—the one concerned with concepts of God while the other is wholly occupied with the personal relation to God. But we know too little about type-psychology to draw more than hesitating inferences; and the types grade into each other so closely that, apart from

[1] *Conversion: Christian and Non-Christian* (George Allen and Unwin Ltd.).

religious experience altogether, it is difficult to classify the individual. Whether there are ultimate tendencies inclining one man to be a sacramentarian, another an evangelical, one broad churchman, another anti-churchman will not be our concern. The task we have set ourselves is that of understanding one recognised type of religious experience—the evangelical. There will be no attempt to pit one type against another. The psychologist, as such, must have no preferences. In the study of one type there need be no disparagement of any other type.

There are good reasons, however, for a study of the evangelical type of religious experience. It stands very close to the New Testament Epistles. Its power to change individual lives, to create the 'twice-born' soul is unquestioned. It is the motive power behind the great Protestant Missionary Societies, and its leaders have been foremost in every influential movement for the alleviation of social conditions. Every wave of this type of religious experience that has swept across the world has deepened and widened the channels of social, political, moral and spiritual progress. John Richard Green's testimony to the effects of the Evangelical Revival of the eighteenth century is relevant here: "The Evangelical movement", he writes, "which found representatives like Newton and Cecil within the pale of the Establishment, made the fox-hunting parson and the absentee rector at last impossible. In Walpole's day the English clergy were the idlest and most lifeless in the world. In our time no body of religious ministers surpasses them in piety, in philanthropic energy or in popular regard. In the nation at large appeared a new moral enthusiasm which, rigid and pedantic as it often seemed, was still healthy in its social tone, and whose power was seen in the disappearance of the profligacy which had disgraced the upper classes, and the foulness which had infested literature ever since the Restoration. A yet nobler result of the religious revival was the steady attempt, which has never ceased from that day to this, to remedy the guilt, the ignorance, the physical suffering, the social degradation of the profligate and the poor. It was not till the Wesleyan impulse had done its work that this philanthropic impulse began. The Sunday Schools established by Mr. Raikes of Gloucester at the close of the century were the beginnings of popular education. By writings and her own personal example Hannah More drew the sympathy of England to the poverty and crime of the agricultural labourer. A passionate impulse of human sympathy with the wronged and afflicted raised hospitals, endowed charities, built churches, sent missionaries to the heathen, supported Burke in his plea for the Hindoos, and Clarkson and Wilberforce in their crusade against the iniquity of the slave-trade."[1]

This testimony alone would justify the psychologist in turning to a study of evangelical experience. The psychologist of today cannot stand aside in academic aloofness from the needs of the modern world. The objective sciences have justified themselves, not merely by the light they have thrown upon natural history or the phenomena of nature, but even more so by the fact that the knowledge thus gained has been found capable of application to human needs. Practically every sphere of material activity has been transformed by applied science. The industrial machine has been made so productive that it can produce more goods than it can employ workers to buy its products. What if this economically and morally anomalous position can be corrected only by an influx of another kind of knowledge, a kind of knowledge which helps to change man's motives, his valuations and the ends to which he directs his activities in the industrial and economic spheres? That, apparently, is what the Evangelical Revival of the eighteenth century did for men and women of every class; and for public opinion on great moral and social questions; and, what, from all accounts, Evangelicalism is doing for many individuals through what is known as "the Oxford Group Movement" today. Is there not, then, a justification for the study of evangelical experience as a source of moral and spiritual strength?

[1] *A Short History of the English People*, chap. x.

It is admitted on every hand that we are not only passing through an economic crisis, but also a moral and religious crisis. As we saw in our opening quotation from MacMurray, religion stands at the cross roads. He admits that science, in spite of the benefits it confers, *cannot save the world since it must serve and cannot lead.*[1] It is felt that religion is able to give societies the power to redeem themselves; and its condemnation, in some quarters, arises from the fact that it has not done so. Students of morality are calling attention to the need for controlling motives, and to the moral dangers which arise from the slackening of the old moral restraints. Psychotherapists, becoming more and more concerned with the prevention of the neuroses which are such a feature in our modern life, are laying emphasis upon the necessity for a religious attitude to life because it is through this attitude that the will becomes most strongly organised. Freud, himself, says somewhere that with the decay of religion nervous troubles multiply and deepen. Philosophical ethics is in the position in which the older psychology found itself; just as the latter could give no help in the practical understanding of the mental conflicts which led to the neuroses, so ethics today can give little or no guidance on practical morality. The mere motive of abstract rationality can inspire no great compelling system of morality. Most of the great ethical systems had a practical aim from Plato's Republic to the Idealism of T. H. Green. Even Kant's moral philosophy was practical in its aim, and his "categorical imperative" was meant to give guidance; and indeed today it can elicit more than an academic interest; it can find a response in the psychological springs of behaviour. The Utilitarians, and even Hegel, whose philosophy is the most abstract of all, were practical in their aims. Their main aim was not to make a contribution to philosophy but to outline ideals which states and individuals could impose upon themselves. The barrenness of moral philosophy of the academic kind at the present time is not altogether unrelated to the fact that while the schools are studying one set of

[1] *The Structure of Religious Experience*, p. 10.

problems the world and the individual are compelled to study a wholly different set.

The relevance of the last paragraph is found in the fact that not a few are turning again with a wistful longing and an implicit faith towards and in religion. Is there a type of religion that can provide the spiritual and moral insight which leads to a cleansed and matured personality? Is there a type of religion that can provide motives that will lead to a lasting re-organisation of society in which some at least of the economic, and political contradictions would be resolved? It is not unusual for the preacher to tell his congregation that 'Christ can solve all our problems'; but as one writer has remarked, this sweeping statement is usually made at the end of the sermon; and one longs that the speaker would make it his first point and then tell us how Christ can solve the problems of our time both individual and social.

No one doubts the need of controlling motives in the individual life, and controlling ideals in the state. But the world of today is one in which all the old external restraints have been shed. "The task", says one severe critic of ecclesiastical Christianity, "before us is that of persuading a race of beings who are to an exceptional degree free from external restraints, to impose some sort of voluntary restraint upon themselves. Everybody is able today to do 'as he likes', but what he likes to do is only too frequently something ugly, crude, banal, or positively subversive. The finer values of civilisation are slowly but surely being destroyed. A great wave of vulgarisation is sweeping over the world. Everything tends to be dragged down to the level on which it is comprehensible or emotionally satisfying to the man who has neither purified his perception, disciplined his will, nor cultivated his mind. From one point of view, at least, the fruit of liberalism is libertinism."[1]

Nevertheless, the psychologist must not let moral considerations of any kind confuse his judgment upon psychological fact; but he may hope that the outcome of his labours will

[1] *The Prospects of Humanism*, by Laurence Hyde, pp. 9-10.

increase the power of those whose special task it is to elicit the motives which control behaviour tendencies, and thus help them to give a truer moral and spiritual direction to the younger generation. This need not detract from his main object, namely, to increase our knowledge of religious experience of a particular kind; and thus make his contribution to a better understanding of the nature and activities of the human soul in what are acknowledged as amongst its deepest religious experiences.

Psychology, Psychotherapy and Evangelism

Having shown the importance of the study of the type of religious experience, and also, we trust, given some justification for the study of the evangelical type, we must now attempt to relate our subject-matter.

Little justification will be needed for the application of psychology to the study of a particular type of religious experience, for it is the province of psychology to study all behaviour experiences, whether of action, thought or feeling. Woodworth speaks of the subject-matter of psychology as being, "What the Individual Does", and as long as we realise that psychology is as much interested in what goes on within the mind of the individual as in 'behaviour products', the popular phrase describes the subject comprehensively. The subject-matter of psychology, however, is best illustrated by example. What does the individual do? He attends to something; he becomes angry about something or with somebody; he remembers his past; he feels guilty about that past; he is tempted and falls; he strives to correct his weaknesses; he falls out with someone and 'makes it up'; he desires; he aspires; he takes means of satisfying his desires and of realising his aspirations. Thus the subject-matter of psychology is not simply motor activity or sensory activity, it is all the activities of the individual-mental activity as well as activities involving overt action. We should not go far astray if we were to accept the definition: *Psychology is the study of the mental processes correlated with behaviour.* Such a definition leaves us free from the charge of introducing a theory of behaviour causation, or of assuming certain beliefs about the soul or the self.

No one will deny that religious experience of a particular type is a suitable subject for investigation; for, as we have seen, religious experience may have profound behaviour effects on the individual and society.

But what relation can psychotherapy have to evangelical experience or any other kind of religious experience? The answer is not far to seek. Many of the unfortunate people who seek the help of the psychotherapist seem to express their need in religious terms; and in being cured they undergo a 'conversion', that is a change of attitude in their mind. Psychotherapy helps the individual to change his nature; to react differently to the demands of his nature and of his environment. One psychotherapist of international fame asserts: "Among all my patients in the second half of life—that is to say, over thirty-five—there has not been one whose problem in the last resort was not that of finding a religious outlook on life. It is safe to say that everyone of them fell ill because he had lost that which the living religions of every age have given to their followers, and none of them has been really healed who did not regain his religious outlook."[1] Another psychotherapist speaks to the effect that every *neurotic suffers from a bad conscience; and that every neurotic is religious.*[2] If we are to accept Jung's statement—and he has gone more deeply into the problem of neurosis than either Freud or Adler, because they are more interested in the processes of conflict than in the ultimate question as to why conflict arises at all—then we must believe that "A psycho-neurosis must be understood as the suffering of a human being who has not discovered what life means for him. But all creativeness in the realm of the spirit arises from a state of mental suffering, and it is spiritual stagnation, psychic sterility, which causes this state."[3]

[1] Dr. Jung's *Modern Man in Search of a Soul*, p. 264.
[2] Stekel, *Conditions of Nervous Anxiety and Their Treatment*, chaps. i–iii.
[3] *Modern Man in Search of a Soul*, p. 260.

We must note that Jung uses the concept 'spirit'. Such a concept is foreign to psycho-analysts, and to many who attack the problem of moral and psychological conflicts from the purely biological or physiological points of view; but there should be no doubt in the mind of the unbiassed observer that all these neurotic conflicts have a spiritual factor. Twenty years of study and nearly that time in actual treatment of the psycho-neuroses have convinced us that we shall not make progress in the treatment of mental conflicts until we have taken full cognisance of the fact that there is a factor involved in all conflict in the moral and spiritual spheres which is not covered by the Freudian topography of personality; there is more involved than a conflict between the *ego* and the *id*. But more of this anon. At the moment we are concerned to discover what illumination the findings and practice of psychotherapy can throw upon the religious experience we call evangelical. In the first place, psychotherapy will throw light upon the conflicts which often lead to the evangelical experience of conversion. These conflicts are not different from the conflicts which compel the individual to seek the psychotherapist's help. James's definition of conversion implies that the soul is divided, and as a consequence is unhappy and inferior. It is the divided soul that sends the unhappy victim of 'nerves' to the psychotherapist.

There is, however, a fundamental difference between the repentant soul that seeks to end its divisions in surrender to God and the unhappy soul who seeks release at the hands of the psychotherapist. The latter is unaware of the conflicting elements which divide his soul. All neurotic conflict is the outcome of unconscious factors. The real causes of the unhappy state have been *repressed*, to use the technical term; they have become unconscious. The causes manifest themselves in symptoms of anxiety, loss of the feeling of God's presence; there is a sense of unavailing prayer; the futility of life; and often an impulse to perform actions wholly contrary to conscious ideals. (I am confining myself, now, to cases of neurotic trouble whose symptoms are psychological and not physical. There are, of course, cases of functional disorder which manifest themselves in physical symptoms to which whatever anxiety is present is referred.) The light which the knowledge of the unconscious mind, and the tendency to repress whatever threatens the integrity of the organised personality have thrown upon the normal spiritual struggles, temptations, backslidings and the loss of spiritual faith cannot be over-estimated; for the tendency to repression is present in the most normal; and the influence of the unconscious is universal. The whole field of spiritual conflict, spiritual failure and spiritual victory has been lit up in a way that would have astonished even the pioneers of the psychology of religious experience. Certainly the field is far from being fully explored; but as the methods of exploration become more exact our knowledge will grow. Yet the little we do know about the unconscious mind, and the unconscious mental processes, such as repression and its causes, is of tremendous importance for the understanding of evangelical experience.

It will not be out of place here to elucidate the meaning of the terms *unconscious mind*, and *repression*. To do so it is not necessary to enter into the controversies which occurred when the concept of the unconscious mind was first formulated. It was most unacceptable to the academic psychologists and philosophers who studied man as a purely rational being. They took little or no cognisance of the non-rational tendencies which motivate so much of our behaviour. They assumed that all behaviour was motivated from the conscious field; and as Dr. Drever has said, their problem was to find out why man ever acted irrationally;[1] whereas the modern psychologist has to find out why he ever acts rationally. While there are differences among psychologists themselves in regard to the concept of unconscious mind, they are in general agreement on certain fundamental points. We may quote from Dr. William Brown: "Anyone who has undertaken long analysis is certain of the unconscious mind as something with positive, not negative characteristics and qualities only to be understood by

[1] *Psychology of Everyday Life*.

prolonged investigation. Such observers regard the unconscious mind as continually active, continually manifesting itself in indirect ways, betraying itself in dreams, slips of speech, in involuntary actions, in what Freud calls *the psycho-pathology of everyday life*. It manifests itself with great force in mass movements under the influence of mass suggestion, by which, only too often, conscious criticism and control are cancelled out that the unconscious factors may ride free."[1]

The criticism which is often brought against the unconscious mind is that unconscious ideas are a contradiction of terms. But such a criticism is based on inadequate psychological knowledge of the process known as *ideation*. For long many writers believed that all ideas were the outcome of thought or of some kind of reflection. This, however, is wholly untrue. *We do not think ideas, we think with them.* We cannot consciously create an idea; we only become aware of ideas which have already been generated. When we think or reflect we really compare ideas, evaluate them in relation to the purpose we have in hand, analyse them and accept or reject them on this ground or that; but we do not *think* them; we find them ready to our hand. Reasoning and ideation are two different processes, the one conscious and the other unconscious, the latter dependent upon dynamic, purposive elements in our mind, and the former upon purely intellectual processes, and acquired knowledge as well. All ideas are unconscious before they are conscious.

This leads at once to the concept of *repression*. Repression is often confused with suppression, and Dr. Rivers used the term suppression as equivalent to repression. The two processes, however, are quite distinct and should by no means be confused. Suppression is a conscious act—Dr. Rivers recognised this when he spoke of 'witting suppression',[2] that is to say, the conscious process of trying to shut out something disagreeable from the consciousness. Repression, however, is an unconscious process; it is an unconscious refusal to admit

[1] *Psychology and Psychotherapy* (3rd edition), p. 3.
[2] *Instinct and the Unconscious*, p. 17.

an idea, already generated, into the conscious mind. As Dr. David Yellowlees has written, *it is a refusal to see something, not a refusal to do something*[1]—a very valuable distinction and description of the process.

Illustration will convey the nature of the unconscious and repression better than definition. Dr. Frink gives an illuminating illustration of the unconscious. A friend consulted him about a young girl, the daughter of a widowed mother who was very fond of her and did everything possible to make her child healthy and happy. The girl seemed to be equally fond of the mother. Nevertheless, in spite of the girl's protestations that she really desired to relieve her mother of the many burdens which her illness caused, and the actual attempts she made, the results were invariably to make things worse. At one time the girl was really laid aside by a physical illness, and to relieve the mother and to give the girl a real chance to get her health restored, the doctor ordered her to go to the country. To her mother's delight the girl improved rapidly; but then insisted on coming home because she was continually worrying about her mother's health. She had to come home, she asserted, to help her mother, to relieve her of the strain and to avoid expense; and her own health she averred was nothing to her compared with her mother's.

Actually, the result of her coming home was to throw an extra burden upon the mother; she caused more work and more worry and more expense. The comment upon the case of Dr. Frink's friend was, "The girl acts as if she *wanted* to make trouble at home, as if she hated her mother and was not satisfied to let her have a moment's peace or happiness. But to say such a thing is absurd, for I've told you how fond she really is of her mother."

What misled the friend in this case was that he took notice of the conscious mind alone and its assertions of affection for the mother. If instead of saying that she acted *as if* she hated her mother he had said that she *unconsciously* hated her mother

[1] *Psychology's Defence of the Faith*, chaps. ii–vi.

he would have been correct. The 'as if's' of the girl's conscious mind were really the *is* of her unconscious mind.[1]

An illustration of the process of repression comes to hand in the case of a young girl of fifteen we were asked to see because she was giving a great deal of trouble to her stepmother and her father. Dishes were carelessly broken, she was slow in all she was asked to do for her mother; and there was a tendency to rebellion. Yet she protested her affection for her stepmother. Nevertheless, analysis showed that when her father married again she repressed her resentment and seemed to be overjoyed at his re-marriage; we found that the stepmother attempted to teach ways of doing things which were quite different from those of her own mother; and this was felt as an implicit criticism of her own mother. All this was perfectly unconscious to the girl; she refused to see it, but it all came out in her dreams, and when it was made conscious the girl faced it, and realising that she was not likely to be happy with her stepmother, found work in a distant town. There she has been perfectly happy and her occasional visits home are looked forward to with pleasure.

What we must note is that whatever is repressed into the unconscious retains its dynamic element. The girl's resentment, as that of the girl in the previous illustration, determined her behaviour. How important this is for the study of evangelical experience will be shown at the proper place. Enough here to show and to justify the significance of psychotherapy for our study. All that makes it difficult for us to 'Unite our hearts to fear His name' is studied daily by the psychotherapist, and cannot but throw light upon our problems.

In using the knowledge which the treatment of mental conflicts has laid to our hand, there will be no necessity to ally ourselves with any particular school of psychology. All schools have made their contribution to the understanding of the human soul, its conflicts, its unification, its manifestations in outward form in behaviour, and, above all, its need of religious experience. That the type of individual who needs

[1] *Morbid Fears and Compulsions*, pp. 39-40.

the help of the psychotherapist is not very different from the type who enters the evangelical experience may be shown by the fact that by far the greater number of neurotic troubles is found to arise in those who have been brought up in our Protestant Evangelical churches. We ourselves have been amazed at the large proportion of evangelically brought-up individuals who have sought our help, and equally surprised to find that the greater proportion of those come from certain denominations. Dr. Jung says: "I have treated many hundreds of patients, the larger number being Protestants, a smaller number of Jews, and not more than five or six believing Catholics".[1] Is there something in the evangelical atmosphere which influences the individual towards repression? Whatever the answer may be, it would be almost a dereliction of duty on the part of the psychologist to attempt to study Evangelicalism without taking into account what psychotherapy has learned about the conflicts of the soul and their resolution.

[1] *Modern Man in Search of a Soul*, p. 264.

CHAPTER II

The Meaning of Evangelicalism

BEFORE we pass to the analysis of evangelical experience it will be well for us to understand what is connoted by the adjective 'evangelical'; and to whom we are to look as types of that particular kind of religious experience. The task is by no means easy; for 'the evangelical' is not a sectarian; his theology is not necessarily 'fundamentalist'; he is not one of a 'peculiar people'. It is true that the adjective was first applied as a term of opprobrium and that evangelicalism as represented by the average 'evangelistic mission' is more or less fundamentalist; it is also true that there are various small sects with an extremely conservative theology; and perhaps it would not be untrue to say that even the 'Liberal Evangelicals' in the Anglican and Free Churches are the more conservative theological elements in the Protestant communions.

Nevertheless, it would be a mistake to identify Evangelicalism with particular views of theology or of the Bible, or to think of Evangelicals as unprogressive in thought. From the psychological point of view, at least, there is nothing that binds them to any particular regulative creed. Indeed, *freedom*, as one of them has said, *is the keynote of Evangelicalism*. Always they have demanded *freedom before God*, although that has often been interpreted as a desire to be *free from God*. Believing as they do, that 'they have the glorious liberty of the children of God', and that with free access to God, they would deny that they need to be restricted in their interpretation of God's revelation to men. We must not forget that it was Luther's Evangelicalism that demanded freedom from the decrees of councils and the 'arrogant' assumptions of the Roman Hierarchy. There is always a tendency for doctrine to harden, and evangelical doctrine has not escaped this universal tendency. Hence, whatever conservative elements we may find among Evangelicals, Evangelicalism itself is not necessarily conservative.

From its earliest stirrings the Evangelical Movement claimed men and women of varying cultural and social position. Alongside Newton, the converted slave-trader, we have the gentle Cowper and the Countess of Huntingdon. We have Wesley with his strong High Church tendencies and Whitefield the 'pot-boy' of a Gloucester Inn. It is even so today. Bishop Barnes is proud to belong to the evangelical tradition, and although it is difficult to imagine him delivering one of his trenchant addresses on the Keswick platform, he would not fail to make contact if he were speaking at a convention on personal religion. The late Professor Burkitt of Cambridge, and Canon Grensted of Oxford may seem to have little in common with the Plymouth Brethren, but there is one passage at least in the former's address on *The Importance of the Historical Element*[1] to The Modern Churchmen's Conference which might have drawn forth applause in a Brethren conference; while the latter's volume on *The Person of Christ* is as evangelical as anything the Brethren could wish.

Church Polity gives us little help in our attempt to get a clear idea of Evangelicalism. "The Evangelical Alliance" claims members in every one of the reformed churches. Only one denomination has used the term to designate its specific position—The Evangelical Union of Scotland—and it is now merged in Scottish Congregationalism.

The Distinguishing Marks of Evangelicalism

It has been said that the real mark of Evangelicalism is not so much a new doctrine as a "new emphasis on ancient doctrine, and in particular, a new fervour". It is undoubtedly true that the leaders of the eighteenth-century Evangelical Movement did not differ in regard to theology from their less enthusiastic

[1] *The Modern Churchman* (Conference Number), October, 1928.

brethren in the Church. As Dr. Gillie has put it: "Bishop Butler and Wesley had no quarrel on theology".[1] There is a vast difference, nevertheless, between the religious attitude of the man whose main interest in the articles of the creed is that they are dogmas which can be logically justified, and that of the man to whom they conceptualise a living and present experience. One may hold firmly the dogma of the Incarnation without ever experiencing fellowship with the living Christ; that God will forgive sin may be truly believed in an intellectual manner although the believer does not realise either his need of the forgiveness of his sins or the creative relationship which the forgiveness of sin effects.

An illustration from psychotherapy may help us to get a clearer knowledge of a distinction which appears to us to be vital. We are accustomed in psychotherapy to distinguish between a *knowing and a knowing*,[2] to use Freud's phrase; or between *recognition* and *realisation*,[3] to use Dr. Hadfield's attempt to differentiate between two different forms of knowledge. The *knowing* of Freud, the *recognition* of Hadfield is something less than cognition in the full psychological sense. It lacks assimilation; it lies over against our knowledge or the 'apperceptive mass', and never enters into it modifying our existing beliefs and attitudes. We may recognise something without realising its meaning for us; in other words, there is no assimilation, and therefore no modification of the subjective attitudes. "Realisation" implies the assimilation of the truth, the fact, the knowledge or belief; realisation always brings a modification of our reactions both from the point of view of an inner experience and outward behaviour. In the early days of psycho-analysis, Freud tells us, he thought it was sufficient to tell the patient what conflicting tendencies were the cause of his particular complaint. Alas! he found, as every psychotherapist finds to his cost, that it is one thing for the analyst to know what is wrong with a patient and another thing to

[1] *Evangelicalism*, p. 9.

[2] Freud, *Introductory Lectures on Psycho-analysis* (George Allen and Unwin Ltd.).

[3] *Psychology and Morals.*

elicit the intuition from the patient, so that he *realises* it. There is no technique for eliciting this intuition. We convey to the patient what we have found; he believes what we tell him, but it makes no difference. Why? Because really he only believes a certain thing is wrong with him; he does not *feel* it is so. Until there is psychological insight into their own processes patients get little relief from their trouble. They must get what the philosopher calls *knowledge by acquaintance*, and not simply *knowledge by description*.[1] In other words, the repressed ideas or tendencies must show themselves in consciousness, and be dealt with there before the patient gets relief. There is little or no attempt on the part of the psychotherapist to convince the patient from the intellectual point of view as to what is wrong; he must wait for the offending complex to come into consciousness in the form of a dream, or a memory, or an actual experience. Some psychotherapists, such as Dejerine, use a good deal of persuasion. But the ultimate change in the personality which is synonymous with a cure comes about by the elicitation of an intuition. It is not the truth of an idea in the intellectual sense of that term, but the realisation of an experience which alters the psychological attitudes.

If then we may use this distinction between *recognition* and *realisation*, *knowledge by description* and *knowledge by acquaintance*, then *realisation* or *acquaintance* brings an experience of an immediate kind. The knowledge is immediate; and Whitehead argues that all such immediate knowledge is infallible.[2] It is in the realm of knowledge by description that error occurs. The Evangelicals emphasise knowledge by acquaintance; they believe because they have an experience; they realise Christ rather than know Him; experience Him rather than believe in Him. The experience of the forgiveness of sin for example is not reached by methods of ratiocination; the assurance of salvation is knowledge by acquaintance. Strictly speaking, the reference of their experience to God is outside

[1] *Problems of Philosophy*, Bertrand Russell, chap. v.
[2] *Symbolism*, p. 7.

knowledge by acquaintance; but it is not outside the psychological experience of realisation. The experience, whatever reference it may be given, is real.

It is this experience, this realisation, this knowledge by acquaintance which the Evangelical emphasises, and which the great leaders of the Evangelical Movement attempted to evoke. They elicited an intuition of sinfulness, a need of forgiveness, a need of saving power from sin; these needs were referred to God and His Grace for satisfaction. It is this experience which the evangelical preacher attempts to secure today. When Paul spoke of having faith in 'the Son of God who loved me and gave Himself for me' he was describing an experience primarily, and not uttering a dogma. 'If any man is in Christ Jesus he is a new creature', is again the description of an experience which is immediate. Hence when it is said that Evangelicalism was a new emphasis and a new fervour, it must not be interpreted as meaning that the Evangelical believed a little more deeply or more intensely than his non-evangelical brother, or that he gave greater importance to certain dogmas. The emphasis was upon the experience which the doctrine conceptualised. The contention of the Evangelicals was that what the doctrine conceptualises must be experienced anew by every believer. Their fervour came, not merely from the greater intensity with which they held the central doctrines of Christian faith but from the depth of the experience which the doctrine describes.

It would be easy to multiply quotations to show that the Evangelical is distinguished from other types by his experience, and not by any intellectual emphasis. Speaking of Christ's power to atone for the sin of the world, Karl Heim makes it clear that the grounds for this fact of forgiveness which the Atonement makes possible is experience: "Whether", he writes, "Jesus actually possesses this power, as eternal high priest for men before God; and whether He has the right to speak of Himself in these terms, cannot be decided by reason alone. The answer to these questions does not depend on the authenticity of isolated words and narratives. Forgiveness, the deliverance of the soul from its burden of guilt, the birth of a new personality which is reconciled to God, is something which is unique, and to be understood only by intimate communion of the soul with God. The inward deliverance of the soul from the burden of a deed; this bursting of the fetters which we have fastened on ourselves, is something different from the cancellation of the consequences of a deed which is open to the eyes of the world. It is only about the latter that we can form scientific theories. This inner resurrection, looked at historically, is invisible and independent of all tangible consequences."[1]

Here we have the experience and its reference to the power of Christ Jesus. In so far as any cognitive reference is common to all Evangelicals it is this reference of their experience as having its source in Christ.

Clearer still is the definition by Dr. Dickie in his volume, *The Organism of Christian Truth:* "A Christian in the full evangelical sense of the word is not simply one who accepts as true certain propositions about God and the world, man, sin, redemption and the other topics which are ordinarily set down as belonging to the cycle of Christian Doctrine. He is one who has made the Christian salvation his own, and thus knows himself as reconciled to God through faith in our Lord Jesus Christ, and knows God as reconciling the world unto Himself. . . . A man is not a real Christian, however correct his views upon all these subjects, unless he has this personal knowledge of the Christian salvation of which God is the Author and Christ the Mediator. . . . For Christianity has always lived and functioned in the world, not as a body of ideas or doctrines but as *a religion,* that is a felt personal relationship to God."[2]

Here again the emphasis is upon the experience and it is linked with Christ as the Mediator of that experience.

Enough has been said to show that the distinguishing marks of Evangelicalism are not to be found merely in theology.

[1] *Spirit and Truth,* pp. 66–7 (Lutterworth Press).

[2] See Introduction to *The Organism of Christian Truth.*

What unites all Evangelicals, indeed enables them to be classed as one type of religious devotees, is an experience which they believe to be of God's grace mediated through an experience of Christ.

Theological Emphasis of Evangelicalism

Although it is this experience which distinguishes the Evangelical from the other types of Christians, and although it is the type of religious experience we are to analyse, it will help us to get a clearer idea of the Evangelical and Evangelicalism if we note their theological emphasis. That emphasis may be summed up in the statement that The Person of Christ and His Work and the Authority of the Bible are the axes round which their theology and ethics revolve, as well as their experience. There are great differences, it is true, in the interpretation of both those central themes of the person and work of Christ among Evangelicals themselves; but both are accepted as crucial. The Work of Christ, they believe, implies man's desperate need, and the all-sufficiency of His redeeming Work. Through Christ they believe they have direct access to God, and the freedom and power of the Indwelling Spirit. It must be kept in mind, however, that although all these positions are the content of specific dogmas, the emphasis is upon the direct experience. However great the differences in the interpretation of Christ and His Work, His centrality is held by all. In the same way, in spite of the theological differences in regard to the Bible between the Plymouth Brother and such liberal Evangelicals as Canon Raven or Canon Storr, its authority is central for all and to a large extent final. Likewise Evangelicals differ among themselves in regard to the interpretation of the Cross; but all hold that it is crucial for the evangelical experience of sin, the need for atonement, and the mediation of forgiveness.

Evangelical and Humanistic Views of the Person of Christ

Although it is psychologically true that the evangelistic experience is more fundamental for Evangelicalism than the theological expressions of that experience, it does not follow either psychologically or logically that the beliefs do not affect the experience. They give the emotional tone to the experience; they tend to elicit new intuitions which may enrich and deepen the experience; and it is always through the utterance of the beliefs that the experience is elicited through intuition. That does not mean that no one can experience the forgiveness of sins, the indwelling of the Spirit or a sense of at one-ness with God unless he accepts the evangelical doctrines involved in the phrase 'faith in Christ'. At the same time there can be no doubt that there is a psychological difference in the religious experience of the man who accepts Christ as having the *value of God* and one who does not.

Hence no thorough understanding of the evangelical experience is really possible unless we take into account the place of Christ in that experience. To get that understanding we cannot do better than contrast the Evangelical and Humanistic points of view in relation to Jesus.

The distinction between the two has never been better brought out than by the late Dr. P. T. Forsyth, a theologian of subtle intellect, of deep religious experience and with a sure touch in these distinctions. He writes: "Christ is regarded as central by all who regard Him in any serious way. But central to what? One class of mind sees the whole cosmic issue in human history, all history centred in that of the soul, and the grand symbol of the soul and its meaning set forth for our reverence in Christ. Christ is the spiritual centre of a system of things which is spiritual at least or nothing. He is the grand register of man's confidence in his own spiritual destiny and his power to realise it, the chief symbol in a long history which can offer the soul no more than symbols of itself. The symbolism of rites becomes in Him the symbolism of personality. He is the great illustration of the truths and ideas which must always shine by their own light, and guarantee to an intuition their own power and permanence.

"But another class of mind does not begin with the cosmic problem, even as history, nor with ideas self-luminous and self-sufficient. It begins with the moral problem—of course on a historic scale. It begins with the purpose of God, the Word of God, and man's historic treatment of it. It begins not with the problem of history, but with the revelation in history, not with a problem that revelation may solve, but with a crisis that revelation creates. Its problem is not Adversity, but Guilt. It starts with Christ, not as the symbol of man's aspiration, or the Hero of his resource, but as the Incarnation of God's purpose, or at least the Prophet of God's will. He is the centre of a system of Grace and Sin.

"For the one class Christ is the centre of spiritual humanity; for the other He is the centre of the will and grace of God."[1]

Forsyth did not believe that these two views were incompatible or irreconcilable. He believed that the latter view included the former. On the other hand, he was emphatic on the point, "that we can and must choose whether Christ is the transfiguration of spiritual humanity, with its eternal destiny still unsure as a great surmise; or whether He is the foregone achievement of that destiny, as the incarnation of God's will and grace for the creation of the New Humanity. Is He man's spiritual ideal projected and cherished, or man's eternal consummation presented and guaranteed? Is He there for our admiration as our highest self, or for our appropriation as God's highest boon?"[2]

There can be no doubt as to the answer of the Evangelical. He sees Christ not as a point which humanity may one day reach, but the creator of the new humanity. He is not the projection of man's highest hopes, but the objective power of God towards the consummation of His purpose for men.

Alongside this quotation from Forsyth we put another in which the humanistic position in regard to Christ is well

[1] See Preface to *Faith, Freedom and the Future.* [2] *Ibid.*

stated by the Rev. Boys Smith, the well-known Modern Churchman. It is taken from an address of his to the Modern Churchmen's Conference on *The Significance of the Historical Element in the Doctrine of the Incarnation.* The lecturer argued that "Christianity is absolute, not in the sense that it is without analogy, but in the sense that it is the highest point in a continuous gradation; and salvation wrought by Christ is not catastrophic intervention, but a supreme revelation of what is henceforth seen to be the ideal for all things in which it is already in some sense manifest".[1] Speaking of Jesus, Mr. Smith quotes Troeltsch to the effect that it is difficult to believe that there is a single point in history central for all mankind: "That is in religion", he continues quoting directly from Troeltsch, "what geocentrism and anthropocentrism are in cosmology and metaphysics. To these two centrisms belongs by its logical nature, Christocentrism also."[2] Both Troeltsch and Smith are afraid of 'discontinuities'. Just as the scientist and the historian refuse to allow a break in the continuity in events, so these two theologians shrink from seeing Christ as a 'discontinuity'; Christ is continuous with the past and the present and has effects in the future, but He is not absolute, without analogy. Such a position logically implies the possibility of a greater than Christ, and Mr. Smith is not afraid to accept the possibility. He writes: "It is possible—can it be otherwise?—that when the intervening period has become long or (more important) the discontinuity in civilisation sufficiently great, Jesus Himself may come to mean less to men of that distant age. His influence, of course, will not have vanished; but its source, perhaps, will no longer be recognised. And may we not go further again? Can we say that it is impossible that somewhere, and somewhen, there should live another man who would do as much for the world, and be to it as much, even as Jesus. I see no grounds on which it can be called impossible."[3]

The above shows the full humanistic view of Christ, and

[1] *The Modern Churchman* (Conference Number), October, 1928, p. 379.
[2] *Ibid.*, p. 386. [3] *Ibid.*, pp. 388–9.

helps to bring out clearly the vital distinction which we saw Forsyth had drawn between it and the Evangelical. To the former Christ is our noblest example, but not crucial either for history or for the individual; for Forsyth and the Evangelical everything radiates from Christ; He is central and final both for history and the individual.

A quotation from Brunner's *Mediator* shows how closely Forsyth is to the modern evangelical theologian: "The fact that Christ is the centre of the Christian message does not mean that the central element in this message is no longer the Eternal Truth and the Eternal Being of God. Nothing is more foolish than to try and play off 'Theocentric' and 'Christocentric' standpoints against one another. As if it were not this very 'Christocentric' message of the Gospel in which God is absolutely central! If Christ means anything at all, it is simply and solely because through Him God is revealed, the eternal and Unchangeable God, in very Being. This is all that matters; nothing else counts at all. If we make a hole in a dark wall through which the heavens become visible and the sunlight streams in, we do not say that this window is opposed to the heavens and the sunshine. Jesus Christ is the window through which we can see God. When the Christian message says with emphasis, 'Look to Christ', it does not mean 'look away from God', but 'look away to God where God really is', for if God is contemplated apart from Christ, if Christ is ignored, then God is not seen as He really is. Zeal for Christ is zeal for the true God; the exclusive element in the Christian creed: 'in no other is there salvation . . .' is simply the exclusiveness of Divine Truth. Because the truth of God is one, and one only, and because in order to see this truth we must stand at a certain point, is the reason why we must make such exclusive claims for Christ."[1]

Enough evidence has been given to show how central Jesus is to the Evangelical, and how crucial He is for Evangelicalism. He is to them, not the point of highest revelation, but an unique revelation beyond which revelation cannot go.

[1] *The Mediator*, pp. 400–1.

To quote Brunner again: "Christ is really simply the window through which 'the eternal Light streams in'; this is His significance, and His alone. Because in Him the Word which was from the beginning became flesh—for this reason, and for this alone, He is the Christ".[1] Such a position is wholly different from that of Boys Smith or Troeltsch.

The psychologist, however, as such, is interested in these theological differences only in so far as they are likely to be correlated with different types of spiritual experience; and one does not need to be a psychologist to recognise that the spiritual attitude of Troeltsch will be very different from that of Brunner or Forsyth. All of them may acknowledge Christ as moral example; but whereas Brunner or Forsyth finds that He mediates his religious experience, Troeltsch believes that Christ's moral example and religious experience can be transcended. For the Evangelical Christ is the definitive revelation of God to history and to men. Even Boys Smith admits that to accept Troeltsch's view, which coincides with his own, involves serious consequences for Jesus as a teacher. For the psychologist, however, the difference will be one of spiritual experience, both from the subjective side and from that of behaviour products. For Troeltsch and the humanistic interpreters of Jesus, religious experience in so far as it is related to Jesus, will be a fellowhip of ideals, hopes—moral and spiritual, much as a lover of Plato has fellowship with Plato; for the Evangelicals, on the other hand, it will be a fellowship with what they believe to be 'the living Christ', an incarnation of the living God. In whatever sense we allow the Humanists to speak of having an experience of Christ, the vital distinction remains. To the Evangelical, every religious experience he enjoys, every promise he appropriates, the experience of that grace that covers his sin and is sufficient for every need, his assurance of salvation in time and in eternity, come through *saving faith* in Christ as Son of God. "The faith of the Son of God who loved me and gave Himself for me", is to the Evangelical the very organ of his knowledge of

[1] *The Mediator*, p. 401.

divine things; it is through his faith he believes, intuits divine truth, and experiences divine grace.

In that remarkable book, *Father and Son*, by Edmund Gosse, there is an apt quotation from Archbishop Leighton which Gosse uses to distinguish his own experience from that of his evangelical father's 'saving faith'. "This", says the Archbishop, speaking of divine truth, "a natural man may discourse of, and that very knowingly, and give a kind of natural credit to it, as to history that may be true, but firmly to believe that there is a divine truth in these things, and to have a persuasion of it stronger than on the very thing we see with our eyes; such an assent as this is the peculiar work of the Spirit of God, and is certainly saving faith."[1] As Sir Edmund Gosse realised, this difference is very real, and he knew it was the difference between himself and his evangelical father; and that it went much deeper than that between two men who could not accept the same conceptualisation of religious dogma; it went down to the deepest experiences of the soul.

EVANGELICALS AND THE AUTHORITY OF THE BIBLE

The same gulf which divides the Humanist from the Evangelical in Christology separates the evangelical view of the Bible and that of those to whom the Bible does no more than contain messages of "abiding value and interest". That difference will be clearly seen when we come to analyse evangelical experience. For the present let us mark the attitude of all Evangelicals, whatever the colour of their theology, to the place and authority of the Bible.

There is a wide series of divergencies in interpretation ranging from the " verbal inspiration" of the fundamentalists to Professor Burkitt's position that "there is in the Gospel history—the history of what led up to it—an element which Christians cannot discount if they are to remain Christians".[2] Practically all the Evangelical churches feel the need for a

[1] Pp. 201-2.
[2] *The Modern Churchman* (Conference Number), October, 1928, p. 359.

restatement of the doctrine of the authority of the Bible. The Liberal Evangelicals of the Anglican Church state this definitely as follows: "This (the Bible) still stands in its unique position. The right of appeal to the historical records in order to check the growth of traditional accretion, to correct errors of Church teaching, and to release continually new spiritual movements within the Church, remains as much a part of the creed of the Evangelical as ever. But the authority of the Bible is seen to centre in its relation to the revelation of God in Christ. It is the mind of Christ, not the letter of Holy Scripture, which is authoritative."[1] Such a position leaves ample room for scientific criticism of the Biblical records both as regards history and doctrine. It is realised that we cannot get the mind of Christ apart from the records, and it is believed that both historical and New Testament criticism has given us a truer understanding of Jesus Himself and of the Epistles. We heard Principal David Cairns of Aberdeen, one of the firmest of Evangelicals, sum up the position thus: "The Bible is not the Revelation, but the record of the Revelation; it is not an inspired record of history, but the record of an inspired history". That puts the modern Evangelical's approach to Scripture in a way that leaves the Bible its unique authority, and yet encourages a reverent scholarship.

The Barthians

A word may be permissible regarding the position of the Barthians in their approach to the authority of the Bible. The view of Karl Barth, himself, may not be inaccurately summed up in his contention that history is not revelation, although revelation occurs in history. The authority of the Bible lies, not in its historical events, but in these historical events interpreted by the Holy Spirit as acts of divine revelation. In some respects there is a reversion to the position of Calvin and Luther, but one does not find any idolatry of the letter of Scripture; far from it; it is always the Word inter-

[1] *Liberal Evangelicalism*, see Introduction.

preted by the Spirit. There is no Fundamentalism; Biblical criticism is welcomed. The Bible contains the self-revelation of God, and herein lies its importance and uniqueness. The Old Testament prophets *had* the Word; the New Testament is the record of Him Who *is* the Word, the Self-revelation of God. In the Bible God confronts us, not as object of thought, but with the word of mercy and judgment. Brunner does not believe that history is divine revelation; it rather presents man as in need of redemption. But in history occurred one *unique event*, the Incarnation; the "special revelation" as opposed to the "general revelation". Thus the Barthians are independent of the detailed accuracy of Scripture; although dependent upon the New Testament record for the story of the one unique event—the Word made flesh. Thus the Barthians seem from the theological point of view to meet the position of Troeltsch and the Modern Churchmen in regard to the difficult problem of the relation of Christianity to History. The latter's position is: "How can Christianity which is an absolute religion be based upon history which is contingent?"[1] The Barthian answer, if we read it aright, would be that it is the revelation through these historical events which has meaning; it is on the meaning of them, the theology of them, on which all hangs. To quote Brunner: "Precisely because something super-historical, unique, absolutely decisive has entered into human history, to faith history means something entirely different from its meaning for all other forms of thought. Our relation to history is determined by our relation to Jesus Christ, not vice versa."[2]

It is worth noting that there is a strong resemblance to Dr. Forsyth's position. And when Dr. Burkitt argued before the Modern Churchmen's Conference that it is what is believed about these historical events that is vital to Christianity he followed a not altogether different line of argument. We do not mean to say that either Dr. Forsyth or Dr. Burkitt would accept the Barthian position theologically, but their attitude

[1] See Introduction to *The Modern Churchman*, October, 1928.

[2] *The Mediator*, p. 159.

to the authority of the Bible is not essentially different. All we are concerned with here, however, is to show that every school of evangelical thought accords a unique place and authority to the Scriptures both for life and doctrine. For all, the Bible is regulative.

Evangelicals and the Cross

No clear conception of Evangelicalism can be given without mention of the place the Cross holds in the religious experience and theology of the Evangelical. "Christ and Him crucified", said Paul, was the theme of His preaching; and all Evangelicals unite with him in making that theme central for their message and thought. It is true now, as it was at the beginning of the Evangelical Movement, that all churches hold the Cross as an article of their creed, but the Evangelical alone makes it crucial for the conviction of man's sin and need, and the all-sufficiency of God's sacrifice to meet that need. Here more than anywhere else Evangelicals meet.

Nevertheless, paradoxical as it may seem, here as nowhere else do we see the theological divisions among Evangelicals themselves. The Cross to Evangelicals answers the old question: How can the sinner be justified before God? That is the theological form of the question. Psychologically, the question runs: How can the sinner enter into filial relations with God? The various theories of the Atonement are the attempts to show how the Cross answers this theological and psychological question. Like other attempts to conceptualise experience, the traditional theories of the Atonement have been coloured by the categories of thought prevailing at different historical periods. The 'satisfaction' theory of Anselm which is still current in certain evangelical quarters, the modified form of it held by the Reformers, known as the Penal theory, owed much to the Roman conception of discharging an obligation, and the concept of justice. The more recent 'moral theories' are coloured by the humanistic tendency in thought today. Here the concept of man seems to play a larger part than the concept of God; and there is a tendency to make little of the objective element so marked in the older theories. As far as Evangelicals are concerned the fundamental question has remained the same whether answered by the substitutionary theory of the Plymouth Brother or the refined theories of some modern theologians. All feel that on the Cross *something was done;* and with this *something done* is wrapped up the very meaning of the Gospel. A recent writer who utterly repudiates the 'satisfaction' theory, nevertheless emphasises the Godward or objective reference of the Atonement. He writes: "Several attempts have been made to show the death of Christ upon the Cross was simply a moral appeal to man to give up sin and turn to God, and confiding in His love demonstrated in the death of His Son. In medieval times this view of the work of Christ was put forward by the great Schoolman, Abelard, and in the middle of the nineteenth century Horace Bushnell advocated it in his well-known book, *The Vicarious Sacrifice.* As far as it goes it is a perfectly true theory. The appeal of love shown in the death of Christ does produce repentance. This manward side of His work has been universally recognised by all who have thought about the meaning of the Atonement. But alone it is not enough. Unless the death of Christ was necessary on some other ground it would have no moral appeal."[1]

Here we are brought back again to what we have emphasised all along in our attempt to get a clear view of evangelical doctrine, to the fact, namely, of an inner experience which the doctrine attempts to conceptualise, and of which there are variations of interpretation. As with the doctrine of Christ's Person so here with His work, and His Cross; all schools of Evangelicals *feel* that there is something inevitable about the death of Christ. That position is admirably stated in an address of Professor Burkitt to the Modern Churchmen; the position is stated without any implications of a particular theory of the Atonement. We give his own words: "The whole doctrine centres on Christ, on the career of Christ, and the nature that alone made the career really effective. And the career

[1] *Problem of the Cross,* Rev. William E. Wilson, pp. 26, 27.

of Christ led directly to the Cross; the Christian religion must be a doctrine of the Cross or it is nothing.

"Here again we are faced with a state of things very similar to the state of general Biblical study. The old theory, the old construction, is worn out, and a new religious theory of the Bible is not forthcoming. So it is with the Cross; the old formulation of the Plan of Salvation, of Atonement effected by the Death of Christ, is inadequate for our days. But Christianity, I am convinced, cannot permanently do without one. If the career of Jesus is to have a permanent meaning for us the Cross cannot be regarded as a tragic incident, a regrettable tale, a stormy sunset to an otherwise perfect day. It must be seen to be something inevitable, significant, typical—and I would add, gracious. The *grace* of our Lord Jesus Christ—to Christians this phrase does not mean a state of mind produced by conscious imitation, but involves something that involves a gift, an inspiration from the outside. If this be given up Christianity and the Christian experience is an illusion.

"But this grace, this *charis* has always been regarded by Christians as indissolubly connected with the Death of Christ Jesus on Calvary. The Lord of the Vineyard will not come to reconstitute His estate for anything less than His Son's death; it was not an accident but somehow involved in the inevitable course of things."[1]

We doubt whether it would be possible to produce a finer statement of the emphasis, without doctrinal implications, on the Cross or Atonement. And this same emphasis may be found in every type of evangelical writing or preaching. There is a conviction that the Cross exhibits something objective, something that happens in God as well as in man; it is felt to be more than a supreme expression of the love of God inducing repentance; something was done on Calvary without which there could have been no Gospel. It would be a great mistake to infer that the Evangelical is bound up with any theory of the Atonement, but whether he believes in the literalness of "washed in the blood of the lamb", or the refined theory of

[1] Professor Burkitt, in *The Modern Churchman*, October, 1928, pp. 357-8.

Mr. Wilson, his emphasis is the same in quality if not always in intensity. This is attested by the statement of the Liberal Evangelicals of the Anglican Church: "The modern Evangelical finds salvation for himself and for society at the Cross of Jesus Christ. This is central to his religious experience as it was to St. Paul. He cannot only say, but cannot help saying, 'The Son of God Who loved me and gave Himself for me.' There is no other Gospel for him but that of God's Love in action supremely manifested in the Cross. There, as in the story of Bunyan's Pilgrim, he finds peace, forgiveness, and a new sense of filial relationship to God. His hope for the world lies in the redemptive forces which contact with that love releases in human personality. But the doctrine is no longer related to a primeval fall of man, nor need it find expression in forensic terms. The modern Evangelical is dissatisfied with some of the older and cruder penal substitutionary theories of the Atonement. It is the impact of the Cross upon personality which he seeks to explore. He tries to make it live for men and women today as the great preachers of the Gospel made it live for the people of their own day. He is conscious that his presentation of theological truth will in due time pass like theirs, and that his own sincere effort to interpret the redeeming Love of God in Christ will be replaced, under the guidance of the Holy Spirit, by new efforts in relation to the new modes of thought."

Additional statements or quotations from Evangelical writers could not make clearer the emphasis upon the Cross as crucial to their experience; or the fact that the Evangelical must not be identified with any particular theologically-non-progressive type of religious devotee. It is the conviction that *something was done by God* in relation to sin and its forgiveness, and not *what was not done* that unites into one class men and women of such different cultural, social and theological outlook. This unity of conviction regarding the cross with great diversity of interpretation points decisively to the fact that it is the experience that the Cross evokes—the conviction of sin, its forgiveness, the final breaking of the power of sin, and the removal of the last barrier to free fellowship with God—which is the stable and permanent element in evangelical religion. It is not a concept of sin that is believed, but concrete sinful tendencies which are experienced, and which alienate the heart from God, that divide the soul and burden the mind. The Cross, it is believed by every type of Evangelical, removes the alienation, lifts the burden, unifies the soul, reconciles the soul to God, and thus the sinner and God are at At-one-ment.

In later chapters we shall deal from a psychological point of view with all that is implied both in the experience and the doctrines discussed in this chapter; and in discussing the experience we may be able to throw light upon the theological differences. But our task will mainly be to elucidate the evangelical experience to explain which the whole body of evangelical doctrine has been built up.

PART II

CHAPTER III

Prolegomena to Evangelical Experience

It is not without some trepidation that we commence our analysis of evangelical experience. In the most widespread theological movement of our times, Barthianism, psychology of religion is almost anathema. "In his teaching about God", says one commentator, "Barth does give a substantial basis for theology, and all who have grown weary of interminable books on the psychology and philosophy of religion will turn to him with a sense of relief."[1] Barth, however, is not the only theologian to whom psychology is suspect.

This demand for the objective side of religious experience is more than justified. There certainly has been a strong tendency, as Principal Jacks has pointed out, to speak of religion as though it began from the human side. "How often", he writes, "is the history of religion presented to us in that manner as though it were all the work of the human mind, a movement of human thought seeking a solution to its problems, an explanation of its experience, and then discerning God as the key to the puzzle—a production of human psychology, not necessarily untrue, but if true, having nothing better to rest upon than the validity of human thought."[2]

It must not be thought that psychologists and anthropologists have been the only sinners in this respect. Have not theologians themselves been too eager to draw more from the analysis of religious experience than logic would allow? As Dr. McConnachie, the Scottish interpreter of Karl Barth,

[1] *The Theology of Karl Barth*, by Professor Chapman, p. 23.

[2] *Elemental Religion*, p. 34.

has reminded us recently, "The temptation of theologians has always been to seek the support of outside allies, in philosophy, science or in Nature".[1] In so far as religious experience is a real experience it should need neither philosophy nor science to support the weight of its evidence for the objectivity of its object. Philosophy may help us to assess the value of religious experience for our interpretation of Ultimate Reality; and the sciences of Nature should help us to see the universe as intelligible and trustworthy, and may be a valuable aid to our faith in God; but neither can give us more than an impersonal force behind phenomena. Theologians with a strong tendency to find the basis for their religious beliefs in either philosophy or science would be well advised to remember a sentence from Professor Arthur Thomson's *System of Animate Nature:* "Just as there is a science that knows Nature, so there is a religion that knows God".[2] This tendency of theologians to seek outside support for their religious beliefs is seen at its worst in those writers who seek by the aid of psychology to base religion in a 'religious instinct'; the instinct of 'self-preservation', or in what a recent writer has called 'the incomplete instinct'—we suppose he means by the phrase, 'the urge to completeness'. Apparently such writers do not realise that they are basing religion upon a biological foundation. That there is no specific religious instinct is practically the unanimous conclusion of psychologists. Professor Pratt, who bases religion in the biological innate tendencies, nevertheless is explicit on the point: "There is, then, no specific 'religious instinct'. Yet there is a real truth behind the phrase. None of man's religious acts and feelings is instinctive in the sense in which anger and love are; and yet we may say that, given a being endowed with intelligence and with the dozen or more specific instincts and tendencies of man, such a being is bound to be religious, at least potentially, or incipiently, in the sense of our definition. He is bound, that is to say, to possess at least the possibility or the beginning of some kind of conscious

[1] *The Significance of Karl Barth.*
[2] *The System of Animate Nature*, p. 650.

attitude toward the Determiner of Destiny."[1] Professor Pratt believes that the character of our religious attitude "will be largely determined for man by his instincts—by the specific inborn tendencies which he, the individual, brings with him into the world". No one will deny the truth of what Professor Pratt says in regard to specific inborn tendencies influencing man's religious attitude, but this gives no ground for basing man's religious experience in a 'specific religious instinct'. Man's inborn tendencies influence his attitude to ethics; but no serious thinker would infer that ethics are based on instinct. What is forgotten by Professor Pratt, as well as other writers, is that man as self-conscious being has tendencies other than biological which the biological can never explain. It is as self-conscious being that man is religious; and it is impossible to conceive a religious being who is not self-conscious. The wise theologian, solicitous for his own science, to say nothing about being solicitous for the reality of religious experience, should look with suspicion on the tendency to find a ground for his religious experience in instinct. Without for a moment wishing to trespass on the theologian's territory we do want to stress the fact that religion must find its roots in that which differentiates man from the genus, animal, and that is self-consciousness. Moreover, theologians should remember that even in McDougall the concept of instinct was modified considerably, and in his final volume instinct means no more than a propensity to behaviour. The theologian should resist the tendency to draw theological conclusions from premisses based on psychology or any other science. On the other hand, the psychologist must beware of drawing more impoverished inferences from his data than logic allows.

Our position may be stated in a sentence or two. Psychology will never provide a stable basis for religion. Religion is rooted, on man's side, in the nature of self-consciousness, in that which differentiates man from the animal, and not in his biological equipment. It belongs to man as personality; and thus it would seem to us that theology must always remain metaphysical.

[1] *The Religious Consciousness*, p. 71.

Enough has been said to disabuse our minds of the idea that theology need suspect psychology, whether the theology be Barthian or any other school. Nevertheless, theology cannot dispense with psychology. One must suppose that whether God come to a human soul *perpendicularly*, or in response to some urge within self-consciousness, or in the awakening of a *numinous* disposition, His coming will be an experience. When Karl Barth speaks of *the lost and forgotten image of God* responding to God's grace he is psychologising, whether he is aware of it or not. An awakened soul is a soul having an experience; a forgiven soul is experiencing something; an *enslaved will* is an experience as truly as that which liberates it. There may be a theological dogma as to how a soul is awakened, how it is forgiven, how the enslaved will becomes free; with that aspect the psychologist as such does not deal; but he can help us to understand what is taking place.

Limitations of Psychology

No one more than the psychologist is aware of the limitations of psychological methods when applied to religious experience. For one thing, the objects of religious experience are not open to inspection. Experiment is out of the question. In no laboratory can we reproduce the situation in which a man is experiencing the impact of the Holy Spirit. We cannot stage either the conviction of sin or the forgiveness of sin. Nevertheless, we are not altogether bereft of the means of observing and describing the intimate experiences of religion. Although the psychologist as such can pass no valid opinion upon the theological concept of sin he can observe and analyse the division of the mind which the sinful tendencies create; he can see these tendencies in the morbid form as a psychotherapist; for the sense of sin is a major symptom in many types of illness with which he deals. He can, moreover, get into intimate touch with the experiential phenomena which the individual refers to the Holy Spirit; and although he cannot as a psychologist pronounce upon any theory of the Atonement, he can study the psychological states which Atonement is believed to effect. The behaviour effects of all experienced doctrines can be observed, and illustrated. There is no doctrine common to Evangelicals which has not its inner or psychological aspect.

One of the major defects of Professor James's *Varieties* was his failure to differentiate between the true 'sick soul' and the victim of unconscious tendencies. He concluded too easily that the extreme form was really a true form of the religious experience. Psychotherapy helps us to differentiate clearly between the morbid type of the religious experience and the normal type; and it also helps to explain the difference.

The psychologist may also be greatly helped by his own religious experience. In virtue of it he will have an introspective guide to the understanding and description of the phenomena. It must not be thought that the psychologist who himself has shared the evangelical experience will be less able to give an objective account of it. On the contrary, this alone gives him direct insight into the psychological processes involved. The genius of a Freud in the analysis of the psychic conflicts of his patients lies in the fact that he faced his own conflicts; and thus freed from the repressions common to most of us, he was able to experience, incipiently at least, the conflicting tendencies which in his patients were hidden from consciousness. In a similar manner, the psychologist with an evangelical experience of his own is far more likely to understand and describe the evangelical experience of his neighbour. It may be going too far to say that only the psychologist with an evangelical experience can truly describe it; but at least it is an advantage. Psychotherapists and psycho-analysts insist that part of their training must be personal analysis, so that knowing their own conflicts they will understand those of their future patients; otherwise, they will not merely fail to understand but will in all probability misinterpret their condition. By analogy we may say that we look upon it as a qualification for our task that we have passed through what Evangelicals call 'saving experiences'.

The Task of Psychology as Applied to Evangelical Experience

What then is the task of psychology as applied to evangelical experience? It will attempt to get at the inner side of the experience as well as the behaviour products characteristic of the experience. It will analyse and describe the experiences conceptualised in evangelical doctrine: What is the psychology implicit in the specific dogma? What is the psychology behind specific religious habits, doctrinal emphasis and the belief-attitudes of Evangelicals? Is it possible to find out how evangelical experiences arise; how they develop? What does evangelical experience actually effect? It will not seek to validate the objects of evangelical experience, for it is doubtful whether it has any technique for such a task; yet it must not stop with description but pass to psychological explanation which need not be the ultimate explanation.

Pre-conversion Religious Experience

Most writers on evangelical experience have been content to commence their studies with the phenomena of conversion and the experiences leading immediately up to conversion. The dramatic moments of the conviction of sin, the struggle with the contending forces in the soul, and the final decision, lend themselves readily to psychological analysis. This was the method pursued by Starbuck in his first volume, and also of James in his *Varieties of Religious Experience*. Such isolation of a particular experience is misleading. Continuity is of the very essence of mental life; and to chop off one particular experience as though it had little or no relation to the whole past religious life of the individual is fallacious. If psychotherapy or psycho-analysis has taught us anything it is that all the vital experiences which dispose the mind to stability or the failure to adjust to reality have their origin in our early years, some would say, in our very early years. James made too confident an assertion when he said of the 'healthy-minded' that in many of them 'happiness is congenital and irreclaimable'. Likewise, when dealing with the 'sick soul' he commenced with the symptoms but never reached the real causes which led to the sickness.

It should be kept in mind, that we are born with neither healthy minds nor unhealthy minds; these are both acquired in the course of our mental history. What was once thought to be the outcome of heredity is now known to be due to environmental pressure and personal influence. Childhood is the supreme period for the determination of the mental processes on which character and personality depend; and we cannot doubt but that the same period is vital for the type of religious experience the adolescent or adult will pass through. Dr. Rivers, one of the most objective observers psychology has ever had, states his conclusions regarding the period of childhood in relation to mental health and character in the following words: "Childhood is one long conflict between individual instinctive tendencies and the social traditions and ideals of society. Whether the outcome of this conflict will be a genius or a paranoiac, a criminal or a philanthropist, a good citizen or a wastrel, depends, in some measure, we do not yet know with any degree of exactness in what measure, on education, on the direction which is given by the environment, material, psychological, and social, to the energy engendered in the conflicts made necessary by the highly complex character of the past of our race."[1]

To understand, then, the evangelical experience, as that expresses itself in adolescence or later, we must know something of the growth of the religious sentiment, how it has been conditioned, and what content has grown up within it. Decision or conversion is neither the beginning nor the end, but a particular stage in the growth of the experience. Relativity is a condition of all mental process and must not be neglected in the study of religious experience. The religious sentiment is always prior to the more striking experience with which Starbuck and James dealt. The unexpected and intense

[1] *Instinct and the Unconscious*, p. 157.

conviction of sin, the sudden and dramatic conversion may alter the content of the religious sentiment and does give it a new place in the reorganised inner life, but unless it had been there as a part of the mind's content no religious interest could have been evoked.

The Religious Sentiment

This sentiment—the organisation of impulses and emotions round the religious idea—begins to form in early childhood. The 'numinous' experience is more common in children than we adults usually realise. The 'conviction of sin', self-defence reactions against 'sinful' thoughts or feelings are characteristic of many children although not always recognised for what they are. Before we attempt to teach children religion they are already religious in the sense that the nucleus of the religious sentiment is forming. Bovet, in his admirable study, *The Child's Religion*, is simply stating fact when he writes: "The religious psychology of the child has been less studied than would be believed. One point, however, seems well established, namely, that the great variety of religious experience which surprises us in adults is already discovered in children. The feeling of the sublime when in the grand spectacle of Nature, the mystic intuition of an invisible and beneficent being, the tragic conviction of shortcoming are already present in the inner lives of little children; and in numbers of these experiences we are compelled to recognise with astonishment that we are dealing with original facts, and that imitation plays no part."[1]

No one can read Dean Inge's pages on his daughter, Paula, without being persuaded that the eleven-year-old invalid had a real religious experience. Her desire to leave off saying her prayers to her elders in order that she should be *alone with God* strikes the note of reality. As likewise her answer to her brother who said: "O Paula, I wish you would just get better".

"No, Richard", she replied, "you must not say that. God

[1] *The Child's Religion*, pp. 7-8.

has spared me for a whole year to be with you all, and it has been the happiest year of my life."[1]

There can be no doubting the sincerity of her belief, or the peace and happiness of her experience.

Unfortunately, too many children's early experience of religion is coloured by ideas of God which tend to arouse fear if they do anything wrong. Often this results in behaviour which leads to neurotic habits; sometimes the behaviour is called 'naughty'. We were called to see a child of ten or eleven who could not go to sleep because of 'thoughts which will not go away'. When with great difficulty we got her to tell us what the thoughts were, the little child said that her mind kept saying: 'Damn God, Damn God'.

Here at this early age we have compulsive thoughts similar to those of Bunyan when he had the compulsive thought: 'Sell Christ, Sell Christ'. The explanation of the child's compulsion is quite simple. Impulses of some kind had been blocked by fear, and they were battering against the restraint which apparently the child had identified with God. She must have been taught that God would be displeased or angry were such impulses allowed to express themselves in conscious behaviour. The frustrated impulses were really expressing themselves in the compulsive thoughts.

The sense of guilt is exceedingly common in children whose idea of God is coloured too strongly by fear. Sometimes this leads to what is called a 'ritual complex'. The unfortunate child is compelled by inward tension to perform all manner of actions, such as bowing to every church he passes and saying a prayer; going to school without breakfast; kissing every piece of furniture before going to bed; washing hands so many times; seeing that everything is in a certain position. If any of these acts is omitted the child suffers agonies of fear. In all these cases the unconscious attempt to get rid of guilt is the motive; fear has made the child repress tendencies associated with guilt, and in the effort to get rid of the sense of guilt the child inflicts self-punishment or tries to propitiate the infantile conscience.

[1] *Personal Religion and the Life of Devotion*, p. 91.

We mention these experiences of children because their causes often determine the form and emotional tone of the adolescent and adult religious experiences. Fortunately, in the great majority of children, the religious sentiment grows along with other sentiments, and is not too prominent in consciousness although playing its unseen part in the formation of character and in the religious outlook on life of later years. But there can be no doubt in the mind of the psychologist who is acquainted with children's conflicts through clinical work that ideas of God and what God demands are decisive for the kind of conflicts and the resolution of them which will arise with the beginnings of or later pre-occupation with the religious appeal. In other words, the religious ideas and the feelings which accompany them become part of the content of the child's conscience, and thus determine his reaction to moral and spiritual conflicts. In the child the religious sentiment is scarcely separate from the conscience. It may be, as Dr. Otto asserts, that the idea of the Holy has no moral implications in the dim beginnings of the religious experience of the race; but there can be no doubt that in the child of civilisation, religious and moral ideas act and react upon his religious experience from the first.

Conscience and Evangelical Experience

In Karl Heim's *Spirit and Truth*, a chapter is devoted to the representation of Protestantism by Karl Holl as 'The Religion of Conscience'. The phrase is meant to connote 'the religion which finds its way to God, not by any experiences of an ethically indifferent power or by æsthetic impressions, but by conscience alone'.[1] In a later chapter we shall deal with the sense of sin and guilt as experienced by the Evangelical; at the present stage it will be well for us to understand the psychological source, development and authority of conscience; for there can be no doubt as to its tremendous significance in evangelical experience.

[1] *Spirit and Truth*, p. 115.

In treating of conscience the problem for the psychologist is very different from that of the moralist; and it is very probable that the controversies between Rationalism and Emotionalism in Ethics would have been less acute had either the rationalist or emotionalist attempted to get a psychological analysis of conscience. The problem for ethics, as Rashdall in his *Theory of Good and Evil*, puts it is: By what faculty do we judge that an act ought to be done? Are moral judgments based upon Reason or upon Feeling? Wherein lies the authority of the *ought?*

The psychologist's problem is not the validity of the *ought*, but the source of the feeling of moral obligation and the specific feelings connected therewith. *Ought*, as Rashdall admits, is an ultimate feeling, and he contends that if any individual denies that he has any sense of ought or obligation one can do no more with him except, perhaps, to try and show him how his denial lands him in all sorts of contradictions. But the 'sense of ought' differs from the judgment of ought. The judgment is intellectual, and it differs in different people; whereas the feeling of obligation is purely psychological. We may put it another way: the feeling of obligation is elicited; the intellectual judgment is demonstrated. Laird has said that the moral ideal implies the obligation to realise it; and we think that is true; but it is not the same thing as saying that, when an individual believes a moral ideal to be the right one, he experiences any sense of impulsion to realise it. Obligation or impulsion to perform a moral action, or to right a wrong, arises from within the individual, and the authority of the ideal is felt within and is not imposed from without.

As we see it, the problem of the authority of the moral ideal has three separate aspects. There is (1) the philosophical aspect which will deal with the objectivity of the ideal, its self-consistency, its coherence with other values and knowledge, its pragmatic value, according to the criterion of truth we employ. Then (2) there is the metaphysical aspect, namely, as to the nature of our moral consciousness. Then (3) we have the purely psychological problem as to why we should feel obliged or compelled to obey the ideal.

In passing we may note that here we get a problem analogous to the problem of error in philosophy; we may mourn our inability to feel the sense of ought towards a line of behaviour which intellectually we know to be right. The problem of our moral life is not simply a matter of knowing what we ought to do, but of both wanting to do it and of being able to do it.

These are purely psychological problems. And here we must deal with the psychological problem alone as we are concerned not with the right or wrongness of this or that moral ideal but with the sense of guilt—a problem with which the moral philosopher never deals at all.

Definition of Conscience

It will be readily admitted that the feeling of obligation and the sense of guilt, as well as the emotion of shame, derive from conscience. Professor Laird [1] is doubtful as to whether there is any single emotion which is peculiarly moral. He believes that we have single emotions that are never *unmoral* but always *immoral*, such as *malice* or *envy*. He is not on such sure ground, however, when he speaks of being ashamed of a club-foot, a rounded back or a small stature. Shame, as he uses the term, should be equated with inferiority feelings. A better illustration would have been that of the person who makes a *faux pas*. Nevertheless, the inferiority feelings engendered by some physical impairment or by the making of a *faux pas* differs *toto coelo* from the feelings consequent on falling into some evil habit, or succumbing to a temptation. Nor do we believe that he helps his own theory of the regulation of conduct by conceiving of conscience as no more than the organisation of our moral sentiments. He roots the authority of conscience in the claims of beliefs; and the emotional dispositions do no more than accompany and sustain the beliefs. "Conscience", he writes, "has to do with the guidance, control, and regulation of conduct in accordance with the appeal of the best." A psychological analysis of conscience, we think, will give us

[1] *A Study in Moral Theory*, pp. 130–1 (George Allen and Unwin Ltd.).

more than this. On the other hand, we agree entirely with his position, "that no emotional disposition is properly a matter of conscience unless it is subordinate to the discrimination of good and evil".

The difficulty with Professor Laird's view, as it is with Dr. Rashdall's as well as that of McDougall, is that they do not account for that sense of guilt which undoubtedly plays a large part in evangelical experience; and indeed in all religious experience. "Our sense of duty", according to McDougall, is no more than "what is demanded of us by our fellows; and at a higher moral level, it is our sense of what we demand of ourselves in virtue of the ideal of character that we have formed."[1] As a matter of psychological fact, guilt oftens pertains to what is not demanded by our fellows at all, and may be experienced long before we know any of the demands of our fellows; and even long before we have formed any moral ideal. Psycho-pathology has proved without doubt that guilt may be experienced in very young children without their being aware of the source of the guilt feeling. It would seem that there is in operation very early in life "a hereditary or general source of guilt feeling"[2] which has nothing to do with what is demanded of us by our fellows or by our own ideal. It is this sense of guilt from unconscious sources which often explains elements in evangelical experience which baffle those psychologists who study religious experience without a thorough knowledge of what clinical psychology has brought to light.

On the other hand, McDougall is right when he asserts that action is only possible if there is an active conative disposition.[3] Ideas in themselves, even when the outcome of reflection, are not necessarily realised in action. *We react to ideas; we do not act through them.* It is the contention of this volume that Conscience is conative.[4] McDougall would maintain that 'conscience is identical with the whole moral personality, with moral character'. He argues, moreover, that Rashdall's theory in

[1] *Social Psychology* (15th edition), p. 382.
[2] Graham Howe, *Motives and Mechanisms of the Mind*, chap. x.
[3] *Outline of Psychology*, p. 439.
[4] See article by Professor Broad, *Philosophy*, April, 1940.

spite of the latter's denial is one with his own. Rashdall's statement is: "Conscience or (to speak more scientifically) the moral consciousness, may be held to include not merely the capacity of pronouncing moral judgments, but the whole body of instincts, feelings, emotions, desires which are presupposed by and which influence these judgments, as well as those which prompt to the doing of the actions which they prescribe".[1]

As early, however, as Shand's volume on *The Foundations of Character*, the relative ethics of the various moral sentiments was distinguished from that of the 'general ethics of Conscience'. Conscience was recognised as a psychological entity; it could be enriched or destroyed and that in spite of the fact that many other moral sentiments might remain. It is because the Conscience is a separate principle of moral guidance that he can say of it: "That there is a calm joy in fulfilling the dictates of conscience, and a peculiar sorrow in our failure to fulfil them, is familiar to everyone. When we rebel against it, and persist in our evil courses, this sorrow becomes remorse. Its fear is that apprehension of punishment which follows the violation of its laws; and its anger is known as 'righteous indignation'."[2]

Let us now define Conscience, and leave our analysis of it to give grounds for our definition. *Conscience is the innate tendency to co-ordinate and regulate our moral ideas, emotions and conduct according to the moral ideals we have consciously or unconsciously accepted.*

This definition will be seen at once to differ widely from Professor Laird's idea that conscience always acts in accordance with the response to the best. The ideals on which conscience acts, and the ideas which we believe conscience co-ordinates, are *given* to conscience. And yet there may be an exception. It is becoming more generally believed among psycho-pathologists that we are born with an original prohibition of incest[3] as well as an innate tendency to experience a sense of guilt in a premature

[1] See *Hibbert Journal*, April, 1920.

[2] *The Foundations of Character*, p. 57.

[3] This does not mean an innate idea, but only an inhibitive tendency.

experience of sex feeling. Here, however, there is no attempt to say that we have innate ideas; but there may be prohibition to certain experiences without the individual being aware of an idea prohibiting the experience. As one writer has well put it: "It is quite true that the child does not 'know' much about sex, but the mistake lies in thinking that it is necessary to 'know'—i.e. to be conscious of sex, in order to be emotionally influenced by overheard intimacies. The experience is not a conscious one and does not relate to consciousness, but it may arouse a very deep feeling state, which is all the more important because there is no consciousness with which to correct it."[1] The relevance of this is found in the fact that the development of conscience begins in prohibitions and not in positive responses to the best. Our whole moral experience, and not only our evangelical experience, depends on our capacity to pass from the prohibitive stage of conscience to the positive stage when it is a response to what we think to be best.

Let us leave aside for the time being this original prohibition which can give rise to a sense of guilt and simply study the development of conscience. The child has no innate intuition of the rightness or wrongness of impulses, emotions, thoughts and conduct. The approval and disapproval of the parents are the guides of the child's actions. Thus the moral control of the child, at first, is purely external. Its first conflicts are really against external restraints in the literal sense. Morality begins in a 'Thou shalt not', and the prohibitions generate attitudes in the child towards what is 'right' and what is 'wrong'. Attitude is more fundamental for behaviour than belief; the attitude to a line of action may remain after the beliefs have changed.

Let us say at once that there is no other way in which very young children can be trained in conduct than by prohibition. We cannot reason with a child; we may appeal to him to do something 'for my sake', but that is not an appeal to reason but to affection. Not only so, but the prohibitions of the parent are justified. We may prohibit a child not because we think

[1] *Motives and Mechanisms of the Mind*, p. 184.

the action wrong but because looking ahead, which the child cannot do, we are trying to prevent the rise of a habit which may be difficult to break, such as lying, etc., etc. We do not prohibit the child from climbing upon the chairs because we think it is wrong, but because it is dangerous.

But the parents cannot always be with the child, and tendencies to prohibited behaviour may arise when the parent is not present. How then does control come about? The mind *introjects*, internalises the prohibitions; and the child's conflicts now are not simply a matter of self-will rebelling against the will of parents or teachers, but become *endo-psychic*, i.e. within the child's own consciousness. Nevertheless, although the conflicts are endo-psychic, the restraints are still external in the sense that they are not yet assimilated by the child's personality. They are still the restraints of the parents although felt as coming from within; they lie over against the child's personality.

Bergson puts this aspect of moral growth in his own inimitable manner. He opens his volume, *The Two Sources of Morality and Religion*, in the following paragraph: "The remembrance of forbidden fruit is the earliest thing in the memory of each of us, as it is in that of mankind. We should notice this, were not this recollection overlaid by others which we are more inclined to dwell upon. What a childhood we should have had if only we had been left to do as we pleased! We should have flitted from pleasure to pleasure. But all of a sudden an obstacle arose, neither visible nor tangible; a prohibition. Why did we obey? The question hardly occurred to us. We had formed the habit of deferring to our parents and teachers. All the same we knew that it was because they were our parents, because they were our teachers. Therefore, in our eyes, their authority came less from themselves than from their status in relation to us. They occupied a certain station; that was the source of the command which, had it issued from some other quarter, would not have possessed the same weight. In other words, parents and teachers seemed to act by proxy. We did not fully realise this, but behind our parents and our teachers we had an inkling of some enormous or rather some shadowy thing that exerted pressure on us through them. Later we would say it was society."[1]

We are not concerned at the moment with the objective source of the authority. What we want to point out is that in the experience of us all there is exerted a pressure of authority from within which is not to be identified with the fear of the parent. The authority is exerted by this principle of the mind which introjects, internalises, co-ordinates prohibitions we have received, just as later it will assimilate and co-ordinate the positive guidance to the development of character and personality of a moral kind. It is here we find the source of conscience. Naturally, there is incorporated with the prohibitions a threat; every prohibition involves some kind of threat for its violation, even though no threat has actually been uttered. Here is the origin of Shand's 'fear of punishment at the violation of its laws'.

These prohibitions are what the Psycho-analyst calls the 'super-ego'—super in the sense that they are imposed as it were from above. And this negative conscience whose content is made up of prohibitions can be extremely cruel and demand punishment of the child. In cases of neurotic trouble, as also in psychotic, self-punishment demanded by this internal prohibitive conscience is practically always present. This demand for self-punishment lies, in all probability, at the roots of some cruel theories of eternal punishment as well as being the unconscious ground of some penal theories of the Atonement, of which more anon.

What we must note here is that the infantile conscience can do no more in regulating the conduct of the child than present barriers to the outlet of prohibited tendencies, feelings or ideas. Its importance for evangelical experience lies in the fact that the evangelical experience itself may do no more than strengthen the barriers to prohibited tendencies. In that case the sense of sin is apt to remain, indeed to be strengthened. The evangelical experience in people who have a strongly developed negative

[1] *The Two Sources of Morality and Religion*, chap. i.

conscience gives no deliverance from sin nor in many cases from sense of guilt. The tendencies are left unmodified. "I do try to be good" said a woman brought up in a very evangelical home. In reality she did nothing of the kind. She spent her strength *trying not to do wrong*, which is a very different thing. In the more narrow evangelical sects we, without exception, find this negative conscience with prohibited tendencies unmodified. It makes the individual more afraid to do wrong than eager to know and do the right; and not seldom the prohibitions are confined to certain well-defined tendencies while other unlovely traits of character are left entirely unchanged. The strengthening of the prohibition to adultery does not necessarily modify the tendency to greed, envy, will to power, nor the tendency to exploit others. The implications we may leave until we come to the actual study of evangelical experience. It is enough for us to remember here that if this type of negative conscience remains unmodified during adolescence or before, it will determine the kind of religious experience the individual is likely to pass through, or at least to colour it strongly.

Even in children, however, and without a great deal of instruction, the conscience may of itself tend towards a positive orientation. The spontaneous affection for the parents or the desire to receive their approval may be sufficient to restrain the tendencies without much effort. That desire for the praise of the parents may become the conscious desire to be praiseworthy. Thus prohibited tendencies may give the growing child little or no trouble. Hence the tendency to be 'pulled from in front' may take its roots, and the behaviour tendencies begin to flow spontaneously towards ends which bring no conflicts. Happy is such a child! Happy to have such training! Here is the source of the 'once-born' of James. There is nothing 'congenital' about it; it depends to a very large extent on personal environment, i.e. the moral and religious atmosphere in which the child lives.

Wise parents, however, do not leave the development to spontaneous direction; they attempt through teaching and example to transform the prohibitions into positive directions to behaviour tendencies. The boy in whom there has been elicited the love for honesty has no need to carry an inner prohibition against stealing; the adolescent who has learned to love chastity of thought and deed is free from the burden of carrying within him a policeman to block his impulses from leading him into sexual habits of a dangerous kind. He is not burdened with a sense of guilt derived, not from having done wrong, but from inner unconscious tendencies towards wrong-doing. This is the explanation of that statement of Dean Inge which many found hard to accept: speaking of certain forms of temptation he said that such forms should never enter the mind. Temptation, we must never forget, comes from within; there is no such thing as a temptation from without. A stimulus from without we may have, but it has no meaning psychologically unless there is within us some tendency to respond. The Dean was speaking of a mind whose natural tendencies are accepted and controlled spontaneously by assimilated ideals and ideas.

Here lies the psychological preparation for moral and religious experience of the best type; the positive moral virtues must be assimilated; they must not lie over against our impulses to behaviour; they must be so assimilated as to modify them. Our impulses having a positive outlet in conduct perfectly harmonious with our accepted conscious and unconscious ideas of what is good and right become part of our morally organised personality. They become the disposition to do right; and thus grow up with our personality and tend towards mature outlets, and what we may call reasonable conduct in contrast to that which is the outcome of impulses and behaviour tendencies which have been barricaded at early adolescence or even earlier.

In so far as the negative type of conscience remains it comes into play only as a restraint, a barrier, stimulating fear and sense of guilt when infantile behaviour tendencies attempt to enter consciousness or when they generate ideas of behaviour. This is the conscience that 'makes cowards of us all'.

It should be borne in mind that the tendency to prohibition remains in the fully developed conscience. Its action, however, is not accompanied by fear and guilt. Its function is to restrain us when the morality of some action is uncertain; its action thus precedes deliberation and choice. The positive conscience refuses spontaneously to be driven or coerced by impulse. When the imperious demands of appetite solicit the ego the positive conscience gives the power spoken of as *self-control;*[1] whereas the negative conscience may lead to *repression* and all its miserable sequence. That the perfectly adult conscience may be tempted to abrogate its control of our appetites may be experienced by us all. It is the very nature of our appetites to present themselves in consciousness with attraction; and they may be hard to control; the tension set up between the drive and attraction of the impulses and the regulating influence of conscience may be such as to lead to a moral lapse; but the conscience does not consent; *we may be forced to choose what we do not will.* There thus arises sorrow for sin, a deep sense of shame and guilt; but instead of being paralysed with fear and impelled to self-punishment we are driven in humility to our knees for forgiveness; our self-respect is rehabilitated; we become humble not self-depreciatory; our desire to grow up into the stature of Christ Jesus and to have the same mind in us as was in Him is not checked. "My sins are ever before me" sang the Psalmist; but they were before him as a dynamic urging him to forget the things which are behind and to press on until God's "statutes have become the songs of my pilgrimage". The moral law may become the theme of our music and not simply restraints.

The Psychological Nature of Conscience

As we have seen, McDougall was right in his insistence that ideas are only realised in so far as they are associated with some

[1] This distinction should be kept well in mind. *Self-control* is conscious, *repression* is unconscious. *Self-control* is a conscious refusal to do something, repression is an unconscious refusal to see something. Also see Dr. Wm. Brown, *Psychology and Psychotherapy*, p. 119.

conative disposition. What he failed to see was that the appetitive needs connected with the organism are not the only needs in human personality that have the element of conation. Personality needs are in their own sphere just as dynamic. The "sense of duty" is not the outcome of a fear of being separated from the 'herd' because we have not met 'the demands of our fellows'; in its fully developed form it is the dynamic need for status among our fellows; it is not merely 'our sense of what we demand from ourselves in virtue of the ideal of character we have formed'. Even were it only that, there is nothing in McDougall's catalogue of propensities which could possibly account for this 'higher moral level'. There is nothing in psychology which could be construed as giving grounds for the belief that ethics can be derived from biology. Morality can only be predicated of self-conscious beings. Conscience demands as a right that we fulfil the demands of our fellows, that we fulfil the demands of self-respect to our ideals. It can coerce both the impulses which would rebel against its enactments, and the self or ego which would be allured by the attraction of the pleasure they offer.

It is here that we find the ultimate explanation of repression from the psychological point of view. On its prohibitive side Conscience refuses admittance to consciousness of impulses which would offer a threat to the integrity of the moral personality, and may demand all sorts of self-punishment on the part of the ego for the impulses being active. On its positive side, it gives the direction to the impulses towards conduct in harmony with the organised moral personality. "The moral ideal implies the obligation to see that it is realised,"[1] says Laird. If that ideal is accepted consciously or unconsciously there is a conative urge to see to its realisation; and we disobey at our peril.

Moral philosophers, such as Rashdall, have asserted 'that the desire to act rationally or to do right is created by the intellect', and thus made themselves easy targets for McDougall's

[1] This position is maintained throughout his *A Study in Moral Theory.*

polemics. Had they argued that "Reason as an organic principle in thought, and so far as incomplete but progressive may be termed an organic impulse" with Hobhouse, their answer to McDougall would have been complete. Reason as rational,[1] and not simply intellectual, is the fundamental organ of self-conscious personality; and as such is conative. It strives for unity in its experience both intellectual and moral as well as social. Just as the organism has developed, in its long evolutionary history, organs whose function it is to see to the preservation of the organism and its re-production, so Reason has evolved the Conscience to preserve and further its moral integrity and unity, and the intellect as the organ of its reflective tendency. As Professor Laird has said, "We are inevitably and incurably a reflective species, looking before and after, and pondering invisible principles".[2]

From the point of view of psychology, then, Conscience must be seen as conative, not simply as a capacity to pass moral judgments, but as able to exert power for their fulfilment. Only in this way can we understand its peculiar feelings of guilt, remorse and moral shame.

From whence does it derive its authority which in so many is overwhelming? Like all mental process it has the characteristics of cognition, affect and conation. As organ of the Reason, its cognitive aspect can be easily understod. It is in virtue of Conscience that we discriminate good from evil, right from wrong, and it is from this rational side that we must derive its capacity to form moral judgments. Nevertheless, the grounds of its judgments are never wholly intellectual; feeling may inform as well as re-enforce action. Hence the need to bring its judgments to the bar of Reason. It may compel us to reflect again if it finds itself uncertain in its actions. Nevertheless, its authority, as Conscience, is not altogether derived from Reason. It has its own authority, an authority which is not to be confused with the objectivity of the moral ideal.

[1] Cf. Professor Hobhouse, *The Rational Good*, p. 64, for idea that Reason is a conative tendency (George Allen and Unwin Ltd.).

[2] *A Study in Moral Theory*, p. 130.

That authority lies in the fact that it legislates for the personality as a whole. There are duties, and in a sense a Conscience, inherent in each one of our sentiments. The love sentiment for one's wife will not only re-enforce our devotion to her, but will enjoin constancy, faithfulness, and truth. As Shand has pointed out: "The relative ethics of a certain class of sentiments must be distinguished from the general ethics of the Conscience. For while the former is inevitably partial to its particular object, the latter, unique among all the sentiments in not possessing any private object, is not urged to partiality on that account. However narrow and unenlightened, however hardened by a man's vices, or rendered sensitive through his goodness and virtues, when it acts, within its purview, it acts without prejudice. And as it has no private object so it has no private end; its end being to superintend and regulate other systems, to encourage some, to forbid others, to temper all, to approve or disapprove their actions."[1] If we translate that into terms of the theory enunciated here, the end of that Conscience is to superintend all other systems in the interest of the self as a whole; its task is to preserve the moral unity of the whole. It is this function of Conscience which gives it its authority over all particular sentiments and over all isolated impulses.

The fallacy of McDougall's psychology of character lies in the fact that he found no room for the personality as a whole as distinct from the whole personality in the sense of the sum of our sentiments. The personality as a whole has its own 'prospective aim'. It is when the lesser sentiments or impulses come into conflict with this prospective aim of personality that Conscience comes into operation consciously, and may insist on deliberation and reflection both upon particular lines of behaviour and on the ends themselves. In so far as the Reason can show authoritative ideals, in so far is this inner subjective side of authority strengthened.

The implications of this analysis of Conscience will be seen

[1] *The Foundations of Character*, p. 119.

fully when we come to treat of the evangelical experiences and evangelical doctrine. But if we have carried our readers with us, then it will be seen that the Religion of Conscience is not an unworthy description of evangelical religion. It reaches down to the demands of Conscience as no other religion does; it meets that cry of the self or soul for freedom from its sense of guilt, and for power to realise the demands of Conscience; it brings about the experience of salvation in which the Law, in the form of prohibition is succeeded by the grace in which sentiment and impulse are being directed towards the stature of a man in Christ Jesus.

CHAPTER IV

Salvation and its Problems

THE experience of salvation regarded from the psychological point of view is crucial for the understanding of the psychology of Evangelicalism. The whole drama of Incarnation, Atonement and Resurrection finds its meaning in relation to that experience. Older theologians grounded the doctrine of the divinity and sinlessness of Jesus on the belief that only such attributes could guarantee His fitness for the task of reconciling men to God through His Atonement. Even such a 'modern' Evangelical as Dr. C. J. Cadoux is influenced (perhaps more than he realises) to accept "The Trinitarian assertion of the existence from all eternity of 'God the Son' who became incarnate in the human Jesus", because it is "a method of affirming that the forthgoing Divine life manifestly present in Him *for the Salvation of us men* was as Divine and eternal as that of the Father Himself".[1]

As we have seen in a previous chapter, Evangelicalism asserts the 'need of Salvation', and the efficacy of Christ to effect it. What psychologically is this 'need of Salvation'? How do we become aware of it? What psychological factors are involved in the experience which satisfies the need? Why is it that the need seems so intense in some that only after an experience approximating to a psycho-neurosis is the conflict which the need makes conscious resolved; while in others the need generates a calm decision rather than a catastrophic experience? Why is the sense of guilt so strong in some and but faintly experienced in others?

Finally we must ask what relation, psychologically, is there between the death of Christ and the realisation of forgiveness

[1] *The Case for Evangelical Modernism*, p. 172.

in which the need becomes satisfied? What is the experience of forgiveness; and what is the relation of the 'preaching of the Word' to the elicitation of the sense of need and the assurance of forgiveness? What determines the type of conversion experience?

The Sense of the Need of Salvation

The need of Salvation is a theological dogma; but it is also an experience common to the devotees of every religion. Here we are only concerned with the experience of Evangelicals.

Unfortunately, both religious and psychological volumes have laid an exaggerated emphasis on those whose sense of need approximated to a psycho-neurosis. Many of the experiences recorded and analysed have been of those men and women who have fallen victims to specific sinful habits like Augustine; or of those whose conversion has been accompanied by abnormal phenomena. Evangelicalism may proudly boast of its 'brands plucked from the burning'; its capacity to mend 'broken earthenware'; its long list of 'twice-born' men and women who have become outstanding figures in Church and social history. It is readily granted by all students of conversion that the radical change seen in such is not only psychologically real but has made a deep impression upon the world.

Too little attention has been paid to the experience of those who can look back on no dramatic crisis. It is acknowledged, both by Starbuck and James that the conversion experience may be slow and gradual. James did not deny a real religious experience to the 'once-born', but his interest obviously lay with those who could show abnormal phenomena.

Writers are laying much greater stress upon the 'slow and gradual'; they are realising that our churches depend on such for their best workers. Few psychologists with clinical experience would agree with Professor Leuba when he says 'that violent psychic phenomena by their very emphasis bring to light what remains obscure in less intense and slower events'. Actually our knowledge of what happens in the sudden conversion or in the quick cure of a neurotic patient is gained from the patient analysis of those individuals who have absorbed much of our time.

Whether the process through which an individual comes to be God-centred be slow or gradual, that process is 'conversion'. Canon Raven is explicit on the point: ". . . in whatever form God comes, whether through the slow process of growth or the shattering experience of sudden discovery, the result is conversion. In many, perhaps in most, cases there is no single dramatic crisis: their inward conflict, never acutely recognised, is resolved by a succession of almost unconscious adjustments until gradually the whole centre of interest inclines Godward. To others, and often in proportion to the intensity of their struggle and distress, the change comes in a moment: in a blaze of ecstatic wonder God takes possession of them and the whole orientation of their lives is violently altered. In such instances, whether in the classical cases of St. Paul and St. Augustine or in the multitude of humbler ones, no language seems to be too strong to describe what has occurred."[1]

We think it can be stated without fear of contradiction that by far the greater number of those who are members, adherents and workers in our Evangelical Churches have known nothing of dramatic conversion. In our Presbyterian and Anglican Churches the most loyal and steadfast workers have entered the Church through the catechumen classes. Many of our Congregational Churches are relying more and more on such classes for the recruitment of new members, and to help our young people to a 'decision'; and in the Baptist and Methodist Churches the number who become working members as a result of 'sudden' or dramatic conversion grows relatively smaller.

What is the experience of the sense of need of those who enter our Churches in this way? It may be true that many have resolved their inner conflicts "by a succession of almost unconscious adjustments until the whole centre of interest inclines Godward"; nevertheless, their sense of need is manifested in their hope of a deepening of religious experience as

[1] *The Inner Life*, edited by Rev. Guy Rogers, pp. 68–9.

a result of entering the Church. There are few who join the Church in this way in whom that hope is not actually conscious; and it is this hope that leads to the decision to join the Church. Sometimes the need for a richer spiritual life precedes the decision to join the Church and is then shown in the individual's desire to take up some kind of Church work. Always, however, one finds in those who join the Church or take up some kind of Christian work spontaneously, an attempt and a hope to realise the richer spiritual experience promised by Evangelicalism.

One of the best descriptions of this sense of need without the dramatic and violent conflicts and struggles is given by Dean Inge: "The mystic quest", he writes, "begins in every case with an inward call felt in a moment of vision. It produces a sense of dissatisfaction with ordinary experience, with those superficial aspects of life with which we are usually content. It awakens a great desire and longing to get nearer to the heart of things, and a hope that in doing so we may be rid of some of the discord and limitations and evil with which we are surrounded in this world, and which not only surround us, but infect us, clogging and hampering our freedom and blinding the eyes of the soul. The discord within us is even more painful than the discord without; and we remember that at the moment of vision we seemed to have somehow escaped from it. We escaped from it—so it seems to us when we reflect upon what we then felt—by escaping from ourselves."[1]

That 'moment of vision', that sense of 'dissatisfaction', that "great desire and longing to get nearer to the heart of things", that 'discord within', and 'discord without' reveal the sense of need experienced by the great majority of Evangelical Christians when they set out on the quest for that richer religious life in which all discords would be resolved. There is a felt sense of incompleteness which is stronger than any feeling of wrongness or inferiority. 'Dissatisfaction' may not be the right word for some people; they are unsatisfied rather than dissatisfied, uncontented rather than discontented. Though there is a sense of painful inner discord the individual is not

[1] *Personal Religion and the Life of Devotion*, pp. 18-19.

conscious of having plunged into open sin or of slavery to sexual habits. There is, however, a definite feeling of moral and spiritual ineffectiveness, and of groping after a living vital, religious faith and experience.

The Evangelical Quest Distinguished from other Quests

Our readers will remember that at the moment we are studying those whose conflicts are resolved otherwise than by a sharp, sudden and dramatic conversion. Religiously the sudden conversion is of no more value than the slow and gradual adjustment of the mind and will to the intention of God. There are some people whose sense of need for unity within and without finds its satisfaction along lines which may seem to lead them far from Evangelicalism. James would not agree that their resolution of their problem was a religious one. "To find religion", he says, "is only one out of many ways of reaching unity; and the process of remedying inner incompleteness and reducing inner discord is a general psychological process, which may take place with any sort of mental material and need not necessarily assume a religious form."[1] Undoubtedly James is right in asserting that we may get a new birth away from religion, and from moral scrupulosity, to freedom and license, but there are others who find their souls unified through thought or through adherence to a cause. Their motivation is rooted in the same sense of need for inner harmony or unity.

Let us try to differentiate the quests of the soul. Perhaps we shall find that they are but aspects of the one evangelical quest for God.

'The moment of vision' has constituent moments any one of which may be more prominent in consciousness than the others. If we may use psychological jargon, one of the moments may be at the centre of the field of consciousness while the others are more or less on the margin; and indeed these others may not come prominently into consciousness at all.

A young adolescent may be brought up sharply through

[1] *The Varieties of Religious Experience*, p. 175.

meeting in his studies or in his experience of life some contradiction to beliefs on and by which he has so far lived, but which he had never rationally grounded. We all entered adolescence with beliefs unconsciously accepted when we were younger; and we tacitly accepted them as true until we found that they did not square with growing knowledge or experience of life. Until we received this shock our religious experience may have been real without being intense or very deep. That God is love, that He hears and answers prayer, that loved ones survive death, that sin is forgiven are such tacitly accepted beliefs around which the religious sentiment is formed.

When at the 'moment of vision' these accepted beliefs of childhood receive a shock the religious sentiment is wounded. The effect of this differs from that of the adolescent who has become conscious of a conflict of incompatible tendencies within his religious and moral sentiments. In the latter case the quest is for moral unity within himself and spiritual unity with God; in the former case the quest is to restore intellectual unity which may at the same time have the evangelical motive. Such a quest is likely to lead the young adolescent to the study of philosophy, theology, or science, or he may seek a compensation for the disturbed beliefs in æsthetic pursuits. One well-known professor confessed that his interest in Archæology originated in the shock he received at the University when doubt was cast on the Biblical stories. Many a student of philosophy or theology can trace his interest to such a shock.

The interest, however, is still a religious one; and we agree with Principal Jacks[1] that the search for truth aroused by meeting a contradiction to one's religious beliefs is a religious experience. It is psychologically different from the mere intellectual interest in religion; the motivation is different. We need not confuse spiritual curiosity with spiritual life, and an individual's interest in and search for the truth may be the source of a truly religious or spiritual life. The search may bring the student to conclusions which seem far from the accepted evangelical beliefs which received the shock; never-

[1] *Elemental Religion*, see chap. iv.

theless the whole activity is religiously, though it may be unconsciously, motivated by the urge to validate what he felt and believed about God, the world, the soul, before he was rudely shaken from his tacit foundations.

It should not be out of place here to suggest to those who see in every doubting adolescent a moral conflict, a clinging to some secret sin, that they should be careful not to put the cart before the horse. They may indeed find a moral conflict, or a besetting weakness, but these may not be the cause of the doubts; although they may be intensified by them.

Finding a 'Cause' as the Resolution of Conflict

The 'moment of vision', however, may bring a sudden realisation of the economic or social inequalities in the world —the 'discord without'. Such a realisation may send the individual on a very different quest from the man who sets out to validate his beliefs; instead of seeking objective truth like the philosopher or to understand the ways of God with men like the theologian, he may seek and strive for the Kingdom of God in social, political and economic terms. This man finds a 'cause'; it is a religious quest, motivated by the religious consciousness, and not seldom inspired by evangelical beliefs.

An interesting confirmation of this kind of resolution of the 'discord' felt in the 'moment of vision' as a religious and evangelical experience is given in an article[1] written by Stanley Jones. The article deals with an Evangelical Mission to the State Universities of the United States. Commenting on the attitude of mind of the students addressed by the Missioners he writes: "One thing modern students do not have—they have no Cause. They are all dressed up and do not know where to go. Nothing grips them supremely. And the tragedy is that they do not see it. One youth objected in these words when I said they did not have a Cause: 'But we do have a Cause; we want to succeed'."

[1] *British Weekly*, January, 1939.

Later in the article he asks: "Have we a Cause to give them? Yes, we have. The Kingdom of God! A totalitarian demand and offer to the whole of life. There my message needed no change —The Kingdom of God personalised and offered in Christ is the answer."

Here we have confirmation from one of the wisest of modern evangelists to educated youth that the Social Quest may be motivated in evangelical religion.

We have no doubt that the evangelical mystic experience may remain conscious through life, and enriched by adherence to a Cause, especially if at the moment of vision it has been linked with personal surrender to Jesus Christ. It becomes His Cause. In this case the Cause is linked in the unconscious with the religious motive. The same is true of the individual whose 'discord' led him to philosophy or theology.

In this connection Professor Höffding has a sentence worth pondering: "The more men are absorbed in the task of self-maintenance, or the more they are given up to intellectual, æsthetic and ethical interests, the more strictly religious interest falls into the background—if indeed it does not entirely disappear".[1] Such a generalisation is probably too sweeping; but there can be no question that it contains enough truth to make our ministers of religion ask themselves whether in their preaching they are ministering to the psychological and spiritual needs of this large class whose quest began in 'a moment of vision' not unlike their own. Professor Hocking, from whom we have quoted the statement, answers it by asserting that religion is characterised more by fertility than utility, and that the products of religious experience may become a substitute for religion itself.

Our position is that psychologically the product of the 'moment of vision' will depend on what was most prominent in consciousness at the time—what was the main core of dissatisfaction or discord. It is this that originates and determines the kind of quest on which the soul sets out. But the 'moment of vision' is essentially a religious experience; and the quest is

[1] Quoted in a footnote, *The Meaning of God in Experience*, Hocking.

essentially a religious quest. It is psychologically false to assume that the Evangelical Quest originates only in the discord caused by the sense of sin. We distinguish these quests because they are different ways of finding the resolution of the discord revealed in the 'moment of vision'; they are not alternative 'varieties of Religious Experience' between which we must choose; they are the outcome of the different forms of discord, dissatisfaction, or incompleteness on which the emphasis falls in the 'moment of vision'.

The Evangelical Quest

Let us return to what is thought by many to be the Evangelical Quest proper. Here the 'moment of vision' reveals an inner discord, a need for a deeper spiritual and moral unity within; a sense of inability to attain that harmony by one's own efforts; a consciousness of failure to realise God.

Many of those of whom we are now thinking have been living on their parents' religious capital; but never till now have they been conscious that they have not reached what we may call 'economic maturity' spiritually or morally. They have never made God their own; never appropriated forgiveness; never developed a dynamic faith. Like the "elder brother" they have been content to live under the Father's roof; they are not conscious of having squandered their Father's goods in riotous living. Then gradually or suddenly they became dissatisfied within themselves because they were unsatisfied; discontented because they were uncontented. This class may have no intolerable sense of guilt though deeply conscious of coming short of the Glory of God; they may have no deep-rooted sinful habits whose grip they must strive to break. The emphasis of the 'moment ot vision' falls on the inadequacy of the values they have been usually satisfied to seek. The 'moment of vision' leads them to seek a more vital religious experience; and in the quest of it they make the decision to surrender more fully to Christ. It is a deliberate decision made after a quiet talk with a kindly and understanding teacher or pastor. Their decision is sealed by joining the Church. There is no great wave of emotion, though there may be a deep feeling of calm as they enter the new relationship to Christ and His Church. Made aware of their need in that 'moment of vision' they have set out to have the need satisfied. There is a new birth in the sense that they have made their own values which they had rather taken for granted than experienced; and these values became what James calls 'the habitual centre' from which they act, think, feel. There may, as yet, be no deep experience of the personal love of God for they have never felt the wide alienation from Him of those who have been compelled to eat 'the husks the swine did eat'. Nevertheless they hold fast to their belief in the love of God, and the forgiveness of sin. Their experience is a real evangelical experience; and may in the right spiritual environment be an ever deepening one. Decision is but a beginning not an ending of their struggle.

Let us emphasise again that in the case of the "Once-born" there is a true re-orientation within. Religious values and the religious sentiment take a central place in motivation and in the ordering of their lives.

This, we believe, is the truly 'healthy-minded' type of evangelical experience. Those whose experience we are considering are not afraid to look sin straight in the face; they recognise its power both within themselves and in the world without. Unlike many of James's illustrations of conversion their experience is characterised by a true growth in moral and spiritual harmony rather than a catastrophic escape from sin. From the beginning the direction of their conscience has been positive and not prohibitive. They are not exhausted by their fight with sin, they are 'more than conquerors'—they have strength left over when they have met the contradictions of life, and have overcome their temptations.

Professor James confused the 'healthy-minded' type of personality with what is known in modern psychology as the 'extravert'. He classes the healthy-minded with those to whom "the attitude of unhappiness is not only painful, it is mean and ugly".[1] It is very doubtful whether any truly religious man ever sees unhappiness as 'mean and ugly'. To him unhappiness is always a tragedy eliciting his sympathy and his service. A description of the extravert type of mind will make plain to the reader the class from which James draws many of his illustrations of the healthy-minded.

Dr. Hinkle has described the extravert with precision and insight; she says that he is characterised by the tendency, "to push away all painful situations and unpleasant conditions as far from himself as possible; he turns from the disagreeable situation as rapidly as he can, refusing to face it unless forced to do so, believing that his motto, 'forget it,' is a panacea for his disturbance, and expresses the condition most to be desired. This is a definite effort at repression which may be conscious or unconscious, and is the normal attitude of all extraverted persons who attempt to ignore what is unpleasant and who immediately try to place their attention and interest upon another object . . . (he) merely buries his pain and disappointment in the unconscious, and his forgetting is only a conscious banishment from his own sight; deep in his soul his pain is burrowing, affecting like a dark shadow all his efforts. However, his capacity for losing himself in many objects gives the appearance of successful transference and freedom."[2]

As Dr. Hinkle says, this "successful transference and freedom" is only an 'appearance'; it can deceive the elect as it deceived James. In reality, the blustering type which James confused with the healthy-minded type has little or no inner stability; the bluster is an over-compensation for the unconscious inner instability. Instead of a crust hard enough to resist sensitiveness to sin and contradiction, as James thought, men of this type have an exceedingly thin defence against the onslaughts of real conflict and contradiction, and they usually crack. They provide the psychotherapist with most of his anxiety neurosis cases, and as in an anxiety neurosis the patient is compelled to introvert, that is become pre-occupied with his own thoughts,

[1] *The Varieties*, p. 89.
[2] *The Re-Creating of the Individual*, pp. 176–8.

fears, failings, and emotions, usually has an exceedingly bad time, since introversion is contrary to his psychological type. Moreover, patients of this class are never sure of themselves afterwards, unless the cure has been accomplished through a thorough and religious re-orientation.

James was wrong when he assumed that such a religious experience as that of Dr. Everett Hale, whom he quotes, is to be accounted for by 'the presence of a temperament organically weighted on the side of cheer and fatally forbidden to linger, as those of opposite temperaments linger, over the darker aspect of the universe'. Dr. Hale's own explanation is psychologically more true. He accounts for the 'lack of religious or irreligious struggle' within himself, by the fact that he was born into a family 'where religion was simple and rational'. In such a home prohibitions would be few; the prohibitive side of conscience would not be unduly developed. Through teaching and example, and the atmosphere of the home, the natural tendencies to behaviour consistent with a simple and rational piety would be directed to positive ends and as naturally accepted.

Before we pass to a study of those whose struggle to resolve their inner conflicts approaches a psycho-neurosis, let us say a word more in justification of those who find their evangelical experience in the external relations of thought. Their deep and sustained interest in philosophy or theology is not a substitute for religious experience, it is a religious experience. When Professor Höffding speaks of the decline of religious interest in those who give themselves to æsthetic, intellectual or ethical affairs, we are inclined to think that he is confusing religious interest with ecclesiastical interest. Be that as it may, we are convinced that the rationally grounded convictions of the love of God, the providence of God, the forgiveness of sin, the divine nature of our Lord generate as profoundly deep emotions as the 'ecstatic wonder' which accompanies the personal realisation of those great doctrines. These convictions fuse with the personal experience though the rational side is more prominent in consciousness. It will not be difficult to realise the truth of this statement if we remember that the 'moment of vision' affected the need for rational unity more than for moral unity.

Dr. Dale,[1] an intellectual Evangelical if ever there was one, gives us an experience in which we see the intellectual or rational conviction fusing with personal experience. While writing an Easter sermon on the Resurrection he suddenly realised the reality of the living Christ. It produced an intense emotion, the depth of which can only be explained by the fact that he was realising in personal experience what already he believed intensely.

The soul has a need to know as well as to feel. This was one of the psychological facts James almost entirely overlooked in his choice of the varieties of religious experience which he describes. James was too much influenced in his choice by the explicit motive to find empirical grounds for a transcendental scheme of things. He was looking for contrasts that might justify his Pluralism. As Dr. Uren has pointed out, James's assertion "that personal religious experience has its roots and centre in mystical states of consciousness" is too narrow and excludes from religious experience those whose fellowship with God "is objective and external rather than mystical".[2] The forgiveness of sin, the love of God, the efficacy of Christ, the experience of a dynamic faith, steady progress in sanctification are just as real to those who have reached those experiences through the external relations of thought—through the attempt to satisfy the need for rational unity—as those whose experience has come to them through mystic intuitions. 'Synthetic intuition' is as real in religious as in philosophical experience.

No doubt, as Principal Jacks has pointed out, there is a danger of confusing religion with the study of religion; but the danger is not nearly so great for the future of Evangelicalism as the false notion that the root and centre of personal religious experience lies in mystical states of consciousness. It is truly a great experience to feel the throb of God's love, to know through a feeling state the indwelling presence of Christ, the

[1] See volume, *The Living Christ and the Four Gospels*.
[2] *Recent Religious Psychology*, p. 75.

forgiveness of sin; but is it not just as great an experience to think God's thoughts after Him, to rise to a rational understanding of His ways with men, to see His revelation in Christ, His life and His Cross ? There is no greater danger to evangelical religion than the over-emphasis of the specific states of feeling as preliminary to entering upon the Evangelical Quest. How much psychological and spiritual damage this over-emphasis has done none knows better than the psychotherapist, for he treats continually many whose spiritual distress can be traced to the attempt to induce experiences alien to the particular individual. Dr. Jacks has testified how the attempts to bring him into the circle of religious experience of a certain type produced the very opposite effect from what his instructors intended.[1]

The mistake, from the psychological point of view, of many Evangelicals is that they confuse the elicitation of a sense of need with the arousal of a sense of guilt. Nothing can embitter an individual against all kinds of religion like the over-emphasis on one aspect of religious experience; in many cases it produces a tragedy.

Dr. Jacks gives an illustration of the tragic consequences which may result from this over-emphasis.[2] We give one from our own clinical experience, of an intelligent woman who nearly gave up all religion.

She was a worker with the Quaker Social Mission in Greece. Although she was not brought up as a Quaker she had answered the appeal for social workers.

"I am one of those", she wrote, "whose religion has never once risen into the realm of (personal) experience. I can only say that years ago I made what I intended to be a very definite surrender to God; and followed that up with two years at a Bible School of an intensely spiritual character. Here I did the things I most shrunk from, and hoped it would act as a spiritual forcing house. I fear it did not in my case. I left as I went; feeling that as far as personal experience could testify there might be no God. In spite of much time being set apart for

[1] See *Elemental Religion*, chap. iii. [2] *Ibid.*

public and private prayer, I was never conscious of being in touch with God."

When she came under our notice she was on the point of giving up the whole thing; and said that she could understand a very honest aunt of hers who swore that she never felt such a relief as when she gave up her religion, or rather the attempt to convince herself that she had religion.

Fortunately she was far too intelligent and strong-minded to suffer any psychological damage from the attempt to force a certain type of feeling experience. But how rich her religious experience could have been had she realised from the beginning that she could have fellowship with God through thought, love and service. Her sense of need did not arise from a feeling of guilt, or a stimulation of mystical states of consciousness, but from a desire for objective grounds for the God to whom she was willing to surrender all, and a deepening of the faith that her work of sympathy and service was a work of and for God.

Professor Fearon Halliday has drawn attention to the large number in our Evangelical Churches whose religion is real, whose beliefs are Evangelical and who, nevertheless, have not experienced the 'mystical states of consciousness' by which James defines personal religion. "There are many", he writes, "in the ministry and in the churches, who while believing in God, and indeed believing in Him with a conviction which they would not yield, have yet no sense of His reality. We have known people who have prayed for twenty years and more without any sense they were praying to One who heard. These people are often in a position of responsibility in religious work. They speak about the love of God, the Father, with great intensity. They are not dishonest when they say that they are sure that that love is a fact, but the joy that comes from personal realisation, from the drawing out of the feeling interest, they do not know. The numbers of such cases would seem very great, and the causes which produce this lack of feeling in them will often account for the apparent irreligion of others."[1]

[1] *Psychology and Religious Experience*, pp. 32-3.

These are what we would call the non-mystical type of Evangelical; and they are probably in a majority in our churches. The conviction with which they hold their beliefs is just as real as that produced by the mystic intuition though it may lack the emotional warmth. They are, as a rule, among the most loyal and dependable of members; and many of them are our leading administrators. The spiritual unity of their lives is rooted in the rational and moral need; and generally this kind of unity gives a more comprehensive harmony to behaviour tendencies. Having had no deep plunge into sin, all their behaviour impulses tend to be incorporated into their organised personality; and the objects of desire are predetermined by upbringing and religious ideals. On the other hand, in those who have plunged into sin there is nearly always found a tendency to give the bodily appetites which led them into sin a subordinate place in their psychic makeup. It is true that the experience rooted in feeling gives a more subjective certitude; but it is more liable to ebb and flow than the religious experience whose foundations are in the need for rational unity.

James, it would seem, should have taken account of this large class of believers. Many of them are among our best philosophical and theological thinkers; and it is they, we believe, who provide the thought element in evangelical religion which preserves it from the dangers of hysteria. In evangelical thinkers the feeling element may be rich and deep, but it is connected more with the convictions of objective realities than with the sense of personal relations. Dr. Uren would class with this type the Old Testament prophets, and such stalwarts of Evangelicalism as Calvin, John Knox, and even Jonathan Edwards.[1] In the same class we would place the Anglican theologians of strong evangelical cast of mind, Dean Matthews, Canon Quick, Canon Raven, and Canon Storr. Dr. Dale, whose volume on the Atonement held the field so long, must also be placed here.

We are anxious to guard against the exclusion from evangeli-

[1] *Recent Religious Psychology*, p. 75.

cal experience of Salvation, of the Cross and the Risen Christ, those whose experience of the central facts of evangelical faith did not begin nor culminate in a dramatic crisis due to sin. The struggle with doubt is just as real as that with sin, and may be as exhausting; and the victory of a faith rooted in thought is as deep and real as any recorded in the annals of evangelical revivals.

Nothing that we have written must be taken as in any way an attempt to belittle the 'trophies of His grace' held up by writers on Conversion. The power of evangelical religion to 'make the vilest clean' is too well attested for anything we have written to rob these triumphs of their glory. In our own experience we have seen too many of these 'miracles' of grace to permit of the slightest doubt of their reality, and in our next chapter we shall deal with them. All we desire to emphasise is that there are varieties of evangelical experience; such varieties as to make us believe that Evangelicalism is comprehensive enough to meet the religious needs of all.

CHAPTER V

Salvation and its Problems: Conversion

IN our last chapter we studied the experience of those whose 'moment of vision' is followed by no dramatic struggle; but whose re-orientation is found either in the quest for truth, for social re-construction, or in a deliberate decision to seek a more effective moral and spiritual life in association with the Church. In few of them was there found any deep sense of guilt, or melancholy feeling of alienation from God. They escape from themselves almost entirely and become increasingly object-centred; and their thought, service, and worship increasingly more objective.

It is not our object to go over the well-worn ground of the sudden and dramatic struggle approximating to a psycho-neurosis in those whose 'moment of vision' has lit up their alienation from God; or revealed some deep cleavage in their hearts; or made them aware of incompatible motives struggling for the mastery of the whole personality. In their case conversion gives them an entirely new personality in the sense that their whole attitude to God, the World, and the Soul is permanently changed. We desire to get at the psychology of the sense of need, the conviction of sin, the forgiveness that brings to the soul peace, the beliefs on which the new life comes to rest, and the processes by which sanctification becomes a reality.

Nevertheless, a chapter must be given to a spiritual experience which if not so frequent as in the period from which Professor James drew his illustrations is still frequent enough to demand some kind of psychological explanation. Much water has flowed under the bridge since James wrote:

"Now if you ask of psychology just *how* the excitement shifts in a man's mental system, and *why* aims that were peripheral become at a certain moment central, psychology has to reply that although she can give a general description of what happens, she is unable in a given case to account accurately for all the single forces at work. Neither an outside observer nor a Subject who undergoes the process can explain fully how particular experiences are able to change one's centre of energy so decisively, or why they so often have to bide their hour to do so. We have a thought, or we perform an act, repeatedly, but on a certain day the real meaning of the thought peals through us for the first time, or the act has suddenly turned into a moral impossibility. All we know is that there are dead feelings, dead ideas, and cold beliefs, and there are hot and live ones; and when one grows hot and alive within us, everything has to re-crystallise about it. We may say that the heat and liveliness mean only the 'motor efficacy', long deferred but now operative, of the idea; but such talk itself is only circumlocution, for whence the sudden motor efficacy? And our explanations then get so vague and general that one realises all the more the intense individuality of the whole phenomenon."[1]

If all that James meant by this statement was that we are still ignorant as to how to bring about a conversion in a particular case, then the statement still holds true. We do know more, however, about the mental processes involved. The doctrines of the Unconscious and Repression have outdated many paragraphs in *The Varieties of Religious Experience*. Nevertheless, how to elicit the intuition that turns the 'dead feelings, dead ideas and cold beliefs into hot and live ones' is still beyond the technique of psychology or psychotherapy. Here psychology must give way to theology for the present at least. Here, if anywhere, the doctrine of the Holy Spirit, as we have it in John's Gospel, is our only explanation.

Freud tells us, with his usual candour, how when he began psycho-analysis, he thought he had just to tell the patient what was causing his distress for the patient to understand and the

[1] *The Varieties*, pp. 196-7.

symptoms to disappear. Alas, he learned, as we all had to learn, that it is one thing for the psychotherapist or the minister of religion to know what is wrong in the life of a soul, and another thing for that soul to know it. Freud says there is a *knowing* and *a knowing;* knowledge may lie over against our personality without modifying it in the least. Not only so, but the deeper researches of psychological practice show us that an individual may not be suffering so much from a complex as from a totally wrong attitude of his personality as a whole to moral and spiritual reality.

An illustration from Dr. Jung's *Modern Man in Search of a Soul* will make our meaning plain. He is explaining the postulate of modern analytical psychology that the patient must be treated as a whole and that a thorough cure cannot be expected from a treatment restricted to the trouble itself.

"I am reminded", he says, "of a case which is very instructive in this connection. It concerns a highly intelligent young man who had worked out a detailed analysis of his own neurosis after a serious study of medical literature. He brought me his findings in the form of a precise and well-written monograph fit for publication, and asked me to read the manuscript and to tell him why he was not cured. He should have been according to the verdict of science as he understood it. After reading his monograph I was forced to grant him, that if it were only a question of insight into the causal connections of a neurosis, he should in all truth be cured. Since he was not, I suppose this must be due to the fact that his attitude to life was somehow fundamentally wrong—though I had to admit that his symptoms did not betray it. In reading his account of his life I had noticed that he often spent his winters at St. Moritz or Nice. I therefore asked him who paid for these holidays, and it thereupon came out that a poor school teacher who loved him had cruelly deprived herself to indulge the young man in these visits to pleasure-resorts. His want of conscience was the cause of his neurosis, and it is not hard to see why scientific understanding failed to help him. His fundamental error lay in his moral attitude."[1]

[1] *Modern Man in Search of a Soul*, p. 223.

Thus it is not enough to talk in terms of 'dead feelings and dead ideas and cold beliefs and hot and live ones'; the personality as a whole is involved. Our problem even in psychotherapy but always in Evangelism is how to awaken the personality as a whole. The personality as a whole—which must not be confused with the whole personality—is what evangelical theology calls the Soul. It is to the personality what life is to the organism; it permeates the mass of impulse, emotion, thought and desire, it is not an entity standing over against our personality; it is the principle that gives unity to our psychic make-up just as life gives unity to the organism. It is the man. It is the Subject of which alone character can be predicated. Sentiments are not character, not even the sum total; neither singly nor collectively can we predicate character of the sentiments; the Subject alone has character as James Ward pointed out long ago.

It is this Subject, this Soul, this personality as a whole, that is involved in conversion. Conversion is not simply the eradication of a complex or the correction of a few faults. The whole attitude to moral and spiritual reality is changed. Conversion, whether slow and gradual or sudden and dramatic is a New Birth in the literal sense of the term. The very Soul comes to birth; the biological and perceptual levels of mental life are transcended; behaviour patterns whether innate or acquired become subject to the soul's purposes and spiritual ends. As we shall see later we may have 'conversions' which really do not involve the personality as a whole; the inner organisation may change but the attitude of the soul remains almost unaffected.

The Sense of Need and Reconciliation

We have spoken of the Sense of Need as arising in the 'moment of vision' when discord, dissatisfaction, the ineffectiveness of our lives are experienced. The sense of need is for a felt harmony of experience with feeling. Every 'moment of vision' reveals some disharmony, and the mind is spontaneously driven to seek unity. The sense of need therefore is truly connoted by the phrase 'The Need of Reconciliation'. The individual whose 'moment of vision' revealed a disharmony between his beliefs and knowledge or experience sets out to find a reconciliation between belief and knowledge, between experience and belief; so the individual who sets out on the social quest to seek a form of society that will reconcile his belief in a 'kingdom of God' with an actual social order. Reconciliation with Reality in its various forms is what the thoughtful, the lovers of men, and those who find a more effective life in the Church are ever seeking. The religious term, Reconciliation, covers every form of seeking.

In modern psychology, the term 'adjustment' is used for this same experience. Psychotherapy itself, might be defined as the therapy whereby the unadjusted or mal-adjusted are helped by psychological methods to become adjusted to reality as it expresses itself in our environment or in the imperious demands of our nature. But to be adjusted to reality is not simply to tolerate what we cannot escape. It is a positive acceptance by the personality of the necessary conditions in which we must live our lives. The individual has to know himself, and to accept himself, and he has to adjust himself to the various forms in which reality manifests itself—political, social, moral and spiritual. He must adjust himself—become reconciled—to certain limitations of his freedom if he is to live comfortably in a politically ordered society; he must adjust himself—become reconciled—to equating his desires to the demands of his moral consciousness if he is to enjoy the respect of others and respect himself; he must adjust himself—become reconciled—to whatever he believes lies behind this universe if he is to experience no alienation from God, and indeed if he is to have real stability of will. This adjustment to God is becoming more important in modern psychological theories of the development of personality. It is now realised that it is this last adjustment that is the most vital.[1]

[1] See *Psychological Medicine*, by Drs. Rees and Harris; chapter on Personality.

In many ways, the term reconciliation is more fitted than the term adjustment to express what we all seek and need. To be unadjusted does not necessarily imply any element of rebellion within the psychic make-up against the necessity of adjustment; indeed many who seek the psychotherapist suffer from ignorance of life and themselves rather than from divisive elements in their minds. These patients can be made aware of not fitting into things, and the removal of their ignorance clears the way for a perfect psychological adjustment. But those whose sense of need arises in a felt discord or dissatisfaction always have elements within them that are opposed to the reality with which they must become adjusted if they are to be free from conflict or realise a more effective spiritual life. 'The carnal mind is enmity against God' is no mere cant phrase; it expresses a psychological reality with which every psychotherapist has to deal. There is an element which resists adjustment. In the psycho-neuroses these rebellious elements are as a rule unconscious, and it is the work of the psychotherapist to bring them into consciousness and then help the patient to make an adjustment in which the incompatible motives will be reconciled. In other words, the patient has to become reconciled to reality; his opposition must be broken down; his attitude to the restraining processes within himself and the sanctions which enforce the restraining forces must be changed. It is better, however, to allow psychotherapy to use its own terms, and a colourless term like adjustment with no religious significance or associations is more suited to science than reconciliation.

Reconciliation expresses accurately what must happen in those whose sense of need gives rise to a deep sense of sin. In saying this we are not speaking theologically. Dr. Denney says truly: "The need of reconciliation is given in the fact of alienation and estrangement. Man requires to be put right with God because, as a matter of fact, he is not right with Him." Here we have psychology and theology together, the first sentence being a purely psychological statement, the second a theological. We are only concerned with those whose sense of need lies in the fact that they are *conscious* of estrangement and alienation from God; and in this chapter with those who feel that their estrangement is due to sin. The psycho-neurotic patient may be wholly unconscious of the fact that he needs adjustment; more often he feels that the environment needs to be changed rather than himself. But the soul made aware of the discord, a discord due to a cleavage within himself, is conscious of guilt, conscious that in one way or another he is himself responsible for his condition. The incompatible motives that rack his will and tear his feelings are conscious. He is conscious of that 'body of death', of 'the flesh warring against the spirit and the spirit against the flesh'. He is not only conscious of the alienation and estrangement from God, but of the factors that create the alienation.

Here we have the fundamental difference between the psycho-neurotic and the truly religious conflict. The psycho-neurotic patient has always unconscious elements; he is always trying to escape from his conflict. Unconsciously, he is seeking the *pleasure without the guilt*;[1] and this the prohibitive conscience will not allow. The religious patient is seeking to *resolve his conflict*, to renounce the pleasure which the sinful tendency offers; he is not so much seeking to hate the evil as to love the good. The psycho-neurotic on the other hand is seeking to escape from his symptoms instead of from the offending tendencies. Many seek the psychotherapist in the hope that he will condone the offending tendencies; and great resistance is set up when he tries to make them realise that the offending tendencies are inconsistent with psychological growth or an enlarging personality.

To understand this fundamental difference between psychological illness and the truly religious conflict that precedes the more dramatic forms of conversion we must digress and explicate the concepts of Repression and the Unconscious.

[1] Stekel, *Conditions of Nervous Anxiety and their Treatment*, Introductory chapter.

Meaning of Repression and the Unconscious Mind

Repression has been defined simply by Dr. David Yellowlees as a 'refusal to see something and not a refusal to do something'. It is an active process of the mind whereby something unpleasant is kept from the focus of conscious attention. *The attention is diverted to something else.* We are all familiar with the conscious act of diverting our attention from some source of worry in order to get on with our job; of attempting to forget something that tends to bring anxiety or guilt into our conscious mind; of turning our minds away from some memory tinged with regret, pain and even guilt. If we analyse what is happening in such a process of conscious diversion of the attention, we find that the emotion, idea or memory from which we try to divert the attention tends to force its way into consciousness spontaneously; in other words, it is dynamic. The doctrine of repression asserts that although we may divert the attention, we do not rob the emotion, the idea or memory of its dynamic nature. Suggestion or Christian Science or Faith-healing may help us to divert our attention from the symptoms of an active physical disease, but the pathological process is not altered; the disease will still ravage the organism. In the same way the repressed element in the subconscious mind is not altered; it still strives to enter consciousness and attract our attention. It is not simply a matter of an element in the unconscious being active; the mind is also active in diverting the attention. There is thus an upward force from the element striving to enter consciousness and attract our attention; and a downward force keeping it from consciousness. If we analyse further we find that the mind is not only active in keeping the repressed element from consciousness, but the act of diverting the attention is twofold in its nature—it exerts energy to keep the element down and to keep the conscious mind away from it. Here is a simple illustration: We may be in a tram-car and we see someone we think we have seen before; we look at him for a minute or two, and then become conscious that we might be thought rude in staring at a fellow-passenger. We look away from him;

but we are conscious that conation is involved; there is the impulse to keep looking. Thus the mind represses the emotion, idea or memory; the repressed element strives to enter consciousness; and the mind keeps diverting the attention.

In the psycho-neuroses this process of repression has become unconscious; the conflict of keeping the element out of consciousness and diverting the attention is as active as ever and indeed tends to become more active with time. This is the conflict which causes the whole trouble.

It was the discovery of this process more than the discovery of what is called the Unconscious Mind which is Freud's great contribution. As Professor Laird has pointed out, we have always been more or less aware of the unconscious mind, in the sense that we *knew* 'facts of our nature which are of a different character from that which, when we think of it, we take ourselves to have'. Laird, however, confuses this kind of unconscious when he argues that much of the doctrine of the unconscious of Freud does not differ from old opinions. He instances a statement of Dr. Ernest Jones whom he quotes as follows: "It is the people with secret attractions to various temptations who busy themselves most with removing these temptations from other people; really they are defending themselves under pretext of defending others because at heart they fear their own weakness". "This," says Laird, "has been known for a very long time, and has been expressed quite sufficiently. Thus, take King Lear: 'Look with thine ears: see how yond justice rails upon yond simple thief. Hark, in thine ear: change places; and, handy-dandy, which is the justice, which is the thief?' . . ." Again he quotes:

> "Thou rascal beadle, hold thy bloody hand!
> Why dost thou lash that whore? Strip thine own back;
> Thou hotly lust'st to use her in that kind
> For which thou whipp'st her. . . .
> Get thee glass eyes:
> And like a scurvy politician, seem
> To see the things thou dost not."

Dr. Laird's comment is: "As is plain from these quotations, three things may be meant by argument of this species: first, that like the hangman, we know the fact well enough; second, that although it is true, we do not know it and could not acknowledge it.

"The first of these is conscious hypocrisy and needs no special mention. Instances of the second variety in their extreme form, may very well be hypocrisy, and perhaps a commoner form of it. For the most part, however, what is meant is a degree of self-deception that is 'indifferent honest', and normally to be expected. . . .

"The third of these arguments seems much more revolutionary, for it maintains that these secret inclinations are necessarily concealed from the agent himself."[1]

Now, Professor Laird is right as far as he goes; but we think he misses the essential idea of Dr. Jones, and indeed in other writings on the unconscious, we think Dr. Laird has failed to give full value to the discovery of repression as an unconscious process having a definite positive influence upon behaviour. It is perfectly true that many a magistrate who rails at the thief before him is no better. But that fact is not a source of conflict within the magistrate's mind! So many a beadle might lust after a woman whom he is paid to whip, but again that is not a source of disturbing conflict within him. Secret inclinations we all may have; but they are not held down by an opposite tendency; our attention is diverted from them because they are contrary to something in our personality. They may be waiting their time when they need not be secret.

The people Jones is thinking about *must* remove temptations from others as a method of diverting the attention from the fact that they have the same tendencies themselves. The magistrate is not on the bench to keep him from thieving, nor even to hide the fact that he has thieving tendencies; nor is the beadle whipping the woman to prove to himself and others that he has no lust.

Freud's doctrine of the Unconscious cannot be understood unless the process of repression is fully realised. Freud's

[1] Laird, *A Study in Moral Theory;* see whole of chapter vii.

contribution here is, that tendencies which the conscious mind refuses to face, which have even been repressed before they entered consciousness, are still striving to express themselves in the unconscious mind, still striving to enter consciousness and attract attention to themselves. The repressing force is not merely another tendency like fear; it is the action of the personality as a whole. It is the soul's attempt to preserve its morally organised personality.

The Unconscious,[1] then, is not to be confused with latent appetite, feelings or impulses. Latent in us all there are memories of the past, appetites, which for the time being are quiescent; potential feelings which may flare up at the touch of some stimulus; sentiments and interests which are the potential sources of behaviour. They are potential because, for the time being, they are not linked with any kinetic purposive behaviour in which the mind is engaged. They are latent, not dynamic.

The Unconscious of modern psychology, however, is dynamic; the impulses are striving to attract attention through feeling or idea. The mind refuses to see them, represses them, refuses to acknowledge them. The dynamic energy is then diverted into physical, mental or spiritual symptoms. The diversion is purposive; it is a means of defence against the intrusion into consciousness of the ideas, emotions, temptations or the self-condemnation which the repressed elements would arouse if present in the conscious mind.

Illustrations will help us to understand why we repress and how the repressed elements show their activity.

We were asked to see a young woman with a functional tremor in her arm. Medical examination had showed no lesion of the nervous system. Her father, a devout Roman Catholic, had given her a book of a devotional and moral kind in which it was stated that there was one part of the body which should not be touched except for purposes of cleanli-

[1] See *A General Selection from the Works of Sigmund Freud*, pp. 54–62. Also *Introductory Lectures on Psychoanalysis: The Freudian Wish*, by E. B. Holt.

ness. For a long time the woman had indulged in masturbation apparently without any conscious guilt. She suddenly felt supremely conscious of guilt and fear regarding the habit; the temptation to self-stimulation overcame her again and again, and there was a deepening of guilt. Apparently she was unable to deal with the habit in consciousness and repressed the tendency. Her arm later began to tremble, until finally she practically lost all use of it. She was overwhelmed with anxiety, guilt and fear although there had been no masturbation for a long time.

What had happened? The impulse to masturbate was still dynamic; the tendency was still unconsciously striving to enter consciousness; the upward force of the tendency and the downward thrust of repression, inhibited the normal use of the arm, and anxiety about the arm diverted her attention from the offending tendency. When the young woman was helped to realise what was happening the use of her arm came back spontaneously; and her confessor helped her to deal with the temptation in consciousness, and use her religion to resolve her conflict, and to give her a new attitude to the demands of her own nature.

A married woman who had been very happy in her home near London had come to a comparatively dull town in the Midlands. Her husband had been active in municipal life and as a consequence her interests had been widened owing to social contacts with people of greater culture than herself. She had also left a married daughter who had added interest of a different kind. Not long after her husband was transferred through promotion to the Midlands, she developed a severe cold with throat symptoms which made it difficult for her to swallow. The cold cleared up. As far as her medical adviser could observe the inflammation in the throat had disappeared and he could not find any obstruction. But she still found difficulty in swallowing; and began to worry and become anxious. Two or three specialists examined her but could find no signs of physical disease to account for her difficulty. She was sent to us.

We found that often her husband, while in the old home near London, had told her of applications of the men under him for a transfer to another district owing to the ill-health of their wives. What connection had that piece of information with her trouble?

The connection was unconscious; but nevertheless effective. If she could prove that the district did not agree with her constitution, her husband would be sent back to London or near. Naturally it would be exceedingly unpleasant for her to acknowledge that her private desires were impeding her husband's advancement. The desire to get back to London was not a mere regret that her husband's promotion had deprived her of many things she liked but active. Had she acknowledged the deprivation and adjusted herself to it, or even kept it conscious in the hope that he might get another promotion and transfer back, there would have been no trouble. She did not desire to be ill; but her desire to get back to London could, she thought unconsciously, best be realised by her illness. The desire for the change was the repressed motive of her illness. She had to become adjusted to the fact that she could not have the advantages of her husband's promotion and dictate where she should live.

This is not the place to deal with all the objections which have been raised against the concept of the Unconscious. It may be objected that these two women got more unhappiness out of the way they attempted to resolve their conflict than the original difficulty could have given them. That is perfectly true. But the Unconscious is not oriented to reality. Nevertheless, its action is perfectly intelligible and in a sense logical. The first woman could not bear the guilt of what her Church calls mortal sin; yet she was unable to endure the tension set up by the temptation. The refusal to see her temptation meant for her conscious mind that it was not there. But the impulse remained unmodified and dynamic; its energy reached consciousness as symptoms; and the guilt of the active impulse, which itself was not conscious, was there in her mind though she could not refer to it. These inferences seem inevitable

From the second illustration must we not conclude that the woman's excessive anxiety and worry about the trouble she was giving her husband—which was far greater than the natural anxiety caused by her difficulty in swallowing—was due to the unconscious awareness, if we may state a paradox, of her ego-centricity which preferred her private comfort to her husband's welfare?

Psycho-Neurosis and Conversion

A psycho-neurosis is one way of dealing with a conflict between incompatible motives; conversion is another. They must not be confused. Conversion resolves the conflict; a psycho-neurosis is an attempted escape from the conflict; it is a consequence of *the refusal to see* that the conflict must be resolved. In conversion the Soul is actively concerned to resolve the conflict; in a psycho-neurosis the personality is acting on the biological and childish psychological level—it is meeting a danger and not a challenge. In the psycho-neurosis the infantile prohibitive conscience is playing the dominant part; in Conversion the adult positive conscience is the main director.

If we contrast the conversion of Augustine with a psycho-neurosis caused by identically the same incompatible motives that divided his heart, this fundamental difference between a psycho-neurosis and conversion becomes clear. Augustine was perfectly cognisant of the incompatibility of his relations with his mistress with the peace of mind he sought. His adult moral consciousness gave no uncertain judgment regarding the morality of the association and the incompatibility of his Ego-centric lust with the service of God to which his mother urged him. The lust set up a conscious tension; the woman offered an immediate release and accompanying pleasure. While no modification of the impulse and desire took place, the activity of the desire and the presence of the attractive pleasure pushed every controlling idea to the margin of his mind, and the pleasure was indulged. Once the appetite was quiescent his moral consciousness set up another kind of tension—the tension of guilt, self-condemnation and the disturbance of his spiritual relationships with his mother, and with God. While his moral consciousness held the field, he was conscious not only of guilt, but of rebellion against God and a lack of power to deal with the rebellious tendency that brought his temptations and stimulated his lust. In Augustine there was no attempt at repression; there were alternative states of consciousness in which either the lust or the conscience held the forces of attention. While free from the attraction and looking at himself objectively, he was able to realise his weakness and the need of forgiveness, power and a new heart. It was the lust he desired to escape, not its consequences. And then came the moment of clear vision in which he saw his sin in its true perspective and realised its inconsistency with the moral aspirations of his soul. He made his decision, trusted God, felt His power, and was converted. His mind now became full of gratitude for the deliverance both from the sense of guilt, and the lust which aroused it. The impulses now became associated with this gratitude; the forgiveness created a new relationship to his sinful tendency, and in that new relationship he was able to seek holiness.

Here is a man who has been living with a woman not his wife. He had been brought up in a Christian home; worked in the Sunday school. He was unable to reconcile his life with the moral and religious standards he had consciously and unconsciously accepted. Instead of heeding the judgment of his moral consciousness, he tried to defy it; he attempted to convince himself that 'sex was just a convenience'; and refused to see that there was any conflict in his mind. He developed hysterical symptoms in the form of migraine, anxiety and fear; he felt he was not doing his job; blamed himself for many things which were of really little consequence. His sexual desires practically disappeared from consciousness.

This individual had the same conflict as Augustine; but he escaped from it into a psycho-neurosis instead of resolving it. When he refused to obey his adult conscience, his negative conscience came into power and repressed the incompatible motives—the motives of lust and self-respect. Though the infantile conscience could repress the impulses it could not modify them. His guilt expresses itself in his anxiety, fear, self-condemnation, inferiority feelings. His dreams were as lustful as his conscious life had been previously. He attempted to resolve his conflict on the psychological level; whereas a moral conflict of this kind can only be resolved on the moral level.

To those who have had practice in psychotherapy there can be no surprise that some psychologists have classified conversion with the psycho-neurosis. The conflict is identical; the incompatible motives, the sense of guilt, the sense of alienation from God, the sense of inferiority are similar in both. That is why Stekel can say with truth, "Every neurotic suffers from a bad conscience". There is that in his psychic make-up inconsistent with the moral ideals with which he has identified himself in the unconscious. His identification we designate for want of a better term as negative. His ideals are standards against which he must not sin; they are not ends he has assimilated or chosen. Hence Stekel's accurate description that the neurotic is always seeking the pleasure without the guilt. In many cases the patient is not only failing to assimilate the moral ideals his negative conscience prohibits him from violating, but positively rebelling against them. The rebellion shows itself in diverse ways in consciousness as well as being active in the unconscious. In the religious convert the positive conscience is more fully developed, and there is more assimilation of the moral ideals. The dramatic struggle is the outcome of the attempt to repress one of the incompatible tendencies, either the conscience or the offending or hindering impulses. Repression cannot take place, the positive conscience is too strong so that it compels the candidate for conversion to face his tendencies and resolve the conflict on the conscious level. An intuition is elicited which gives insight not only into the nature of the conflict (the resistances to and the attraction of Christian life), but to the grace, patience, mercy and forgiveness of God. The resistances are overcome; the new life is spontaneously adopted. The convert *sees* the better way, acknowledges it, embraces it; and though the solicitations of old impulses may continue for a time, steadily sanctification becomes a reality and the attraction of the old sins becomes no more than a memory.

A simple illustration may help us here. Let us suppose an inspector of schools is watching a teacher at work, say, giving a lesson on history. Detecting a faulty plan of presentation, he explains to the teacher how he would teach history. The teacher may feel that his own way is better and resent the implied criticism. But on the headmaster's instructions he is asked to teach his subject in the manner illustrated by the inspector. He does so, because he is compelled. Let us suppose, however, that while the inspector is illustrating his way of teaching, the teacher *sees* that it is a better way than his own; he teaches by the method showed him, not now because there is compulsion, but because he *sees* it is better.

The length of the dramatic struggle would seem to depend on two things. In the first place the stage of development of the positive conscience. To the degree that the conscience is negative and prohibitive resistance will be strong and prolonged; there will be a tendency to keep the offending and hindering tendencies out of consciousness altogether with accompanying guilt and fear. The positive conscience on the other hand will attempt to force them into consciousness in order to resolve them. The function of the positive conscience is not only to direct but to bring into consciousness and to the bar of moral judgment any tendency to behaviour contrary to the assimilated ideals. But the prohibitive conscience can do nothing but attempt to keep the offending tendencies out of consciousness. It is as if the prohibitive conscience afraid lest the offending tendencies coming in might mean temptation and a fall would prevent this by refusing them entrance.

In the second place, a good deal must depend on the time taken in the elicitation of the intuition. In so far as the individual passing through the struggle has the help of some understanding soul, the process will be quickened; but as we said above there is no technique by which we can elicit the intuition of God's mercy, grace and willingness to forgive. All that the best helper can do is to present the fact in this way and then in that until spontaneously the mind intuits the means of its own salvation and peace, and the difficulties which prevent the consummation.

Abnormal Phenomena in Conversion

Most writers on conversion have dealt at length with the abnormal phenomena which often accompany the experience of the dramatic struggle, and resultant experience of conversion. James thought that the phenomena were only found in persons of a psychopathic temperament. This psychopathic temperament, however, is not due to any neurological defect; it is caused by the emotional disturbances and unconscious conflicts which may have been repressed early in childhood. In most, if not in all those who have the psychopathic temperament, there will be found a strong prohibitive conscience. The tendency to repress will be unduly strong; and although repression is unsuccessful, the threats and fears and sense of guilt generated by this type of conscience, cause fearful distress. There can be no abnormal phenomena unless there is repression to some degree. The repression may not be exerted against offending tendencies to behaviour, but, as in St. Paul's case, against the intuition through which he would *see* that his whole system of beliefs and life was wrong. When we remember Paul's strong prohibitive conscience which made him a Pharisee of the Pharisees, there can be no doubt that his tenacious adherence to the Law was a defence against tendencies to behaviour contrary to the Law, which were for the most part unconscious in his pre-Christian days, but perfectly conscious after his experience on the road to Damascus. The compulsion of that negative conscience kept him strictly to the Law. It was the schoolmaster leading him to Christ; but it was also a policeman daring him to violate the Law. The Law lay over against Paul's personality; and one may be certain that the war between the flesh and the spirit which he can acknowledge in his converted days, was largely repressed in his preconverted days. Naturally, one who was a leader of the Pharisees, and an acknowledged leader, who had even persecuted the Christians would resist the intuition that his whole attitude to life was wrong, and that his zeal for the Law was no more than a self-defence. His prestige was at stake as well as self-regard. There was a strong tendency to repress what his intuition was forcing upon him. Hence the auditory and visual hallucinations. From the psychological point of view, they were the organic language of the unconscious. Once the resistance was overcome, and the intuition allowed to work its work upon his mind and soul, Paul passed from the purely negative form of conscience to the purely positive. Not the Law, but the principles of the Law, became the spontaneous direction of his behaviour tendencies. He walked in the spirit of the Law, and thus there was no fear of the tendency to fulfil the lusts of the flesh. The Law by which he had guarded himself rather than guided himself instead of being compulsively complied with, was now obeyed as a son obeys his father whom he trusts and loves. 'Love is the fulfilling of the Law'. If one loves honesty one needs no law or fear of the law to keep one from stealing; the idea of theft simply does not enter the mind. If one loves chastity, one needs no commandment against adultery. Just because the Law had lain externally over against his personality, the slightest variation from it would bring guilt and fear. Once it was assimilated, and had become incorporated in his positive conscience, a violation of it would bring shame but not fear, repentance and not morbid guilt, because his mind had not consented to the violation. He could acknowledge whatever tendencies warred against the spirit, for he was not now afraid of them, believing that Christ was able to save him to the uttermost, and to keep that which he had committed unto Him.

But the experience of Paul, however, would need a volume to itself, and fascinating as it is to attempt to understand Paul in the light of the newer psychological knowledge, we must resist the temptation. All we are concerned with at the moment is the abnormal phenomena that accompanied his conversion.

It would be a mistake to explain the struggle so severe as to produce hallucinations in Paul simply as a struggle to resist the intuition, or as an outcome of the tendency to preserve his prestige with his fellow-Jews. If we are right in thinking that there was a strong repressive tendency in his make-up, then he would really be afraid to be free, afraid to trust Christ's grace and power to control his behaviour tendencies; he would really, albeit unconsciously, tend to trust the prohibitive conscience. Paul's moral personality was strongly organised before conversion, although it was narrow and gaunt. Hence his struggle, unlike Augustine's, was not a struggle between a strongly-knit-together personality and rebellious lusts offering pleasure. Nevertheless we should not say it was a happy personality. His was an unhappy holiness rather than the holy happiness which characterised his Christian life. It is doubtful whether he could have said before conversion, "We are more than conquerors". No doubt his firm allegiance to the Law gave him a strong capacity for negative self-control; but not to experience the glorious victory expressed in the phrase, 'more than conquerors'.

It is probable that to this particular psychological change we must look for the explanation of Paul's later contrast between Law and Grace. If we are right in thinking that Paul's Pharisaism was of the nature of a self-defence reaction against behaviour tendencies to which the sense of guilt had been attached, these tendencies would set up a tense conflict within the unconscious, because they would be striving to enter consciousness. To divert his attention from their compulsive entrance he had to concentrate his energy on the insistence of the Law as that from which there must be no deviation. In preaching to others he was in reality saving himself. The inner demand of his prohibitive conscience that he keep the Law was projected upon others. He must shut out of the conscious mind his own contrary tendencies, but they had their revenge by compelling him to busy himself with the Law. What enraged him in the disregard of the Law by others, was in reality his own instability in regard to the Law. Persecution is always the outcome of an inward fear of the very ideas that enrage us; the persecutor of heretics is always an unconscious arch-heretic. Paul's zeal for the Law was strictly correlated with inward fears of tendencies contrary to the Law. Paul was a prisoner of the Law, not a freeman by the Law. He could not sing with the Psalmist: "Thy statutes have become my songs in the house of my pilgrimage". As we have said, the Law lay over against his personality restraining it but not modifying it. To the Psalmist, the Law gave both motive and direction to his behaviour tendencies, in Paul the Law simply barred the outlet of his offending tendencies.

Paul's conversion liberated him from the unconscious fear of the Law. His behaviour tendencies, instead of being held in leash by its external authority, became modified and controlled by his personality as a whole, or as he would have put it: he was indwelt by Christ: "I live, yet no more I, but Christ liveth in me". Paul referred to this change as due to Grace. Law and Grace denote the two forms of behaviour control; the former is compulsion exerted by the prohibitive conscience re-enforced by fear; the latter is motivation and direction by the positive conscience re-enforced by love. The intuition that the latter is the better way, that he had not been really obeying the Law, but had only been unconsciously compelled to guard against breaking it, came to him as a self-liberating revelation. No one who has seen a soul struggling, as Paul struggled, to keep the Law can fail to understand his amazement that the Galatians should go back to the 'beggarly elements' when once they had known the freedom from the Law wherewith Christ made them free. Law is the symbol of the prohibitive conscience that compels the individual to keep every 'jot and tittle' of the Law; Grace is the symbol, not of sitting loose to the Law,—which was the attitude of Anti-nomianism—but of adjustment to and whole-hearted acceptance of the Law.

The Phenomena Accompanying Paul's Conversion

To understand the phenomena accompanying Paul's conversion, or indeed those accompanying any conversion, we must acquaint ourselves with the process of defence against the admittance to the conscious mind of unacceptable tendencies. We have already seen how the process, known as Over-compensation, accounts for Paul's zeal for the Law; the process we are now to consider is named Projection, and it plays a great part in the accusations, with which many are attacked, in the pre-conversion struggle as well as in the phenomena of visual and auditory hallucination.

Over-compensation diverts our attention from tendencies within ourselves by fanatical activity against these same tendencies in others. Projection is the process by which we tend to attribute to other people our own repressed mental content. Illustration will help us here.

We had to see a young man with auditory hallucinations. Sometimes he heard voices from his neighbour's house accusing him of immorality; at other times the voices would urge him to some rash act. On hearing the voices he would tremble, become pugnacious and shout back. He had the further idea that people could tell what he was thinking. The trouble began in France, during the Great War.

Analysis showed that the temptation to sexual indulgence was strong, and after one experience of this kind he began to worry about his sisters. He repressed the whole sexual experience; it became dissociated entirely from his conscious mind. The auditory hallucinations were explained by projection—the accusing voice of his own conscience which he had refused to hear, and the guilt which he could not bear were projected upon the outside world.

This illustration could be multiplied many times. The self-criticism we refuse to accept we project upon others; and if the repressed tendency has strong guilt attached to it, it will come back in the form of *delusions of reference*, accusing voices, threats of punishment, or the feeling that we are forsaken of God.

The repressed voice of self-reproach comes back to us through this process.

Such a process helps us immensely to understand the abnormal phenomena which so often accompany conversion, or rather the struggle towards it.

Let us return to Paul. As we saw there were various contending elements. There was strong resistance to the intuition which his quick intelligence could not fail to grasp, had there been no resistance. The strong light and the blindness indicate the strength of both the conflicting tendencies; there was the tendency to see and accept the intuition as a veritable light from heaven; there was the functional blindness, the organic language of his refusal to see the truth. The 'Saul, Saul, why persecutest thou me?' is the projection of his repressed guilt regarding the persecution of the Christians; while the 'it is hard for thee to kick against the pricks', if genuine—it is omitted in some versions—is the projection of his own state of mind regarding the throwing off of the urge to cast in his lot with the Christians. The truth he was afraid to see, the repressed guilt of his conduct, the unconscious struggle to surrender to Christ, all came back to consciousness through the process of projection. The combined resistance of his self-regard, and the strong tendency to trust to his prohibitive conscience as his behaviour control rather than the Christ of whom the Christians spoke, were the strong factors of the repressing forces. As we have already said, he was afraid to be free, an exceedingly common state of mind in those who have long been under the compulsion of a negative conscience.

Although the intuition was accepted, Paul's struggle did not cease; and we can be sure that in Arabia to which he retired almost immediately after his experience on the Road to Damascus and the recovery of his sight, the victory was finally won. There the intuition would be grounded, made a part, as Professor Stout would say, of the *apperceptive mass;* his changed views regarding the Law as the instrument of Salvation would be assimilated; and the transference of his unconscious faith in the power of the prohibitive conscience to the power of Christ, which is Salvation from the psychological point of view, would be accomplished.

That Paul's rebellious tendencies were strong, that the prohibitive conscience could still exert itself even after his conversion may be shown from various sayings in his Epistles. "Who shall deliver me from the body of this death? I thank God through Jesus Christ, our Lord." Sometimes he was afraid that the flesh warring against the spirit would be too much for him, for does he not fear, "lest having preached to others I myself should be a castaway?"

From the psychological point of view Paul became more and more self-possessed with the increase of faith; in religious language he became more sanctified. In other words, his behaviour tendencies, his intellectual and emotional resources became increasingly at his disposal to send outwards on his task of winning men for Christ. From the theological point of view he became more Christ-possessed; his Ego-centricity became wholly Christo-centricity. To the end he was conscious of what the struggle had meant to him; his behaviour tendencies apparently often aroused his prohibitive conscience; but at the last he could say: 'I have fought a good fight'. The intuition does not seem to have wavered, however, after the first struggle to resist it. His statement, 'I was not disobedient unto the heavenly vision' indicates that the 'will to believe' had to be exerted even to accept that.

Paul's conversion is one of the most interesting to the psychologist. It is the conversion of an educated man; a new intuition had to be elicited and accepted; his strong condemnation of what was contrary to the Law had to be replaced by a Law assimilated—the Law of Grace. Unlike St. Augustine, he does not seem to have been much troubled by the appeal of bodily appetite; but it is possible that he had attached to sensual appetite what in psycho-analysis is called 'unpleasure', that is why the sensual appetites had no appeal for Paul; they called up unpleasant emotions rather than desire for their satisfaction. Nevertheless, their physiological activity would be experienced by Paul and would set up some degree of psychological tension.

It is this association of 'unpleasure' with his sex that accounts for his attitude to that activity and not a repressed sex complex as some have asserted.

Over-compensation and Projection will account for most if not all the phenomena we meet in these dramatic struggles to religious harmony. The compulsive ideas, like Bunyan's 'Sell Christ', are really the projection of the ego's resistance to the surrender of its pleasure to the control of either the prohibitive or positive conscience. Such compulsive thoughts terrify the 'sick soul' for they generate the beliefs that they are past Salvation. We find in all such, periods when they can experience no love for God, no desire for Salvation, and yet simultaneously the awful fear that they have either sinned against the Holy Ghost, or that God has cast them off for ever. On the other hand, there seem to be periods when they can control their pleasure tendencies; the prohibitive conscience retires to the background, and the freedom from its threats and fears gives them a negative happiness. But these periods are short-lived. Not until they acknowledge the pleasure tendencies and surrender them do they find peace of conscience and positive happiness. The psychotherapist deals with many of these patients. They are the type that Dr. Jung had in mind when he wrote: "But what will he (the doctor) do when he sees only too clearly why his patient is ill; when he sees it arises from his having no love, but only sexuality; no faith, because he is afraid to grope in the dark; no hope, because he is disillusioned by the world and by life; and no understanding, because he has failed to read the meaning of his own existence?"[1] It is of the same type of patient he writes in the following passage: "Among all my patients in the second half of life—that is to say, over thirty-five, there has not been one whose problem in the last resort was not one of finding a religious outlook on life. It is safe to say that every one of them fell ill because he had lost that which the living religions of every age have given to their followers, and none of them has been really healed who did not regain his religious outlook."[2]

[1] *Modern Man in Search of a Soul*, p. 260. [2] *Ibid.*, p. 264.

Quasi Conversions

This chapter has far exceeded our original intention, but before we say a final word about conversion, it will be well for us to note that not all conversions lead to a happy result. There are many whose offending tendencies are only displaced and not modified; and there are many whose 'conversion' only strengthens the prohibitive barriers to wrong-doing instead of breaking them down and giving them a new form of control. In these latter cases we may have a definite change; the converts become puritanic where they were lax, but they never know the freedom wherewith Christ makes us free.

Displacement of tendencies is a commonplace phenomenon to the psychotherapist. We may take away a particular fear today, only to find that the patient has migraine tomorrow. The patient is changed but not improved.

This tendency is well brought out in an illustration which I borrow from Dr. Northridge. He tells of an open-air preacher he often passed "whose facial expression would commend religion to no one. He is bitter and cynical in the extreme. His only Gospel is one of fire and brimstone, and he regularly declares that God has commissioned him to preach this and no other Gospel. It is difficult to understand how a man can take such evident pleasure in the eternal torture of the souls of others, but psychology furnishes the explanation. Before his conversion this man was dominated by irrational hatreds. The change that he experienced did not involve the removal of these impulses. They continued in a new form. For bitterness and hatred are the same whether they express themselves in the guise of religion or not.

"What happened in this man's case was that the natural expression of the cruel impulses was checked, chiefly because they were in conflict with the ordinary standards of social life; but they found a new outlet in the idea of a God who takes pleasure in punishment. In the thought and proclamation of this he finds constant satisfaction."[1]

[1] *Recent Psychology and Evangelistic Preaching*, pp. 63-4.

Here also we find the explanation of back-sliding in those who have been 'converted' at revival meetings. In the emotional atmosphere the rational, controlling forces are apt to be dissociated for the time being. The prohibitive conscience is quickened by fear and temporarily strengthened so as to bring into consciousness an acute but short-lived sense of guilt which motivates a 'decision'. There is no quickened insight into the nature of sin or the holiness of God. For a short time there is freedom from the old temptations and a consequent elation which is mistaken for joy in God and the new life. Then gradually or suddenly the old tendencies and weaknesses assert themselves and because there is no real change of attitude to them there is a quick 'fall from grace'.

Sometimes we find men and women with over-sensitive prohibitive conscience unconsciously seeking for a religion that will banish their offending tendencies from consciousness altogether. They seek retreats, 'house-meetings' or revival meetings, always in the hope of finding some way of eradicating their impulses. The testimonies given in these meetings are often the type that dilate on the sins now swept away. Those testimonies raise the hopes of such seekers shutting out their sinful tendencies, and such may be induced to confess the sins to which they are liable. Again there is the short period of elation and apparent freedom. But all that is done by their decision is to repress more deeply. When the tendencies again become active, they are very apt to repress them, for have they not testified that their old temptations are gone? This repression may have tragic results. Probably there is no psychotherapist who has not had to deal in recent years with many such cases who have been in contact with a well-known evangelical movement, but who unfortunately have been dealt with by some one unskilled in the subtleties of the soul. Repression and not conversion occurred in these cases.

Conclusions

What happens, then, in conversion? Leaving the theological aspect until the next chapter we may, with James, say that there is a "firmer hold of religious realities"; or that there are "dead feelings, dead ideas, and cold beliefs" which become hot and alive. Actually, however, there are no such things as dead *feelings or dead ideas which become alive*, and lead to conversion, or help the individual to get a *firmer grip of religious reality*. The doctrine of repression has shown us that impulses, feelings and ideas which create the conflict of which conversion is the resolution, are hot and alive, and to such a degree that they are ever striving to enter the conscious field, and are only held out by strong downward forces which have to be overcome if conversion is to take place. We may attempt to escape from the conflict; in this case we get a psycho-neurosis, or the kind of conversion described by Starbuck as an escape from sin rather than a plunge into holiness, or a higher ethical life in harmony with what is thought to be God's will.

It is very doubtful whether conversion or psycho-neurosis can be satisfactorily explained unless we take full account of what we have called *the personality as a whole* in contra-distinction to what may be thought of as the sum total of the mental processes spoken of as instincts, emotions, cognition, conation, sentiments, complexes, intellectual processes and memory. The Self or Subject as James Ward argued cannot be identified with this sum total. Ideas are really some one thinking; memory is some one remembering; impulse is some one striving; desire is some one anticipating an end. For convenience we may speak of the Ego, the Id and the Super-ego, but these are not separate entities; they are but conditions of the one Subject. For the purposes of psychological description or psychological explanation we may speak of the prohibitive conscience as refusing to allow some tendency in consciousness, but the prohibitive conscience is not an independent entity conscious of what it is doing and why; it is an activity of the Subject. Why the Subject should be divided against itself, why it should indulge in self-punishment is a mystery that philosophy has not been able to explain. We must remember that we are not simply conscious of conflicting tendencies, but of division within a Subject; that is psychological fact. We are conscious of the self being drawn in opposite directions, and not simply of two contending forces. We are not simply watching a battle; we are engaged in it; although we are spectators of opposing tendencies, feelings, ideas, we are in the same moment conscious that the opposing tendencies are ours; in a real sense they are we. We stand not over against our psychic make-up; it is within us; and yet in some mysterious way we transcend our make-up otherwise there could be no chance of introducing order when conflict arises. We are one of the conflicting elements, for if that were not the case we could not feel ashamed that we had the conflict, or feel responsible for it.

It is this Subject, we believe, that is finally involved in conversion. It is self-conscious, endowed with freedom to order and direct its life; capable of moral valuations, and capable of determining its conduct by those valuations. If psychological determinism were true it would be difficult to see how there could be any candidates for conversion or for a cure by a psycho-analyst, unless we are prepared to say that the urge to conversion or a cure is simply another complex. What should be understood by psychological determinism is that we cannot determine what will come into the conscious mind. If we ask some one to think of a name, he cannot determine which name will first enter consciousness; but he may refuse to tell us what the name was or that he has thought of a name at all. What comes into our mind at any one moment is pre-determined by our personal and mental history; how we shall react to it is determined by other factors than our past. Here it seems to us the intuition of the meaning and value, interpreting these terms in the large sense, of what comes into consciousness is the greatest factor in our reaction, or in determining the influence for behaviour of what comes into the conscious field. This is true, even for reflection. When we are reflecting upon a problem, ideas spontaneously come into consciousness, but in consciousness they are sifted, the irrelevant is thrust aside, the idea that does not fit into our train of thought is rejected. *We do not think ideas but with them.* Else, why have irrelevant or inadequate or false ideas at all? Why not choose the fitting idea at once? Our ideas when reflecting upon a problem will depend upon our previous knowledge of the relevant factors of the problem; and our capacity to weigh the value of the ideas for the specific problem in hand and our intellectual capacity to intuit their significance. But we may resist the intuition unconsciously and even consciously if we have started our problem with pre-suppositions. Hence we may conclude, that thoughts, impulses, emotions, conations, may be predetermined by our personal and mental history; but not behaviour. Whether Freud realises it or not, that is the logical implication of his doctrine. Let us take one passage from his volume *Introductory Lectures on Psycho-analysis*.[1] In his chapter on 'Resistance and Repression' he has occasion to speak of the resistance set up by the patient throughout the 'whole course of treatment'. He recognises that it is an apparent contradiction to say that the patient comes to get well and resists the treatment that is to make him well. "And yet it is so, and if the improbability is made a reproach against us we need only reply that it is not without its analogies; for a man who has rushed off to a dentist with a frightful toothache may very well fend him off when he takes his forceps to the decayed tooth." Freud then speaks of the protean ways in which this resistance manifests itself. But if treatment is to be speedy and certain then the patient must follow the following rules of the technique: "We require the patient to put himself into a condition of calm self-observation, without trying to think of anything, and then to communicate everything which he becomes inwardly aware of, feelings, thoughts, remembrances, in the order in which they arise in his mind. We expressly warn him against giving way to any kind of motive which would cause him to select from or exclude any kind of ideas (associations), whether because

[1] *Introductory Lectures on Psycho-analysis*, pp. 242-3.

they are too 'disagreeable' or too 'indiscreet' to be mentioned, or too 'unimportant', or 'irrelevant', or 'nonsensical' to be worth saying. *We impress upon him that he has only to attend to what is on the surface consciously in his mind, and to abandon all objections to whatever he finds, no matter what form they take; and we impress upon him that the success of the treatment, and above all, its duration, will depend upon his conscientious adherence to this fundamental technical rule.*" (The italics are ours.)

Now, if that passage does not imply that we are free in our reactions, then language has no meaning. The success of psycho-analytic treatment depends on the *willingness* of the patient to observe what is on the surface consciously in his mind, and the further *willingness* to tell that to the psycho-analyst, and to *overcome* any resistance to telling him.

Behaviour, then, mental as well as overt behaviour, is not pre-determined once we are aware of the factors at work. Once the Subject sees what the conflicting elements are in his own mind, and intuits their meaning and value for the Subject, his reactions are determined 'now' and not by what has happened in his personal or mental history.

We have said, 'value for the Subject'. What do we mean? We mean that the Subject has a definite urge to maturity, to completeness, and is capable of intuiting whatever is of value for that maturity and of acting upon it. Here we have the basis of the Socratic doctrine that 'knowledge is virtue'. It is capable of renouncing pleasures which it intuits as hindering the growth to completeness or maturity; it is capable of leaving behind the interests and habits of one period for the interests of the next period of development.

It is of this Subject we can predicate, attitude, character, resolution, faith, love, charity and all the virtues as well as its attitude to vice or to complexes which could give rise to vicious action. It is not to be identified with the vices unless it acquiesces or adopts them. Our impulses and complexes are ours, but they are not we.

Professor Laird has argued that the self or what we call the Subject is no more than a union of its constituents. He uses the simile of the bodily organism: 'The members would not act as they do in isolation, but together they act; and the body, as a whole, cannot be anything additional to the members in their union. It appears to us similarly that the self, 'as a whole' cannot be other than the union of its constituents, and I do not know what these constituents can be if they are not these psychological processes which, in a larger way, we have been considering.'[1]

Our position is that the mere union of the psychological processes will not give the Subject, neither will the union of the bodily processes give the organism. Is not Laird's doctrine a species of Hume's position? Is not the union he speaks of the outcome of some kind of mutual attractiveness like that of Hume's ideas? It is the unifying factor we desire to get at; not simply the union; just as the biologist wants to get at life which gives the union to the bodily members of the organism.

Be that as it may. What we are contending for here is that there can be no understanding of the process of conversion where union or rather unity takes place unless we postulate a Subject who is able to unify the various psychological processes of the mind; nor do we believe that we shall ever understand thoroughly the nature of psycho-neurosis or psychoses unless we take into account the activity of this Subject in determining what will and what will not be allowed to be incorporated as part of its character. It is doubtful if this Subject is active on the lower biological and psychological levels of the life of the infant and young child; it is most active on the rational and spiritual levels; but once it comes to birth it plays an important part in determining what will and what will not be allowed to express itself overtly both in consciousness and behaviour.

Conversion, as we read its meaning, occurs when the Subject is given full control of all his psychological processes. It is literally a new birth; it is the birth, the coming to conscious control of the Soul. In the truly converted man, the Soul takes control; it permeates the mass of impulse and emotion with

[1] *The Idea of the Soul*, p. 83.

itself and its spiritual attitude. It is now conscious of conflicting processes, of solicitations, temptations and even of sin, but the Soul does not *consent*. The strong impulses may compel a man to choose what he does not will, and to will what he is unable to choose, but the Subject, the Soul, does not consent. Hence instead of the fear, guilt, of pre-converted days, or in the psycho-neurosis, there is shame and renewed repentance leading to ever greater sanctification.

CHAPTER VI

Salvation and its Problems: Guilt, Sin, Forgiveness, Atonement

It might be thought by some readers that it would have been more logical on our part had we dealt with the subject of this chapter before conversion. Our justification lies in the fact that we are dealing with these problems from the psychological and not the theological point of view. Psychology is not primarily concerned with the abstract notions of Sin and Guilt, or the objectivity of Forgiveness: it must deal with these as data of the experience of Salvation. It ought to be able to give a psychological explanation for the preference of one theory of Atonement to another by particular types of mind, but it cannot pronounce judgments on the theological or objective validity of any theory on the *modus operandi* of Atonement. In experience abstract reflection upon guilt, sin, forgiveness, and atonement comes after the 'moment of vision'.

The Meaning of Guilt, The Sense of Sin

The sense of sin is an experience not confined to evangelical religion; it is characteristic of all religions. Whether it is an illusion, a moral disease, a morbid perception or an objective reality is irrelevant to the psychologist, as such; to him it is part of the data of religious experience and must be studied as far as that is possible apart from any pre-suppositions of any concept of sin he may actually hold.

Psychologically sin is different from crime, or immorality; and thus we would expect to find the sense of sin different. The sense of guilt is the sense of having broken the law of the land; and in so far as the criminal is conscious that motive and intention entered into his act he will feel responsible, he will experience fear, and will have an apprehension of punishment. But he may not experience the sense of sin although he be held to be guilty. He may have broken the law intentionally from the desire to arouse attention to some anomaly in the law, as in a recent case in England where a highly respected gynæcologist performed an operation which is illegal in order to draw attention to the state of the law relative to abortion. Passive resisters refused to obey the law; they were held to be guilty, and their goods were distrained, but they experienced no guilt.

Morality has to do with how we *ought* to conduct ourselves in relation to our fellows; and how we *ought* to order our motives and dispositions relative to vice and virtue. It implies responsibility for our acts, motives, emotions and dispositions. The moral law is not to be confused with statute law; it is written on the 'tablets of the heart' and there alone. It is the measure of what is right and wrong, virtue and vice, good and bad for the individual, and whether it has objective validity or not is matter for the moral philosopher rather than the psychologist. That measure of right and wrong, virtue and vice for the individual may be identical with the customs of the primitive tribe or the moral opinion of a highly civilised nation, but the sense of subjective responsibility is correlated with what the individual believes he ought to do or not to do. "Ethics", says Professor Laird, "has to do with the justification of imperatives"; and the moral life would thus be one in which the imperatives are obeyed because they ought to be obeyed, and for no other reason. They would be seen to be necessary conditions of social and individual welfare. The imperatives are intuited as imperatives, and thus are felt to be obligations. But what are seen and felt to be imperatives differ at different times, and in different peoples, and even vary in individuals themselves. Hence an individual may be held to be immoral and yet experience no sense of culpability; he may even feel it is his duty to break with what is held by his fellows to be the moral law. Only what the individual has accepted consciously or unconsciously of the 'imperatives' gives content to his conscience and exercises subjective authority over him. He can feel ashamed of his immorality only to the degree in which he has behaved contrary to what he believes to be moral.

Just as the immoral man can only feel conscience-stricken to the degree in which he has acted contrary to his moral consciousness, and the criminal guilty to the degree in which he has violated the just law of the land, so the sinner can only have a sense of sin to the degree in which he acknowledges God's Holy Love, and God's Holy Will. Theologians are entitled to say with Paul: "We have all sinned and come short of the glory of God", but the psychologist must be content to take into account only those who have the experience of having sinned. The 'sinner's' (using the term in the theological sense as we use 'criminal' in the legal sense, and 'immoral' in the sense of moral philosophy) sense of sin is relative; and in many is not found at all. 'Hell-deserving sinners,' and 'guilty sinners', we may be, but the psychologist must confine himself to the *experience* of being such a sinner, and must leave alone the judgment, 'All have sinned'.

What, then, is this *sense* or *conviction of sin?* How is it related to the sense of guilt? Are 'guilty', 'conscience-stricken', and the 'sinful' synonymous terms? That there is something common to all of them may be inferred from the fact, that a crime may be a sin, an immoral act a sin; but there are sins which are not accounted guilty in the legal sense, and sins which the moral philosopher ignores even if he does not deny that they are immoral.

Space will not allow us to deal with all the psychological questions raised by the theological concept of sin. Sin, however, is not only a theological dogma but also an experience. The Fall, Original Sin, its cosmic implications are all outside the sphere of individual experience, and therefore, not within the subject-matter of psychological judgments proper; nevertheless, the psychology of evangelical experience must relate itself to evangelical dogma.

In his *Essays on Christian Philosophy*, Dr. Leonard Hodgson writes: "In ordinary Christian teaching the matter of sin and its remedy is commonly stated somewhat as follows: Sin is defined as conscious disobedience to God's will, a definition which implies belief in God whose will is discoverable, and in the possession by man of freedom to obey or disobey it. When sin has been committed, it leaves the sinner in a position in which by himself he cannot undo or make good the evil that has been done. This deadlock is met by the doctrine of the Atonement regarded as an act of God making possible the neutralising of the evil effects of sin, both those which linger on in the state of the sinner's soul and those which remain elsewhere—*God was in Christ reconciling the world unto Himself.* What is required of the sinner in order that he may benefit by this act of God is repentance—that is to say, sorrow for his sin, confession of his sin, and purpose of amendment. When he repents, God sees to the rest. This is the fundamental message of Christianity, that as a result of the act of God in Christ sins repented are sins forgiven."[1]

A more explicit evangelical view of sin is contained in the late Professor H. R. Mackintosh's volume, *The Christian Experience of Forgiveness*. He writes: "The wrong attitude of the will (that we do 'not simply reject the Higher Will; we discover that to accept it gladly is beyond us') is called *sin* by all who acknowledge its reality, and what is distinctive of the Christian religion in this area is not so much its recognition of sin as the new estimate placed upon it. Recognition there has always been. It has not usually been denied that men do steal, or lie, or hate, or indeed that in the main human history has been a record of tragic failure. St. Augustine and Huxley, leagues apart as they may be, are in agreement here. But the religion of the Bible is original and final in its contention that the distinctive quality in sin lies not chiefly in its antagonism to our higher life, or to the welfare of society, but in its antagonism to the will of the living God. That will was fully disclosed through the compassionate love of Jesus.

[1] *Essays in Christian Philosophy*, p. 15.

Accordingly we detect and measure sin by its unlikeness to the spirit of Jesus; we know sin by its unlikeness to the spirit of Jesus; we know sin when we see its difference from Him. Men had other serviceable criteria of sin before His day, but these are antiquated now. It is in the light of Christ that we see sin clearly and can in some real degree understand how it looks to God above, whose estimate of it we are bound to share so far as we discover it. In proportion as man grows familiar with the fact of Christ and lets the illumination of that pure spirit fall on his own soiled nature, he will become more sensitive to the horror of sin; also with growing insight he will discriminate more surely what sin is from what it is not.

"Historically, we can scarcely overrate the importance of the fact, that every closer approach to true knowledge of God has been accompanied by deeper insight into sin, though not by any means, as some thinkers have supposed, by an increase of attention given to sin. We are wise if we shut our eyes 'from looking upon evil', and decide that it is unprofitable to meditate on our own wrong-doing. But apart from this practical reason, it remains true that every growing apprehension of God's reality and its meaning for our lives brings us to a profounder realisation of the sheer evil of all that exiles us from Him and from blessedness. And here the limiting case, to repeat it once more, is the effect upon us of Jesus, who shows us God and therefore *ipso facto* shows us ourselves. In His light, we begin to understand what sin is and also why it is sin. Moral evil instantly ceases to be something arbitrary and incomprehensible, as it is in many religions, and even at times in the Old Testament, where the worshipper cannot tell why certain things are wrong and need pardon in the sight of God, because the commandments he is bidden to keep have no intrinsic or self-evidencing rightness. All such arbitrariness is at an end for the man who has met with Jesus Christ. If, as He has taught us, to be one with God means confiding in the Heavenly Father with unqualified trust and in the service of His children, it follows that sin means every disposition and action which lack faith and love. Sin, essentially, is selfish failure to trust and obey God.

"In technical language, the predication of sin is a judgment not merely of existence, but of value. It asserts both a fact and a character. What conscience is expressing in such a judgment is condemnation of an attitude or act as exhibiting a certain kind of will or person. . . . Though colloquially we use it more broadly, sin strictly is a religious term, as is indicated by the fact that when condemning anything in ourselves or others as sin we assume without reasoning that we are dealing with it as 'in His sight'. It has been done against Him; He sees it in its real colours; our judgment, if sound, is an echo of His. . . . We are sinners in His eye, though before men we might be without reproach, and even our heart may not condemn us."[1]

Both these writers are theologians and we believe belong to different schools of theology, but their definition is essentially the same. In Professor Mackintosh's we have a good deal of reflection and explication of what is meant by sin as disobedience to God's Will, how we know it is sin, and some explanation of the sense of sin.

When the psychologist comes to study the experience of sin he finds that it does not altogether coincide with the definitions or reflections of Dr. Hodgson and Professor Mackintosh. The sense of sin is relative to the experience of sin; that must be the psychologist's standpoint. Both writers lay emphasis upon conscious 'disobedience' or 'antagonism' to the Will of God, as the essence of sin, and the cause of the alienation, but neither lay sufficient stress on the fact that the sinner experiences just as strongly, conscious antagonism to his sin. He is conscious of being compelled to choose what he does not will and to will what he cannot choose. Professor Mackintosh does hint at this when he says we find that to accept gladly the higher will is felt to be beyond us; nevertheless, 'antagonism,' the word which Professor Mackintosh uses, is a strong word going further even than Dr. Hodgson's

[1] *The Christian Experience of Forgiveness*, pp. 53–6.

'disobedience' and the qualification does not meet our objections.

Nor does either of these writers, or 'ordinary Christian teaching' if it is correctly interpreted in the first quotation, take account of the fact experienced by the sinner, that his real sin is that he has outraged the love of God. It is here, we believe, that theology is apt to be divorced from experience and that theories of the Atonement are sometimes out of touch with reality. In the first quotation we might easily substitute Kant's moral law for God without altering the meaning of the definitions. Undoubtedly the individual under the conviction of sin does feel that he has been consciously disobedient to the Will of God, and many experience what we may describe as antagonism to the Will of God; but they experience a great deal more. The theologian tends to identify the sense of sin with guilt, as though all that was necessary to participate in the 'act of God' through which sin is forgiven is an experience similar to what the criminal feels. That is why the psychologist refuses to lay the emphasis upon sin or guilt as defined by the theologians. When Sir Oliver Lodge uttered his now hackneyed statement that people were not now worrying about their sins, he was really thinking of sin and the sense of sin as defined by many theologians. When the emphasis is laid too strongly upon the Will of God as the object against which we sin, unintentionally it may be, but nevertheless truly, we are taking a legal view of sin; and such a view has least appeal to the ordinary man. The emphasis is *ipso facto* laid upon guilt. It is perfectly true that the sinner cries out, as we have seen in our study of conversion, about his disobedience to the Will of God, that he deserves eternal damnation for his sins; but that is not the central moment in the experience. The central moment in the experience of the conviction of sin is not guilt, but the sense of alienation from God, and the longing to be reconciled to God, to be at one with the Will of God, to be in fellowship with God, to love God. "Lord, Lord, forgive me, and I shall sin no more" is not a *quid pro quo;* it is the implicit acknowledgment that 'Love is the fulfilling of the law'.

Psychologically, guilt is not the accurate term to apply to the emotional and ideational content of the mind prerequisite to repentance. The content of the experience of guilt is not only a sense of responsibility for what has been done, but an emotion of fear and the fear is referred to the idea or apprehension of punishment, and a conational striving to flee from the punishment; whereas the antecedent to repentance is simply a vivid realisation of the *Mea Culpa*, with no fear. What we must grasp is that while guilt is experienced repentance is absent. A deep humiliation is the true condition which leads to that repentance which, unlike guilt, precedes the resolution of the conflict instead of escape from it. In the repentance itself, we have the shame and sorrow at the outrage of God's love. It is not the violation of the Will of God which is most prominent though very prominent in some, and consequently not the apprehension of punishment, but the alienation from God, the idea that *God cannot love me*. Is it not well expressed in the hymn of that undoubted evangelical theologian, Theodore Monod:

> Oh the bitter shame and sorrow,
> That a time could ever be
> When I let the Saviour's pity
> Plead in vain, and proudly answered,
> 'All of self, and none of Thee'.

When Peter said, "Depart from me for I am a sinful man", it was not because he was conscious of guilt or of having violated the Holy Will of Christ, thought of as some abstract entity standing over against him, but because he had been presumptuous, ego-centric and mistrustful of Him who loved him. When Nicodemus, who had been seeking for the living God and found nothing but dead traditions, lifeless ceremonial, creeds which had lost their meaning, a Church whose vitality had gone, spiritual observances from which all the spirituality had evaporated, sought Jesus, he was bewildered by the fact that Jesus demanded no new addendum to the law, or to what he had already believed, no new ceremonial observance to be more punctiliously performed. Instead of a new belief, a new observance of ceremonial, he was met with the challenge of a new birth, a new spirit; and the ground Jesus gave for this demand was not the old Jewish, 'Holy is the Torah', but 'God so loved the world'. Again, when the light shone upon Paul, he cried: "Lord, what wouldst Thou have me to do?" He was still clinging to a personal relationship to God through the keeping of law, he still refused to see that we love the law because we have learned to love God, or as Paul himself put it, we know that He loves us. It is not a guilty fear, then, which is the pre-requisite of forgiveness, but the humble and contrite heart of repentance.

Let us not be misunderstood; the sinner is perfectly conscious of his sins, and he does refer the alienation from God to them; but it is the alienation which is most prominent in his consciousness. He knows intuitively that if he could but be forgiven, restored to God, he would be done with his sin. After all, it is our unconscious alienation from God, in the first place, that gives the chance for sinful habits to get their grip, and the pleasure experienced in sin gives a wrong attitude to our lives. The mere lack of sin defined as 'conscious disobedience to God', or freedom from conscious antagonism to the Will of God, neither guarantees forgiveness, nor the approval of Christ. Need we remind our readers of the psychologically significant parable of the Pharisee and the Publican: "I thank Thee that I am not as other men, extortioners, etc. . . . or even as this publican". To be free from any conscious disobedience to God's Will, or antagonism to it, may and will result in a freedom from guilt, but may have as its concomitant, self-righteousness.

A sense of guilt, then, we must insist again, is not a pre-requisite of forgiveness any more than the lack of it is a sign that we are forgiven, or have no need to be. That many who have been truly converted, and reached sainthood and even saintliness experienced guilt strongly both before and after conversion no psychologist could possibly deny. But the fundamental fact psychology reveals in this connection, is that we get no complete and true change until the guilt is removed. The attitude to sin must change from guilt to spiritual shame, humiliation, contrition and even remorse, the remorse implicit in Monod's hymn.[1] The sense of guilt is almost always referred to the wrong source; it is apt to be displaced upon the wrong thing; and in those who have done nothing criminal, psychology today would trace it and does trace it to early experiences of childhood which have little or nothing to do with the present life of the individual seeking salvation. Analysis of patients racked by guilty fears concerning the past are always found to be suffering from the repressed tendency to repeat the past. The sense of guilt hides the true extent to which we have become the slaves of sin. It is always a fear of the violated law, except when it can be traced to the original guilt source mentioned in the section dealing with the growth of conscience. There is the fear of the angry God, the judge who punishes, and never of the shame and sorrow that reveal our real wickedness. The sense of guilt is not a moment in the upward movement of repentance, but an emotion experienced in the downward thrust of repression; it reinforces the striving to escape the conflict, and never helps to a resolution of the conflict. It is generated by the infantile prohibitive conscience, and not by the adult positive conscience. It is very largely associated with some form of concupiscence or sexual aberration, or with acts that might lead to social ostracism, or police proceedings. Shame, sorrow, contrition, remorse because love has been refused, and outraged, is the true moment in repentance that leads the sinner to seek forgiveness, and reconciliation with God.

Professor Mackintosh is right when he says, that "All guilt is destructive of that fellowship with the Father which pardon alone can re-create". That is true; but until we have first removed the guilt and replaced it by the true repentance in which there is no craven fear, the soul never knows the 'joy and peace of believing'. While guilt remains, our consciousness of God is coloured and vitiated by the ascription to Him of judicial functions alone, or at least these are prominent. Actually what is happening psychologically when we ex-

[1] Note we are speaking of the psychological sense and are not discussing the objective reality of guilt; guilt as objective reality is a theological question, not a psychological.

perience guilt in relation to God is that we are projecting upon Him the threatening of our own infantile conscience; of making God our policeman and not our Father: we are not yet conscious of Him as seeking us in love, or grieved at the sin that keeps us from His fellowship. Professor Mackintosh has confused the *bad conscience* of the neurotic with the repentant soul of the sinner when he writes, "It appears to be psychologically true to say that the bad conscience inevitably produces what we can only describe as resentment or enmity against God . . . and therefore finds it impossible to conceive of Him as other than menacing and hostile". That is what the psychotherapist finds in those who are repressing their inner perception of the meaning of what they have done, or resisting the impulse to be reconciled to God, or refusing to accept the necessary limitations upon their pleasure impulse.

Before the true conviction of sin leading to repentance, forgiveness and salvation can be elicited, guilt has to be replaced by repentance, and then "the light which shows us our sins can be the light that heals us".

There is much in Professor MacMurray's pages in *Creative Society* on this subject which is worth pondering even though we may not be able to agree with all he says about sin and forgiveness. This passage, at least, is true. He writes: "The doctrine of the forgiveness of sin has been almost more completely parodied by pseudo-Christianity than any other. A great deal of Christianity has actually so perverted the plain teaching of Jesus as to conceive that its first duty was to arouse and deepen in men, by all the means in its power, the sense of guilt. This is, of course, one of the subtlest means of destroying the spontaneity of any individual and making him amenable to the control of others. The whole problem for religion, as Jesus clearly saw, was to reverse this process; and so to create the kind of men who could not be imposed upon by authority through their own sense of guilt, but would spontaneously create from a sense of equality and freedom."[1]

Illustrations from psychotherapy could be multiplied

[1] *Creative Society*, p. 69.

indefinitely for our position in regard to the place of guilt in human life. Practically every psychotherapist will agree with Dr. Wm. Brown that before we can help the masturbator we must remove anxiety and the sense of guilt. Any condemnation but strengthens the already strong prohibitive conscience and increases the trouble. When a patient comes with an anxiety-neurosis really traceable to some moral lapse, he may be unconscious that this particular lapse has anything to do with his trouble. He is full of fear and apprehension of something going to happen to him. Before he can be helped psychologically the sense of guilt has to be removed. Once that is done he will be psychologically able, to a large extent, to resume his work, his social contacts and his ordinary daily life. But he will not be cured. Cure only comes when he has taken a new attitude to what was done and to the tendency to do it again. If a married man has committed adultery, the fear of being found out and of the consequences of his act has to be replaced by a true realisation of the love he has outraged, the children he has let down even though wife and children may never know anything about the lapse. If he is to be cured religiously he must realise that he has outraged the love of God. Merely to remove the sense of guilt will not make the patient either a better man or even a safe man. Indeed, he may become a worse man; he may reconcile himself, not to God, nor the necessary limitations upon his appetites, but to indulgence. He will be cured of his neurosis but at the price of becoming un-moralised.

That is the danger which is feared by many religious writers on the significance of psycho-analysis or psychotherapy for religion. It is a real danger. It makes many understanding people hesitate before advising any kind of psychological treatment. It is especially dangerous to the moral personality if the analyst or psychotherapist feels no responsibility to help the patient to get a moral attitude to his offending tendencies. Illustration may help us here.

One psycho-analyst gives the case of a patient, a male, whose trouble was due to a "mingled hypochondria and anxiety-neurosis. The patient was formerly an onanist and then practised *coitus interruptus* with a widow whom he must not impregnate. He dared not go to a brothel for fear he might have a 'stroke' there, and then everybody would know of his vicious life. A speedy recovery was brought about by the use of a condom in his sexual relations."[1]

We doubt if the patient's trouble was due to *coitus interruptus;* we believe it was caused by the fact that he could not incorporate his behaviour tendencies into the moral personality he did have. There was resistance from the moral personality even though it was only through the medium of the prohibitive conscience, or his *super ego*, as Freud would put it. The 'cure' was not a resolution of the conflict, but an un-moralising of the patient's conscience; it may be that the conscience was only repressed; in that case we should expect a later neurosis of a severer kind than Stekel 'cured'.

It must not be thought, however, that all psycho-analysts or psychotherapists are concerned merely to relieve their patients of the sense of guilt and other symptoms. Our quotations from Jung must have already shown that there is a large school of psychological experts who recognise that the great majority of the neuroses have their roots in the moral and spiritual side of our personality. Even Stekel has to admit that these patients suffer from a bad conscience; and he writes also: "Every neurotic is religious". Dr. Wm. Brown states the position of the great majority of those who deal with functional nervous troubles when he says: "Psychotherapy should be spiritual as well as mental reclamation; the individual must be born again, achieve a new view-point and a stronger will".

What we want to emphasise is that spiritual and moral reformation can take place only when the sense of guilt is removed. But the personality is not healed psychologically or spiritually unless the true emotions, repentance with its deep sense of alienation from God, and the implicit seeking to be reconciled to God are awakened. To feel alienated from God is only possible to the soul who is consciously or unconsciously seeking Him; who is seeking to be reconciled to Him, that is

[1] *Conditions of Nervous Anxiety and their Treatment*, p. 96.

to say, seeking to become adjusted in mind and attitude of soul to what is consistent with God's love. "Love God and do what you like" said that wise psychologist, St. Augustine. There can be no fellowship with God when some sinful tendency is secretly indulged or unconsciously repressed.

We have written at length on this differentiation between the true sense of sin which involves repentance, and the sense of guilt which is always the outcome of repression and must be removed before repentance and forgiveness can take place because the emphasis upon guilt, the attempt on the part of many to deepen this sense of guilt not only does damage to the personality but is a hindrance to evangelical Christianity. What troubles the true seeker after God is not that he has committed this sin or that, but that he *could* do it. He knows he is not suffering from a 'complex' but from a state of soul that can only be met by a new relation to God.

The Meaning of Sin

If the sense of sin is not to be equated with the sense of guilt neither can sin itself be equated with guilt. We remember a professor beginning a lecture on the Theology of Sin with the words: "Gentlemen, Sin is Guilt". But sin in the true psychological sense of the term as an experience should be entirely separated from judicial concepts. There is no need to apply the term guilt to sin in order that we may not forget that the human heart is sinful. Paul does not exaggerate the sinfulness of the heart in the first chapter of Romans; nor does Freud paint a darker picture than the reality. The wonder is that either Freud or any other psychologist who knows the human heart—the self-deceit it can consciously or unconsciously practise, the lusts and perversions which corrupt it, the cruel phantasies it can harbour and indulge—can believe it can ever be changed without a birth from above. But the human heart is sinful not because it has lusts and attitudes contrary to the law of God, but because these can destroy the spiritual relationship to God, and the human relationships within which our personality must enlarge or shrink. It is the power of sin to disturb every spiritual relationship which differentiates it from criminality. Certainly every one of these lusts and attitudes are contrary to the moral law and the Will of God, and most of them are contrary to statute law of any civilised country. No revelation is needed to make that known to us. Neither social life nor moral life would be possible if limitations were not placed upon human lusts. But their sinfulness does not consist in what is contrary to statute law; what makes them sinful is that they alienate from God, our neighbour, ourselves, from beauty, goodness and truth; from love, faith and charity; from the true service of God and man. When a man commits adultery he may or may not have violated the statute law of the country, but *ipso facto* he has alienated himself from God, he has disturbed his moral relations between himself and his partner in sin, and every moral and spiritual relationship in his home.

It is outraged love of God and the alienation from Him it entails which is central in the experience of sin. However prominent the sin, as act, is in the conscious experience, the alienation from God occupies the focus of consciousness.

What makes the conviction such a poignant experience is that *we* have alienated ourselves from God—*Mea Culpa*. The emotions and ideas in the experience of the conviction of sin are totally different from those we have when we make a mistake, or when through ignorance or want of thought we do harm. We may indeed blame ourselves for our mistake, ignorance or want of thought, but regret is the prominent feeling tone of this experience, not the conviction of sin. The sense of responsibility for what we have done; the inner perception that we sinned and knew what we were doing intensifies the humiliation, sorrow and shame of repentance. Even when our motives have been but sub-conscious and only in the light of the consequences are seen in their true colours, there is no mitigation of self-blame, no excusing of ourselves.

Moral Disease and Sin

At this point it will be well to take note of a distinction made by Dr. Hadfield between moral disease and sin. Many of the moral perversions, obsessive thoughts and compulsions, such as homo-sexuality, impure thoughts, or the obsessive intrusion of one specific word with an evil content, or sexual phantasies, or the compulsion to theft or to exhibition of the genitalia are classified as moral diseases. The patient's will is unable to keep the tendencies from entering consciousness or to keep them when they are present from what to the layman seems deliberate acts. A patient is compelled to 'Damn God', to say that the Holy Spirit is of the Devil, that Christ was not born of a virgin. Although he resists the tendency to utter the 'blasphemy' he is filled with dread. The utterance of these thoughts gives relief to the psychological tension set up by the tendency to indulge them, but that is now succeeded by the sense of guilt with its apprehension of punishment or the fear of having sinned the unforgivable sin. The patient feels, and will even argue that he did it deliberately. So those with impure obsessive thoughts find no excuse for themselves. In many cases of kleptomania and exhibitionism and homo-sexuality, there is the same sense of compulsion, but in these cases or at least in all but one, we have found that the patients have time between the impulse and the act to pull themselves up. In many of these we find the process of rationalisation by which they persuade themselves of some 'good reason' for doing as they have done. Many homo-sexuals, however, attempt to justify themselves on the ground that they are as entitled to their form of gratification as those who have the normal attraction for the opposite sex.

These are the people who are said to be suffering from a moral disease and not sin. Dr. Hadfield justifies his use of the apparently contradictory term, 'Moral Disease,' on the ground that the acts or thoughts are those generally considered within the sphere of conduct, yet being uncontrollable and due to unconscious causes must be classified as diseases. The patients feel they are doing wrong, yet apparently can do no other.

Hadfield attempts to make a clear distinction between these behaviour tendencies and sinful tendencies in the following manner: "Sin", he writes, "is due to *wrong sentiments*, moral disease is due to morbid complexes giving rise to uncontrollable impulses. The full and efficient cause of sin is a deliberate and conscious choice of the will moved by a 'false' or wrong ideal. The sinner and the morally diseased both see the ideal: but whereas the former does not, the latter cannot, under ordinary circumstances respond to it."[1]

This should not, however, be taken to mean that although the patient is not to be held responsible for the present compulsion, perversion or symptoms that some degree of ultimate responsibility should not be attached to him for his condition. In many of the compulsion cases we have seen the symptoms could be traced back to a period when the acts were conscious and often deliberate. There is a period in our lives when behaviour-tendencies have significance for us though not meaning. They offer some kind of pleasure, but the meaning of the act is not understood and indeed could not be understood at that period. Nevertheless, the fact that these acts should not be indulged is of significance to the child. Temper, cruelty, sexual curiosity, sexual play with his little friends, all these have a moral significance even to the young child which cannot be mistaken. The prohibition from within, which we mentioned in our quotation from Bergson, comes early into operation. Repression follows upon its heels. Often the repression lingers until the acts or state of mind has meaning. Hence there is the same degree of responsibility for the acts or condition of the present as the moral philosopher attributes to the victim of habit. On the other hand, many of the symptoms of these patients seem to have their roots in behaviour-tendencies whose significance was never allowed to enter consciousness; they are repressed while still sub-conscious, or to use Freud's word, 'pre-conscious'.

It is an undoubted fact, however, that many of these patients do feel a degree of responsibility and some a very great degree; and certainly every psycho-analyst and psychotherapist acts on the assumption that they are responsible for co-operation with him in the cure; and as we saw in the quotation from Freud the

[1] Hadfield, *Psychology and Morals*.

treatment is strict. In spite of all that is said about the non-responsibility of these patients for their 'moral disease', no one can read the literature of psycho-pathology without feeling that although the psychologist does not blame the patient he does write as if the patient were blameworthy. As we shall see later, in this he is justified.

Without entering into the theological concept of sin, the psychologist can agree with the theologian that sin is no mere slavery to habit, no single act of deliberately perverse behaviour, but something that must be predicated of the personality as a whole. To say that sin has its roots in instinct or sentiments is to evince an inadequate understanding of personality and the psychology of moral behaviour. Even if instincts were the semi-independent entities which MacDougall's definition implies—a definition which suits the convenience of medical-psychology and has pragmatic value in psychological practice—they can do no more than solicit the ego. This is true of the sentiments as well. Neither instinct nor sentiments can determine action. "It is a common-place, surely", says Professor Laird in the article quoted above, "that the ordering of our lives is always an ordering of our impulses, instincts and desires."[1] It is for the ordering of our impulses and desires and the *choice* of our sentiments that we are held responsible. As Hocking puts it: "Some innate dispositions we may justly call dangerous; but this does not make them wrong. There is nothing in original human nature which taken by itself can be called evil." Impulse, as he argues, has always its mental environment. Sin has no biological roots; these are spiritual, using the term in its widest sense.

We have seen in Mackintosh that "Sin is, essentially, selfish". Some have defined it as 'selfishness'. Undoubtedly all sins are selfish; and selfishness characterises the sinner. Nevertheless, there is an element in the sinner and in sins which is not fully connoted by the moral trait of selfishness. Hocking has given a chapter to 'Sin as Blindness and Untruth'; but blindness to truth is not Sin; it is effect not cause; it is caused by what in a previous chapter we saw as resistance to the intuition

[1] *Hibbert Journal*, July, 1922.

so that it is repressed. We want to know why we are deliberately blind to the truth; and why we misinterpret the impulse.

The older theologians explained sin by the concept of 'corrupt nature'; and they seem to have referred this corruption to our animal nature. But Hocking is right when he says: "Debasement is not an act; it is a condition of choice resulting from a series of acts. Each abandonment of the effort for complete interpretation makes the next abandonment easier; and what conscience is concerned about is not alone the issue of the act, but also, and primarily, the psychological status which it creates."[1] Older theologians, however, were not fools; they did intuit rightly an element in sin which was the ground of their inference of corruption; though it had little to do with what they thought of as corrupt nature. A corrupt nature as defined by them is acquired, not innate. One may confess the corrupt nature of his lusts, one may abandon the lusts, and yet that which turned normal appetite into lust may remain unchanged.

Can we say, then, where the real root of sin lies? Can we describe the crucial character of a personality that compels us to predicate of it, 'sinfulness'? The refusal to see the truth, the tendency to misinterpret impulse, the refusal of the Will of God, the antagonism to it which many feel, are effect not causes. We resist the intuition, disobey the Will of God, generate antagonism and are alienated from God. We must be reconciled to God.

The recent psychology of character as well as the recent psychology of the neuroses has found that we must look beyond both the instinctive impulses and even the personal history of the individual if we are to find the reasons for the direction character takes in different individuals. Why does one person escape from a situation in life by a neurosis, while another meets the same situation by a conversion? Why do the great majority have neither a neurosis nor a dramatic conversion although they meet the same situations in life which led to neuroses or conversion in their fellows? Even if it were true that all psycho-neuroses could be accounted for by an

[1] Hocking, *Human Nature and its Remaking*, pp. 101-44.

Oedipus Complex the fact still remains, on the Freudian theory, that we all pass through the Oedipus stage of development. Why, then, have some failed to develop sufficiently beyond that stage to a normal development, while others have suffered no ill effects? If with other psychotherapists we attribute the falling ill, becoming a criminal or immoral, to some definite situation, the fact still remains that others have met exactly the same situation without loss of capacity to grow up.

The most significant contribution from recent psychological study of both normal and abnormal persons is the deeper understanding of the meaning and contrast of Ego-centricity and Object-centricity. These two words denote two absolutely different kinds of personality. They are not to be confused with Jung's 'extraversion' or 'introversion'. The saint may be an extravert or an introvert; and the worst sinners are found in both types. Ego-centricity and Object-centricity designate fundamental principles of motivation which permeate the whole psychic make-up, and consequently all our behaviour. Hocking would seem to root sin in the intellectual sphere. On his theory of misinterpretation of impulse, ignorance would account for all sin. It is not in the interpretation of impulse sin lies, but in the motive using the impulse or behaviour-tendencies of the sentiments. When understood, these principles help us to see why our sin is not merely the violation of the Will of God; why sanctification is the task of a lifetime; why a true conversion leads to that consummation; and is not simply the evaporation of a complex or the lopping off of a diseased branch here and there. They help us to understand psychologically the indwelling of Christ—"the Christ in me" of St. Paul.

Ego-centricity denotes the type and the cause of the type of personality which consciously or unconsciously "makes himself his own main purpose".[1] In other words, everything and everybody is just grist to his own mill. He may achieve great things in any sphere, or sink to the level of the beast, and the motivation be the same in both cases. He may be 'holy' but the motivation may be his own self-display; he may win an

[1] Künkel, *What it Means to Grow Up*, pp. 3-5.

empire for his country and the motivation be his own Ego-centric will to power; he may give generously to charity with apparent sympathy but the motive may be self-seeking; he may give because he 'cannot bear to think of people suffering' and yet the motive be Ego-centric; it may be his own discomfort at the thought of suffering and not the fact of others suffering which motivates his 'generosity'. But why go on multiplying illustration? Have we not the exact contrast in Paul's great thirteenth chapter of 1 Corinthians? "Though I speak with the tongues of men and of angels and have not love, I am become as sounding brass or a tinkling symbol. And though I have the gift of prophecy, and understand all mysteries, and all knowledge; and though I have all faith so that I could remove mountains, and have not love, I am nothing. And though I bestow all my goods to feed the poor, and though I give my body to be burned, and have not love, it profiteth me nothing." Or again, take this subtle piece of moral theology: "Sin that it might appear Sin worketh death through that which is good". Ego-centricity,[1] which is *Sin* and not a *Sin* pollutes the whole activity of the individual to such a degree that it is the principle of that individual's personality. What is lust but the Ego-centric desire to use another for the gratification of one's own pleasure? Once the lust is satisfied there is the tendency to turn away from the object which gratified it, or to cast her off altogether. What is greed but the seeking of things that others cannot share? What is the will to power but a desire to get one's own way? In regard to patients who break down because of this particular manifestation of Ego-centricity, Adler says they rule the home from their sick bed. Every neurosis may be interpreted in terms of protecting the Ego-centric self, or of getting it something. Pride, Envy, Anger, Covetousness, Gluttony, Lust, Sloth, these deadly sins of Catholic moral theology, can all be explained without remainder, by the principle of Ego-centricity.

Ego-centricity corrupts everything it touches. It is original sin, for the infant is wholly Ego-centric.

[1] See article in *Expository Times,* April, 1940, by Principal J. S. Whale.

Hocking has the curious passage: "Sin", he writes, "is the refusal to interpret crude impulse in terms of the individual's most intelligent will to power". Surely, the 'will to power', unless object-centred, is anything but lovely if Adler's accounts of his patients are anywhere near the truth. Again, Hocking writes, "Sin is the deliberate failure to interpret impulse so that it will confirm or increase the integration of self-hood". The integration of self-hood is not a moral process in itself. The goodness of an integrated self-hood depends on what moral principle has integrated it. The 'Devil' is the most integrated self in the Universe. An unscrupulous Dictator, or libertine, has an integrated self-hood.

Perhaps our view of sin will be seen better in the perspective of its opposite—Object-centricity. The object-centred personality is motivated by the person, cause, activity in *whose service he is enlisted*. Instead of pressing everything into the service of himself, he *is* enlisted in the service of whatever has captivated him. To change the figure, the centre of gravity of his moral personality is without, not within.

Here we can link up the principle of moral personality and indeed of all personality both with Object-centricity and religion. Professor Grensted has made the thesis of his Bampton Lectures on "Psychology and God" rest on the principle that personality is found without not within. That confirms all that we know about the growth of personality; and Grensted is on firm ground when he argues that this principle is necessary to psychology as well as religion. We grow within but *not from* within; we grow from without.

Even Behaviourism must admit that if there is such a thing as personality at all, it is the result of a stimulus from without—a conditioned response of the whole psycho-physical organism to its total environment. The purpose of the psycho-analyst must be to break up the adhesions of the libido to early *cathexes* that it may be captured by others. Looked at from any point of view the psychology of personality can neither deny nor ignore the principle.

The most object-centred principle is love. The message of Evangelical Christianity is that the principle animating God is

Love, indeed that He is Love. *God gave;* and the very object of His giving was not that *He* might be reconciled to us, but that we might be reconciled to Him. "God was in Christ reconciling the world unto Himself."

If we go back to Paul and examine the constituents of his analysis of love, we find that every one of them is object-centred. "Love seeketh not her own." In love we are enlisted in the service of the loved object. "For *their* sakes I sanctify myself", said Jesus. "The glory which Thou hast given me I have given unto them." Brother Lawrence said that his conversion made no difference to the works he performed; it was the motive that was different. He had passed from Ego-centricity to Object-centricity.

Here we see why the mystics laid great stress upon transcending 'self-love'. It is Ego-centric; hence their *via negativa*—the attempt to eradicate the Ego-centricity of self-love; then the upward climb until possessed by God.

Sin, then, is Ego-centricity; and we are sinners to the degree in which our attitude to life is Ego-centric. In other words, to the degree in which our relation to our fellows and our behaviour-tendencies are consciously or unconsciously motivated not by the self, but *for* the self, we are Ego-centric. Selfishness is only one aspect of Ego-centricity, and is more negative than positive. Ego-centricity is mainly positive. It is the tendency of the self as a whole to subordinate all things to the ends of the self. It tinges our deepest love sentiments, and often our holiest acts. That is why Christ could say, "There is none good but God". He alone is truly loving. What were the temptations of the wilderness but appeals to Ego-centricity; or rather they were appeals not from without, but from within His Ego. God alone is absolutely object-centred.

Are We Wholly Evil?

Most theologians have felt an obligation to answer this question. The psychologist who believes that sin is a principle of personality and is not rooted in any behaviour-tendency belonging to our instinctive nature must not shirk the question. The child begins its life wholly Ego-centric, and in that sense we may speak of 'original sin'. But Ego-centricity before the dawn of self-consciousness has no moral significance except for those whose duty it is to direct the child's behaviour-tendencies towards object-centred activities. Not until there is the dim beginning of recognition of the significance of our acts does Ego-centricity become a principle of personality. But there can be no doubt, as we saw in the quotation from Rivers, that the conflict between Ego-centricity and the limitations laid upon our desires begins early. The moment we are conscious that a prohibition is laid upon some form of behaviour we desire to indulge in, that moment the fight between sin and goodness begins, that is to say, the conflict between opposing tendencies within us.

The question as to whether men are wholly evil has been well put by Professor Mackintosh, thus: "The psychological fact that in repenting the best Christians ask pardon, not only for what they have done, but even more for what they are, signalises the truth that 'sin' is predicable, strictly and in the ultimate sense, of the *self* rather than of isolated acts. *We* are sinful. Does this mean that we are purely and exclusively sinful, untouched by good? Probably some candid minds have revolted against the thought of forgiveness on the ground that to ask for it is implicitly to confess that we are wholly and unrelievedly bad. This unmitigated badness in God's sight they deny, and we must enquire how far their denial is justified."[1]

Belief in total depravity is possible only to those who implicitly or explicitly hold to a purely biological interpretation of human nature. Morality cannot be explained unless on the assumption of a moral consciousness. And as moral consciousness cannot exist apart from self-cónscious being, sin belongs to us as self-conscious beings.

But just as the biological needs drive us outside ourselves for their satisfaction, so we believe the need to realise our personality in personal relationships drives us outside of ourselves towards objects which can draw us out of our Ego-centricity.

[1] *The Christian Experience of Forgiveness*, p. 62.

Spontaneously the child begins to form sentiments. Every sentiment we acquire is to some degree object-centred; for a sentiment is the organisation of impulse and emotion round the idea of some object. In so far as the love sentiment is active, its activity, thought and emotion will be directed by the idea of the good of the object. In addition to the normal tendency of the sentiments towards Object-centricity we have other tendencies such as sympathy and the maternal and paternal tendencies which work towards Object-centricity. It would be difficult to find anyone bereft entirely of the tendencies which correct our Ego-centricity. Nevertheless even our strongest love sentiments may have, and in most of us have, an Ego-centric element. They may be little more than an extension of the *me*, as James pointed out.

It is this fact that the Ego-centricity belongs to our personality as a whole, and thus tends to tinge everything we are and do, that makes us ask for pardon for what we are as well as for what we do. On the other hand, it explains also why Dr. Dale could say that the sense of sin is deepened as we grow in the Christian life. Mackintosh takes the same view when he writes: "Historically, we can scarcely overrate the importance of the fact, that every closer approach to true knowledge of God has been accompanied by deeper insight into sin".[1] It is for this reason that Jesus reveals our sin more than any other. Against His perfect Object-centricity, His perfect object-centred Love, we see the Ego-centric element in our love. The hymn writer who wrote that those are more conscious of sin within who love Him most, had insight into the human heart.

Let us not, then, in our reaction against the idea of the depravity or total corruptness of human nature, go to the opposite extreme and try to take the capital letter from the fact of Sin. The psychotherapist who sees his work as spiritual reclamation as well as mental reclamation knows that he must get behind the symptoms to the personality as a whole. He must strive for a new birth in his patient. In terms of his own

[1] *The Christian Experience of Forgiveness*, p. 54.

science this means a radical change of the personality from Ego-centricity to Object-centricity. In religious terms it means the initial movement from self-obsession to Christ-possession. It is only as the sinner becomes aware of this self-obsession and its consequent alienation from Christ, Whose life was perfect in relation to God and man, that he realises that experience of Forgiveness which becomes one of his most precious possessions.

Forgiveness and its Conditions

To understand forgiveness from the psychological point of view it is necessary, not only to realise the effect of sin upon *our* spiritual relations, but also its effects upon those whom we sinned against.

Sin, as all agree, separates the sinner from the person sinned against. This separation is perfectly spontaneous; it is not caused by the person sinned against. In Dr. Forrest's volume dealing with the Authority of Christ, the question is raised as to how far the penalties of sin are imposed by God, or how far they are automatic. They are wholly automatic. What are often called the penalties of sin are not directly connected with sin as such; the same penalties might accrue from the same behaviour and no sinful motive. These penalties are the outcome of the violation of other than spiritual laws, e.g. disease as the outcome of loose living, prison for criminal offence. The true penalty for sin or immorality is the disturbance and even the undermining of personal relationships. Hence the question discussed by some writers as to whether forgiveness implies or involves the remission of such penalties is an unreal one because they are not directly penalties for sins. It is the sinner that is forgiven, not the sin. "Forgive us *our* trespasses as we forgive *them* that trespass against us." Even the law cannot forgive a criminal; the judge may remit the penalty; but he cannot restore the status of citizenship the criminal had before he committed the offence; the 'conviction' is recorded against him. Only personal wrongs can be forgiven; for it is only against persons that we can sin.

The woman sinned against may forgive both her husband and his paramour, but she cannot condone the adultery—

that is she cannot blot it out as though it had never been. The repentance of her husband, her own forgiveness, may create a new relationship to the particular act of adultery on the part of both, but she will probably hate adultery the more.

Forgiveness is the restoration of the spiritual relationship; the status of the sinner is re-created. To the sinner it seems impossible; indeed if he did not think it impossible, he could never experience forgiveness. The fact that he regarded forgiveness as a possibility would be a sign that he had never truly repented. It is only the intuition of faith that gives us the hope of forgiveness, and as we trust that intuition, the miracle happens. That wayward genius, Oscar Wilde, wrote in prison: "Nobody is worthy to be loved. The fact that God loves man shows us that in the divine order of ideal things it is written that eternal love is given to what is eternally unworthy."[1] If we change 'loved' to 'forgiven' and 'loves' to 'forgives' we have the experience of the sinner as he seeks forgiveness and who is forgiven. Hence the 'ecstasy of wonder' that is experienced by those whose conversion has brought a sudden elicitation of the intuition of God's Grace in forgiveness. Forgiveness, we must not forget, is a moment in the experience of conversion, and is probably the most intense moment in it to those to whom the sense of alienation is felt to have been the most awful effect of their sin. While it is natural to emphasise the change in life which conversion implies, yet the freedom from the sense of sin and alienation, the consciousness that God loves him and restores him to fellowship is the psychological cause of the 'ecstasy of wonder'.

We often get an analogous state of mind in those whose neurosis has for one of its symptoms a sense of alienation from their loved ones. Often they experience a sudden lifting of the barrier that seemed to lie between them and those nearest and dearest to them, or between them and old interests of which the neurosis seemed to have deprived them; for the time being they could almost jump for joy.

The psychological reason has a bearing on the theological reasons, for this sense of the impossibility of forgiveness lies

[1] *De Profundis*, p. 103.

in the fact that we cannot forgive ourselves. By the innate tendency to projection, we ascribe our own unforgiving attitude to God. The child who has done wrong tends to project his own feelings upon the parent. If the prohibitive conscience is strong and the child is afraid of what he has done, he tends to project the cause of the fear upon the parent; ashamed of himself he cannot but think his mother is ashamed of him.

Two Fundamental Conditions of Forgiveness

Two fundamental conditions must be fulfilled before forgiveness is really and truly experienced. Both these conditions are psychological. One applies to the sinner, the other to the person wronged, in this case God. On the human side, as we have already seen, there must be repentance. This is a spiritual condition in which thought, emotion, and will are all involved. On the cognitive side there is the knowledge of what was done, of responsibility for what was done. It is the *Mea Culpa.* Then there is the emotion of shame, humiliation and remorse arising out of the *Mea Culpa* against God. Finally the conational turning from sin, from Ego-centricity to Object-centricity. All this is involved in repentance. To acknowledge responsibility is not the same as *Mea Culpa;* to experience *penitentia* without *metanoia* is not repentance. The whole spiritual attitude must be changed towards sin and towards any particular sins prominent in consciousness. There can be no qualification of this repentance. We may find excuses and extenuating circumstances for the sinner but he dare not seek these for himself. If the individual is ashamed he is hopelessly ashamed; if he is responsible he is wholly responsible. Dr. Denney states a psychological truth when he says: "If man is guilty he is hopelessly guilty". That is the psychological fact, whatever theological inferences we draw from it.

We already quoted *De Profundis* to the effect that nobody is worthy of being loved; "If that phrase", continues the writer, "seems to be a bitter one to bear, let us say that every one is worthy of love except him who thinks he is. Love is a sacrament that should be taken kneeling, and '*Domine, non sum dignus*' should be on the lips and in the hearts of those who receive it."[1] That is the exact position relative to forgiveness. Nobody is worthy of forgiveness: The "Lord, I am not worthy" must be in our hearts. The "God be merciful to me a sinner" of the publican must be made our own.

The Atonement

That, however, is but one of the conditions—the condition of the sinner's heart. What of the other condition. It must be fulfilled by the forgiver. *He must feel the sin as though it were his own.* These are the psychological conditions of forgiveness—repentance of the sinner, the vicarious suffering of the person wronged. We have analysed no case of human forgiveness which has not fulfilled these two conditions. Two simple illustrations may clarify the matter: While a social worker in connection with a Magdalene Home, we had occasion to see the father of a young woman and the mother of another about the same time. The father came in great distress and sorrow. He was a widower whose wife had died in childbirth. The adolescent daughter had given trouble for some time and was away when the mother died. The mother's death seemed to bring about a change in the girl who returned and took charge of the home and the motherless baby. The old temptations were apparently too strong for her, and on the day the father came to us she had gone, leaving the child in the cot. With the tears streaming down his strong face the distressed father asked us to find his daughter—we knew her haunts. He had no angry word for her; he spoke with the sorrow of a man who felt the shame as if it were his own sin he was confessing. He spoke of the heart-breaking sorrow that the daughter would suffer when passion had died down and she had come to herself. One could see that he was passing through a Gethsemane in which his sorrow was for the girl in the awful alienation she would feel. He spoke, too, of the gladness that would be his if she were but completely free from her sin. While she was unrepentant a barrier was between, not

[1] *De Profundis*, p. 103.

of his making, and no fellowship could exist between them while this barrier remained. He was separated from her as well as she from him. The father's broken heart shows what we mean by 'vicarious suffering' of the one who has been sinned against; he was ready, able, longing to forgive, able, ready and longing to restore the old fellowship as if sin had never been. His love sentiment for his daughter was more intense because deprived of its object not only by her sin but by her unrepentant heart.

In direct contrast with the above is the case of the mother whose daughter had been brought to the Home by the police. The mother came to see her. We had to see the mother to arrange some details about her daughter as well as to try and comfort her. She needed no comfort. She spoke with bitterness of the shame the daughter had brought upon her; the trouble and expense she had caused. Her heart was hard against the sin and the sinner. The father could forgive; the mother could not, although the daughter had been repentant enough to come to the Home and try to start anew. The mother could not feel the daughter's shame, only her own; she could neither experience her daughter's sorrow nor sorrow as if the sin were her own.

Dr. Maltby in his booklet, *The Meaning of the Cross*, tells of a Yorkshireman whose son had apparently often gone wrong. He was telling a business friend that the lad had gone off again. "If he were mine", said his friend, "I should send him abroad and cut him off with a shilling." "So should I", answered the father, "if he were yours." Here again we have the condition of forgiveness; the love of his son will not let the lad go. He would strive until his prayer for his son's repentance is answered.

Something has to happen in the forgiver as well as the repentant sinner before forgiveness is a reality to both. The whole problem of the Atonement is what happens in God, and how does it happen? The Atonement is objective else it is meaningless psychologically; for forgiveness is an experience in which two are involved. Let anyone who has truly forgiven someone he loved analyse what happened and he will find that he experienced alienation from the sinner; his love sentiment was wounded deeply. To the degree that his love sentiment was object-centred he would feel the alienation experienced by the sinner while still unforgiven, perhaps still unrepentant; and in virtue of the same fact he would be identified with the sinner and feel the sin as though it were his own. "How could he have done it?" will be his thought.

Hence the psychologists approach the problem of the Atonement from the point of view, not of the Holy Will of God so much as from the Holy Love of God. Many theologians approach the problem as if the law violated by the sinner was objective to God as well as to man, and as though the problem for God was to reconcile His forgiveness with this external law.

Professor Mackintosh is perfectly aware of the difficulty. When discussing the question as to whether there is a remission of the penalty, he writes:

"When we take the problem up into the religious sphere it is to find that so far from forgiveness of God necessarily involving the abolition of all punishment, the truth rather is that over a certain area of experience pardon and retribution invariably go together, because the holy love which constitutes the Father's very being makes anything else impossible. In saying so we must be on our guard against reviving the old misconception which divided the nature of God against itself, by deriving forgiveness from love and the punitive consequences of sin from righteousness. The point is that the Divine character is such that wherever it encounters moral evil, in saint or sinner, it cannot but react against it with repelling and retributive force. Love, that is worthy to be called love, confronts the evil thing with an inevitable and intrinsic purity. If God did not chastise sin in the very act of forgiveness, and in the persons of the forgiven as a sequel to forgiving them, He would not be more loving than He is; He would cease to be God."[1]

Thus the problem for the theologian seems to be: "How ward off the repelling and retributive force?" Who will bear the chastisement of sin which must be exercised in the very act of forgiveness?

[1] *The Christian Experience of Forgiveness*, pp. 54–5.

The history of the doctrine of the Atonement is just the record of how theologians have tried to answer this question; and how others have tried to reconcile God's love and holiness with the experience of forgiveness in which this 'repelling retributive force is absent' and that demands the chastisement of the sinner. The problem to Denney was the same as to Mackintosh; but he states rightly that in the experience of forgiveness in the sinner no dualism is found. Let us quote him: "From a very early time—perhaps from the time of St. Paul himself—the sense that reconciliation was a great achievement, involving effort or tension of some kind even on the part of God, has played a considerable part in theologising on this subject. In forgiving sins, it might be said, God takes sides against Himself; He has a right to exact something from us, and for our sakes forgoes that right. His justice impels Him in one direction and His mercy in another, and in this very act of pardoning men and reconciling them to Himself He must reconcile these divergent attributes. It is certainly part of the experience that God treats us better than we deserve. He does not deal with us after our sins, nor reward us according to our iniquities. . . . But it is not a part of the experience to feel that there is a conflict between the divine attributes of justice and mercy, and that these attributes have to be reconciled to one another before man can be reconciled to God. A good deal of speculation deals with this idea, but it is speculative, not experimental. There is not in Christian experience any antagonism between justice and mercy: they are in active and immutable harmony with each other, and God always—not merely in forgiving sins—acts in unison with both. Mercy and justice never need to be reconciled, for they are never at war. The true opposite of justice is not mercy, but injustice, with which God can have nothing to do either in reconciliation or in any other of His works."[1]

Our contention is that the tension within God is felt not as a tension between justice and mercy, nor between God's love which would receive the sinner and the violated moral law

[1] *The Christian Doctrine of Reconciliation*, pp. 21-2.

which must somehow be satisfied, but between the Holy love which by its very nature separates itself from sin and all that has to do with sin, and the inevitable compulsion of that love which would *draw us sinners in.* Love cannot be but 'hurt' when the loved one has done something which outrages it. *Forgiveness is never spontaneous;* it would not be a moral value unless it cost something; we would not be moral beings unless we could feel; unless something in us was mortally wounded by the sin of the loved one. The tension is not between two divergent attributes, nor between a law external to both sinner and God which God has to reconcile with his loving act of forgiveness. Forgiveness must be both a holy act and a loving act. *The tension is within the sentiment of His love;* something must happen in Him if the tension is to be overcome, and His need of the fellowship of His children, and their need of repentance satisfied. Before reconciliation can take place between God and His loved ones, both God's need and man's need must be recognised. Hence it seems to us that the intuition of the Church from the beginning that there was an objective element in the Atonement is verified; and the struggle of the Church to maintain that objective element in her dogma of the Atonement has been justified. The Cross was not simply a fitting end to a life like Christ's; it was the inevitable end. There is something presumptuous in the idea that God has only to know that His loved one has sinned to be ready to forgive when that loved one is 'sorry' and confesses the sin. It is not our repentance but God's love which brings about our reconciliation and the forgiveness of sin. At the same time our repentance has to be elicited as well as God's tension overcome. What induces repentance? In the human relationship of love, it is the intuition that we have 'hurt' the wronged person, that we have wounded and outraged his love. The wronged one is presented to the consciousness of the wrongdoer as wounded by his transgressions. There is thus an objective element here also; otherwise the whole experience of forgiveness would be a subjective process experienced only in the soul of the sinner and not in the heart and mind of the person wronged. The deeper one digs into this central experience of evangelical religion, the more one feels with Canon Kirk, in his Essay on the Atonement, that the children's hymn,

> There is a green hill far away,
>   Without a city wall,
> Where the dear Lord was crucified,
>   Who died to save us all,

contains solid objective truth.

The Three Great Types of the Theory of the Atonement

Evangelical religion has linked the act of forgiveness with the life and death of Jesus; and three great types of theory have held and still hold the hearts of Christian people.

We can but touch on the relation of these theories to the analysis of the experience as given here. How far do they take into account what we have called the necessary psychological conditions of forgiveness? Can we explain the divergent theories by the fact that it is a tendency of the human mind to stress one element in the experience—the element most relevant to the individual thinker's experience and intellectual outlook? Let us recapitulate for a moment. Sin is an outrage on the Holy Love of God; it alienates God from man, man from God; the spiritual relationship between them is disturbed. Man feels that his sin is *Mea Culpa* and due to something which belongs to his nature as self-conscious personality. To be forgiven repentance has to be elicited; that is elicited by the intuition that he has wronged or 'hurt' God; he feels that nothing he can do can merit the restoration of these violated relations between his soul and God. Within God a tension is set up and that tension is within His Love Sentiment. The Love Sentiment is wounded; it would turn away from the sinner, yet is drawn in the same moment towards him. Something has to happen within God to overcome this tension so that His love can go out freely again to His child. Something experienced or done on His part alone can elicit the repentance. The repentance cannot induce God's forgiveness. Moreover, repentance itself is impossible unless the tension in God is presented to the sinner's consciousness. The something that happened in God which makes it possible for Him to forgive and the sinner to repent is manifested upon the Cross; the Love of God is manifested in the life of Jesus; what sin means to God, the tension it sets up within Him and overcome belongs to the Cross alone.

The Penal-Substitution Theory

In the light of the above analysis what can we say regarding the theory which Aulen has called the 'classical' theory of the Atonement? In spite of Dr. Denney's brilliant pages in which he tries to rehabilitate this theory by stripping off its cruder elements, it is very doubtful whether it satisfied the conditions of forgiveness. There is a real element of truth as we have seen that sin always entails suffering-punishment if you will. That suffering or punishment is not imposed by God, it is involved in the very nature of spiritual relationships.

The attraction of the theory seems to the psychologist to lie in the fact that the violation of the prohibitive conscience always involves a threat; the very nature of that conscience is to demand punishment for its violation. This demand is projected upon God; it is He who is supposed to demand the retribution, and until retribution is made He cannot forgive. But, now, this demand is met by Christ's substitution for us and His death upon the Cross. By appropriating His death the prohibitive conscience is appeased; the threatenings of it are silenced; its own appeasement it projects upon God and the heart is at peace.

We remember a patient, a minister of one of the strict Evangelical churches, recounting his conversion. While a youth, he came under the 'conviction of sin' during a mission conducted in the neighbourhood. He 'feared all the pains of hell', and the night and his bed became a terror to him. Then one evening while still under deep conviction and unable to see how his sins could ever be taken away, the evangelist took up his Bible and put it upon the desk beside him, and said: "There are your sins upon you" to which the youth agreed. Then the evangelist shifted the Bible and laid it upon another desk, and said, "There are your sins on Christ, He has received the punishment; He died in your stead". And said our patient, "In that moment a great burden lifted, my sins seemed to pass away and I could not sleep for rejoicing. The very countryside seemed changed ever after."

There can be no doubt that where the prohibitive conscience is strong and its demand for self-punishment insistent, the penal and substitutionary theory will always make an appeal; and it will give subjective grounds for the faith that the individual's sins have been forgiven. How often does the psychotherapist listen to a patient saying with tears: "Oh that some one could take my conscience, if only for an hour".

Powerful, however, as this theory has been in the removal of the sense of guilt—for that is what essentially it removes—it is inadequate as an objective ground of Atonement or even for the revelation of the nature of *Sin*. It is the *sins* that are prominent in the mind of the individual to whom this theory comes with relief; and the guilt of these particular sins is removed. Unless, however, the theory leads to a growing knowledge of the meaning of sin through a growing knowledge of God, the Christian life grounded in it is apt to be strait and narrow, deep but gaunt. The prohibitive conscience, although now appeased, exercises its negative influence on the individual. The horror of sins and even sin is a very real experience in Christians of this type; but it is doubtful if they ever have the experience of being 'more than conqueror' which is the product of Christian faith. This theory tends to produce the 'puritanic' type if it becomes a resting-place for one's faith in forgiveness.

There is, however, a second objection to Dr. Denney's presentation and to the theory itself. It seems to be based upon a fallacy or what we may term a false pre-supposition, namely, that all sacrifice is offered to some one. "If we say", he writes, "that the death of Christ was an atoning sacrifice, then the atonement must be an objective atonement. It is to God that it is offered and it is to God that it makes a difference."

A priori psychology offers no objection to the idea of a sacrifice being *offered to God;* but it is doubtful whether Denney's view fulfils the conditions of forgiveness or whether a sacrifice offered *to* God is an element in the experience at all. If we say that it is the *grace* of God that grants forgiveness, or that God in His grace *accepts* the sacrifice, it is still the grace and not the sacrifice which is the final and efficient cause of the forgiveness from God's side. If we say that something in God demands the sacrifice, then we are back to the dualism which both Mackintosh and Denney deprecate.

On the other hand, if God Himself offers the sacrifice, if the sacrifice is entailed by the necessity of God entering into man's experience of alienation, if His own alienation and suffering as a result of His children's sin must be presented to the consciousness of the sinner to elicit repentance, then we can say with Denney and the theory he so brilliantly defends, "He died for us". "The death of Christ", said F. W. Robertson, "was the sacrifice of God." It was not a sacrifice *to* God, but *of* God. If, as we shall see later, McLeod Campbell's concept of *vicarious repentance* is psychologically impossible, so it is just as psychologically impossible for Christ, as man, to suffer vicariously for God. The wronged person must suffer Himself if the *tension* is to be overcome.

That a sacrifice had to be endured, that there could be no remission of sins without it, we believe as intensely as Dr. Denney did; but the sacrifice was *of* God and not *to* God. With Denney we can sing the hymn and the Amen to it which both he and Canon Kirk quote:

> He died that we might be forgiven,
> He died to make us good,
> That we might go at last to heaven,
> Saved by His precious blood.
>
> There was no other good enough
> To pay the price of sin;
> He only could unlock the gate
> Of Heaven and let us in.

We believe that everything Denney stood for regarding the Atonement is guaranteed in the above interpretation; the undoubted objective element involved in the forgiveness of sins is retained without recourse to any legalism. The Penal theory will, if accepted, remove the sense of guilt, but it will not necessarily induce repentance in the psychological sense of the term. No theory can reconcile the 'divergent attributes of justice and mercy' if the sacrifice is thought of as being offered *to* God. Denney realised that God could not offer a sacrifice to Himself. The essential idea of the Penal theory is: The death of Christ was an atoning sacrifice through which sin is annulled and God reconciled to man. This position is maintained. *God makes the sacrifice. He does not offer it.* Sin is annulled in the sense that the spiritual relations between God and man are restored by the removal of alienation. It is the *sinner* that is the vital element in the problem, not the sin.

The Satisfaction Theory

Here the central idea is that forgiveness cannot take place without adequate satisfaction for sin. We get the same difficulty here as in the Penal theory, namely, to whom or to what has the satisfaction to be given? Who has to be satisfied before the sinner can be forgiven? Exceedingly crude ideas have been associated with this theory at one time or another. There is one good thing about the theory as enunciated by Anselm. He does attempt, as Dr. Franks has pointed out, to see the problem of forgiveness from a central standpoint "whence all aspects of the Incarnation and Atonement are seen in their proper perspective".[1] But it should be kept in mind, however, that a metaphysical standpoint must not be inconsistent with a psychological one. Like the theories which preceded, the Satisfaction theory of Anselm is based upon the idea that sin must be followed by punishment or its equivalent. As Rashdall writes: "Sin was to Anselm essentially the subtraction of the honour from God involved in disobedience to His commands. Consequently justice requires either that God shall be paid for what He has lost or that punishment shall be inflicted."[2]

The theory has often been called the Latin theory. This is justified by the fact that as Rashdall has pointed out Anselm simply transferred the conceptions involved in ecclesiastical jurisprudence to the transaction between the Father and the Son. It differs from the Penal theory in this, that whereas there Christ is punished for our sins, in the Anselmic theory

[1] *The Atonement*, p. 77.
[2] *The Idea of Atonement in Christian Theology*, p. 351.

He is the substitute for punishment, and His death does not constitute the punishment. Satisfaction could only be made by a perfect life, because God has a right to demand a perfect life from us; there must be 'a second Adam' to the rescue. Hence the Incarnation is necessitated.

What has been said about the Penal theory of punishment is relevant and just as applicable to this theory. But it is psychologically false to assume that forgiveness demands satisfaction; if we are hopelessly wrong or 'hopelessly guilty' no satisfaction either of our own or of another could alter the relation between us and God. Merit cannot cancel a wrong. Only the suffering of the person wronged can 'cancel' sin. Works of supererogation can have no place in the psychology of forgiveness.

'Moral Theories'

We come nearer to a recognition of the psychological conditions of forgiveness in what are known as the 'moral theories'. They go back in Church history to Abelard, and the most recent statement of this type of theory is that of Dr. Franks in his Dale Lectures. Macaulay attempts a reconciliation between Denney and McLeod Campbell. The love of God and its manifestation in the passion of Christ is efficacious to kindle the soul with love for God. Here are the crucial passages from Abelard, as translated by Rashdall: "Our redemption, is that supreme love of Christ shown us by His passion, which not only frees us from the slavery of sin, but acquires for us the true liberty of the sons of God, so that we fulfil all things not so much from fear as from love to Him who exhibited so great favour towards us, that favour than which, as He Himself attests, none greater can be found: 'Greater love', He says, 'hath no man than this, that he lay down his life for his friends'." "To us it appears that we are none the less justified in the blood of Christ and reconciled to God by this singular grace exhibited to us in that His Son took our nature, and in it took upon Himself to instruct us alike by word and example even unto death (and so) bound us to Himself by love."

Abelard refuses to have anything to do with the idea that the Incarnation was necessitated either by the necessity of paying a ransom, or giving satisfaction to God, indeed he would have repudiated any arbitrary compulsion upon God to give or the sinner to receive forgiveness.

Dr. Franks argues that God is always ready to forgive; the message of the Church is forgiveness as is the Sacrament of the Lord's Supper, and forgiveness is "preached prophetically to the child in baptism". The main position of Dr. Franks, if we have not misinterpreted him, is that God is ever ready to forgive; He needs no ransom; seeks no satisfaction, and never forgives in any arbitrary way. The difficulty, it would seem, lies in the sinner; he needs to be made forgivable. Let us quote directly: "What was necessary to make the sinner forgivable was to bring him to accept forgiveness. . . . The Cross makes the sinner forgivable just because it creates penitence and trust, which are two aspects of one and the same process of re-union of the sinner with God."[1]

We believe the Cross elicits the intuition of faith by which the sinner is justified, and that the sinner needs some power that "moves and constrains" but "does not compel" him to accept forgiveness. If Dr. Franks means that the Cross in addition to inducing repentance, also helps the sinner to accept what he has difficulty in believing, namely, that he can be forgiven, then we agree.

It seems to us that Dr. Franks' statement of the moral theory fails because of its inadequate sense of the psychological conditions of forgiveness, as well as what is needed to induce the repentance. What induces the repentance of the sinner and elicits the intuition of faith is not the manifestation of God's love in the life and death of Jesus merely; but the fact that the Cross reveals that God is suffering and must suffer if He is to forgive. He has 'to pay the price of Sin'. Repentance is the condition on man's side of the experience; the suffering which the Cross symbolises is God's side of the experience.

Apart from the above criticisms, Dr. Franks' whole theory

[1] *The Atonement*, p. 70.

is vitiated by the fact that he cannot accept the idea that God can suffer. If the theologians he criticises so keenly are too much biased by the idea that the wrath of God must be propitiated, he himself seems to have allowed his metaphysics to blind him to the psychological condition of forgiveness. It is psychologically impossible for love not to be capable of suffering. Unless God could feel with and for us we could not say "God is Love". There is sheer contradiction in the statement: "The power of the Cross is the power of love that died. I do not say that the suffering of Christ is the suffering of God, any more than I say that God died: the suffering and the death belong to the human revelation of the Divine Love, which Jesus came to make. But I do say that the same love, which in Jesus found expression in suffering and death, is the very love of the Father; it is the power of forgiveness, the grace that saves to the uttermost."[1] If it is the same love, then God must be capable of suffering. We could have wished that, like Anselm whose method he praises, he had linked his conception of the Atonement with the Idea of Incarnation. Anselm was right in this that the two must be connected.

The fundamental truth of the Abelardian theory, whether as presented by Rashdall or Franks, lies in the fact that it does run truly as far as it goes. It does emphasise repentance instead of the sense of guilt. But the objectivity of the Atonement is dropped. Dr. Franks seems to be amazed that anyone should think that the moral theories are not objective. "God, Christ, His Cross and Divine Love", he says, "are objects of human trust" and "responsive love"; hence to trust these gives objectivity. If words mean anything then objectivity does not mean this; surely it means that something happened in God, something that made possible the removal of the alienation in us and in Him caused by the sinner's sin. Otherwise forgiveness would be spontaneous, and worthless. The theories speak as though forgiveness was easy. But not even to the saintliest of men is forgiveness easy. Luther was not far from psychological truth at least, when he said that forgiveness was 'a task fit for a God'. The something that happened in God lay in His capacity to

[1] *The Atonement*, p. 169.

feel the sin as though it were His own, to feel the alienation of the sinner from Himself and His own spontaneous alienation from him; and to overcome the tension within His love sentiment by the suffering manifested in the Cross. He suffered for our sins. "God was in Christ reconciling the world unto Himself." It was God in Christ whose sufferings heal our wounds, and whose suffering reconciles us unto Himself.

One word, only, can be given to McLeod Campbell's theory of vicarious confession and repentance, a theory which has had a deeper influence on subsequent writers than is always realised. He did realise that a thorough repentance alone can break us from sin and create that condition of soul capable of receiving forgiveness; and he did realise that we are incapable of making a full repentance. Our capacity for repentance is relative to our experience of the love of God; hence Dale and Mackintosh's statements that the sense of sin deepens with our knowledge of God. The difficulty with McLeod Campbell is that as Denney has said he has a tendency to regard sin as misfortune rather than a fault; sympathy with the sinner is apt to lapse into an extenuating or condoning of sin. He still speaks in terms of the wrath of God. "He (Christ) responds to the divine wrath against sin, saying, 'Thou art right, O Lord, Who judgest us'." There we have the perfect confession of sin. Again: "That response has all the elements of a perfect repentance in humanity for all the sin of man—a perfect sorrow—a perfect contrition—all, excepting the personal consciousness of sin, and by that perfect response in Amen to the mind of God is the wrath of God rightly met, and that is accorded to divine justice which is its due and could alone satisfy it".[1]

Apart from the fact that no account is really taken of the suffering of God entailed by forgiveness, the theory must fail on the ground that one cannot repent for another, although he may experience his sin as though it were his own. In thus approaching the problem from the psychological side, McLeod Campbell began a movement of thought regarding the Atonement which is likely to increase in the future.

[1] *The Nature of Atonement* (2nd edition), pp. 136–7.

In closing this chapter it is well to remind ourselves that all theories of the Atonement have been preached with effect. The Penal theory will always have an appeal to those whose 'repentance' is strongly tinged with guilt, whose punitive conscience is stronger than their moral conscience. The moral theories will have among their supporters those whose 'moment of vision' did not contain any deep conviction of sin, that conviction growing with their Christian lives. The satisfaction theory can only grip those who can believe that the merit of one can cancel the sin or punishment of another. In any case souls have come to a realisation of sin and repentance through every theory. That is true, because it is not the theory which elicits the intuition but the preaching of the word of reconciliation. Theological dogmas are not merely the embodiment of intellectual concepts, they are also the expression of an experience. Every theory holds some aspect of truth, though the "formula", as Whitehead would put it, may become "secondary to its meaning. . . . The formula sinks in importance, or is even abandoned; but the meaning remains fructifying in the world, finding new expression to suit the circumstances. The formula was not wrong, but it was limited to its own sphere of thought."[1] The 'meaning' in this case of the Atonement, which has remained permanent and continuous, in thought is the Need for Reconciliation, and the power of God to accomplish it. What we have done is to analyse the experience of forgiveness and reconciliation; we have not enunciated a theory. We have tried "to marry old truth to new fact" which James thought all truth should do. To formulate a theory of the Atonement with anything like adequacy is, in our view, only possible if that is linked up with the doctrine of the Incarnation; that in its turn will depend upon a metaphysic. Although the psychologist is not entitled to 'make' dogma, he knows the value of dogma; it embodies meaning, which in psychological terms is experience. Whatever theory of the Atonement may be prevalent at any particular period, the experience of forgiveness and reconciliation will remain the same. As our thought of God becomes

[1] *Religion in the Making*, pp. 121–2.

more refined, and our knowledge of the processes of the human soul more profound and exact, repentance will be more adequate and the cruder features of what God does demand will be outgrown. But preachers who think that they can preach the forgiveness of God with effect without some formula make a profound mistake. As Whitehead has very well said: "Every true dogma which formulates with some adequacy the facts of a complex religious experience is fundamental for the individual in question, and he disregards it at his peril. For formulation increases vividness of apprehension, and the peril is the loss of an aid in the difficult task of spiritual ascent."[1]

NOTE TO CHAPTER VI

After this volume was completed, and indeed in the hands of the printers, our attention was drawn to Bushnell's volume, *Forgiveness and Law*, by Dr. Cairns, who thought there was a similarity between Bushnell's later conception of the Atonement and the theory outlined here.

Bushnell's volume arose from a feeling that in his *The Vicarious Sacrifice* he had conceived the whole 'work of Christ as a reconciling power on men', and had taken little cognisance of the necessity of something happening in God before forgiveness could be a reality. He found that forgiveness is a two-sided affair. Forgiveness, he argued, involves 'the making of cost' on the part of the one wronged. He is not too clear as to the meaning of 'the making of cost', but his illustrations point to the necessity of the Forgiver doing something for the sinner before he could be At-one-ment with him. The main object of 'making cost', if we understand him aright, seems to be the recovery of the sinner to God. The Cross would thus be God 'making cost' for us.

Any likeness between Bushnell's theory and ours arises from the fact that we both approach the problem of Atonement through a psychological analysis of forgiveness. Bushnell realised in this later volume that forgiveness always involves suffering on the part of the one wronged. If anything, Bushnell lays too much emphasis upon the external acts done for the sinner; we have laid the emphasis upon the inner struggle in God which forgiveness involves, and which the Cross symbolises and expresses in time. It is doubtful whether we should have expressed ourselves differently had we read *Forgiveness and Law* before this chapter was written, but we would have pointed to that volume in support of our contentions and theory.

[1] *Religion in the Making*, p. 122.

PART III

CHAPTER VII

Evangelical Experience and Evangelical Doctrine

A FAVOURITE question of an old professor of ours was: "Who makes our Theology?"[1] His answer was: "Individual experience". Perhaps his generalisation was too wide, unless we take into consideration that the need for unity was a fact in the life of the early Church that necessitated the formulation of its experience in the Creeds.

Walter Rauschenbush,[2] who was a teacher of Church History as well as the brilliant theologian of the Social Gospel, maintained that "Theology has often received its most fruitful impulses when secular life and movements have set it new problems". If we interpret 'experience' in its widest sense, then we can say that theology is always the outcome of the need for rational unity; the need to harmonise our experience with feelings; the need for coherence in our spiritual and intellectual life. Psychologically, "reason is not an arbiter to be appealed to but an instrument to be used", as Dr. Visser 'T Hooft[3] has said. Its function is not primarily *judicial;* and certainly it is never impartial in the sense that its judgments are unbiased by motives. In reality, Reason is a motive, a drive, a rational *endeavour* to find and bring unity into our experience. But its organ, the intellect, is often the slave of both conscious and unconscious motives which blind the intellectual vision, and corrupt pure thought. "There is no

[1] *Hibbert Journal*, January, 1906.
[2] *A Theology for the Social Gospel*, see Foreword.
[3] *None Other Gods*, pp. 20–1.

rational sentiment,"[1] according to James, by which he meant that no one could be in love with intellectual abstraction or theorising for its own sake. We may, however, have a sentiment for the Truth, as we may have one for Justice; but this is but another way of saying that we consciously seek and enjoy satisfying this need for rational unity in every aspect of our experience. "The corruption of reason" is really the perverted use of our intellectual powers in the interest of some motive other than reason. If we substitute the term, 'intellect' for 'reason', then Visser 'T Hooft's words are not too strong when he writes: "Everything depends on the purpose for which reason is used. If used for the wrong purpose and on behalf of a wrong authority, its organising ability, its critical function, its urge to coherence may become devilish. But if used for the right purpose and on behalf of right authority, it is then a great power for truth."[2]

Because theology is the child of experience we have thought it best to discuss evangelical theology in relation to evangelical experience. As we saw in the quotation from Whitehead, dogma is the expression of experience (and in this case of evangelical experience) and the dogma makes the experience more vividly realised. Psychologically, the formulation of experience gives it the sense of objectivity. Hence the function of theology is to make the preaching and the experience of the Gospel effective; but if theology itself is to be continually vital, it must be kept in living contact with the experience of Christian people. It is not the doctrine of the Atonement that comes first in time, but the need for reconciliation and forgiveness; then when that experience is realised the doctrine by which the believer explains and makes it more vivid to himself is formulated, and through the formulation he preaches the word of reconciliation to the world.

The psychological study of evangelical religion must keep the experience and the doctrine in living contact. Just as the

[1] See *Papers in Philosophy* (Dent's edition), "Is there a Rational Sentiment?"

[2] *None Other Gods*, p. 21.

need of reconciliation and forgiveness arose out of the need for moral and spiritual unity within a soul, a unity that had been broken by sin, so the need for a doctrine of the Atonement arose out of the need for rational unity between experience and thought. It will be found, we believe, that all evangelical doctrine has the same genetic history.

Evangelical Experience and the Incarnation

We have seen in our study of Forgiveness that the Evangelical finds his experience centred in Christ and is always referred to Him as its source. That is true of those Evangelical Christians whose religious life had no 'great divide' like those whose 'second birth' was realised in a comparatively sudden and dramatic conversion. It is Christ whom they serve through the Church; it is because the image of Christ is consciously or subconsciously in their minds that their prayers are a vivid experience to themselves of communion with God, and not a 'talking to themselves' or a 'speaking into the void'. Most of these 'once-born' Evangelicals have been brought up in Christian homes, passed through Sunday School, and the name and image of Christ have been associated with their religious experience from the beginning. Whittier expresses this religious fact in the familiar lines:

> Through Him the first fond prayers are said
> Our lips of childhood frame,
> The last low whispers of our dead
> Are burdened with His name.

Martineau says somewhere that always our prayers are spoken to the God we have seen in Jesus Christ. That, we believe, will be found to be psychologically true, in Christian countries, of all who pray, however abstract their ideas of God have become.

Be that as it may, it is certainly true that the experience of the decided Christian is always linked with Christ. It is the 'stature of a man in Christ Jesus' his moral life reaches after; it is the same 'mind that was in Christ Jesus' to which he aspires in his religious striving; it is the 'example' of Christ he emulates; and it is the realisation of His Kingdom that motivates his social and political life.

The Christian life and even the Gospel has often been over-simplified by the statement that it is 'A way of Life'. It is that but a great deal more. Christ is not only the 'way', he is also the "truth and the life" to the believer. He is end and dynamic. In Ethics we speak of the *terminus ad quem* as also being the *terminus a quo*—the end is not simply the ideal we desire to reach and towards which we strive, but also the moving, dynamic power generating both moral energy for, and giving direction to, all our behaviour. The end is present in every moral act; it is power and direction; it is an 'indwelling presence' as well as an objective to be reached.

If we substitute *Christ* for the concept of *end* and assume that Christ is a conscious element in the striving and direction, we have the supreme experience of the Evangelical Christian.

> Yea, through life, through death, through sorrow, and through sinning,
> He shall suffice me for He hath sufficed;
> Christ is the end for Christ was the beginning,
> Christ is the beginning for the end is Christ.

Those lines of Myers' *St. Paul* do not speak too strongly of what the hero of the poem experienced, and what every truly believing Evangelical Christian experiences. It is the 'Christ in me' to which the Apostle refers when speaking of the subjective side of his Christian life. Paul's conscious religious experience is not to be wholly explained in terms of an objective revelation of God's love in Christ's life and teaching. To him Christ was an inward experience; it was God through Christ with whom he had fellowship; it was through Christ who loved us that he is 'more than conqueror'; the 'love of God' from which nothing could separate us, was the 'love of God *in* Christ Jesus, our Lord'. The "I live, yet not I but Christ liveth in me" is an experience and not a dogma, as we pointed out in the introductory chapter.

Paul's experience of 'Christ in me' is the experience of every writer in the New Testament. "This is life eternal, to know God and Jesus Christ whom He hath sent." Even if, in deference to New Testament scholarship, we must agree that the words may belong to the writer of the Fourth Gospel and not to Jesus, that makes our case stronger; it but shows that the experience of the writer did not differ one whit from that of Paul; it was an experience of Christ. We may grant that we have not in the Synoptic Gospels any developed doctrine of the Christ of experience comparable to that in the Epistles; but that may not be because the Apostles were ignorant of the Christ of experience, but because their immediate task in writing the Gospel narratives was to set forth the 'Jesus of History'. We must remember that the motive of the Evangelists in writing the Gospels was not historical; it was not simply to record for the benefit of posterity the story of Jesus with whom they had companied, with whom they had lived in fellowship; to whose words they had listened, whose deeds they had witnessed. It is doubtful whether any New Testament scholar would attribute a purely historical motive to them. What was their motive? Was it not to narrate the story of the 'Jesus of History' because He had become to them 'The Christ of Experience'? Were it only in the Pauline Epistles that we had emphasis upon the 'Christ of Experience' then we should have some grounds at least for saying that Paul theologised the simple life and teaching of Jesus. But every Epistle assumes the 'Christ of Experience' and has few references to the 'Jesus of History' as recorded in the Synoptics. The 'Jesus of History' and the 'Christ of Experience' were one and the same to the writers of the New Testament.

The experience of the Apostles has been repeated by Christian believers from the beginning until now; that experience is a present psychological fact, and has to be explained. The psychologist has simply to accept it. "The Living Christ" of Dr. Dale is not an interpretation of St. Paul; it is an experience of Dr. Dale as well. "The Living Christ and the Four Gospels" is the content of the experience he is expounding. The evangelical experience is an experience of living fellowship with Christ—an experience of loving communion, of power received, of inspiration, of a living presence, of an 'objective conscience', to use a phrase of Dr. Denney's, whose voice says, 'This is the way, walk ye in it'.

It is to this experience of Christ in the heart and life of the believer that we must look for the psychological origin of the doctrine of the Incarnation. We need not doubt for a moment that not a little thinking on the Person of Christ is explained by the necessity that drove Anselm to ask: *Cur Deus Homo?* The sacrificial victim must be unblemished; the substitute must himself have had no sin. But when we have analysed this necessity psychologically, we are still thrown back, not to find what concepts involved other concepts, but upon the experience of reconciliation and forgiveness through Christ. Experience always involves a cognitive reference; that reference is never independent of experience. "Truth grows", says James, "for subjective reasons." In other words, the 'subjective reasons' are simply the experiences which compel us to move amongst the facts of experience until we have found an interpretation of them which will satisfy our own minds. This does not imply, nor did James imply, that the 'subjective reasons' could be the criterion of truth. That the 'subjective reasons' can be a source of fallacy is obvious, but they are the source of thought. "Impulse", writes Professor John Dewey, "is needed to arouse thought, incite reflection, and enliven belief. But only thought notes obstructions, invents tools, directs technique, and thus converts impulse into art which lives in objects. Thought is born as the twin of impulse in every moment of impeded habit."[1] Until experience finds its cognitive reference, it is impeded.

Amongst the 'subjective reasons' there will be found the intellectual necessity for consistency of thought. There will also be found in some a 'subjective reason' of intellectual curiosity. We may study and reflect upon religious experience of Jesus without having any personal experience of Him; we may be motivated by no more than the curiosity aroused by the obvious impact Jesus has had upon history and upon

[1] *Human Nature and Conduct*, pp. 170–1 (George Allen and Unwin Ltd.).

individual lives. The modern study of conversion and revivals and even religious experience as a whole had its motivation here. But it will be one thing to study Jesus and the doctrines which have grown around his Person and Work from the 'subjective reason' of finding an explanation of our own personal communion with Christ, or our own conversion and religious experience, and another thing to study Him and what has been asserted in regard to Him for the 'subjective reason' of intellectual or spiritual curiosity. All that the latter can do is help us to move amongst our concepts; to discern inconsistencies of *thought;* it cannot for a moment validate or invalidate the fact of the experience. It can only validate or invalidate the *interpretation* of experience. "Immediate knowledge", says Whitehead, "is infallible."[1] Error lies in the 'symbol of reference'. And it is only amongst the 'symbols of reference' that the intellectual interpretation can move.

We would be the last to belittle the contribution of intellectual or spiritual curiosity to the interpretation of evangelical experience; but that interpretation is bound to be from the outside. When the motivation for reflection is the subjective need to explain to ourselves at least, "That which was from the beginning, which we have heard, which we have seen with our eyes, which we have looked upon, and our hands handled of the Word of Life", and the capacity for reflection is adequate, we are more likely to find a truer explanation.

Be that as it may, all we contend for here is that "The Way to the Real Jesus" began not in an 'august tradition' regarding Him, but in an experience of Him by whom the soul was so mastered that the disciples could do no other than say with Thomas, "My Lord, and My God"; or with Paul, "The Son of God who loved me and gave Himself for me"; or with John, "We beheld His glory, the glory as of the only begotten of the Father full of grace and truth".

That experience of the disciples and their explanation of it is repeated in the souls of men today. They may not be able to accept the Chalcedon formula of the Incarnation, but the

[1] *Symbolism*, pp. 1-24.

fact that they give to Christ the supreme place in their religious faith gives grounds for the psychologist's contention that the doctrine of the Incarnation corresponds to something in the experience of the believer related to Christ; even more than it gives grounds to the theologians' assertion that the Incarnation 'is based on an irrefragable reality'.

The psychologist would agree with Dr. Neville Talbot that there is a danger in the tendency to displace the centre of gravity of religious experience from God to our Lord. The theological interest must take precedence over the Christological. The Incarnation, if it is an objective truth, must have been necessitated in God. But apart from that, the psychologist must take into account the fact that religious experience is wider than evangelical experience; and also that in the true evangelical experience the believer is always *led to God* through Christ. The experience of Paul was an experience of the Father, through Christ by the Spirit. "For through Him we both have access by one Spirit unto the Father."

Psychology and the Incarnation

Although this is not the place, nor have we the space, to discuss the problems of Christology, we have no doubt that psychology has a contribution to make here even as it has in regard to the Atonement. The problem of the Person of Christ, as we read it, is how two natures, the divine and human, both perfect and complete, could be predicated of one Person. Dr. Cadoux's[1] objections to the Chalcedon formula seem to be that such a theory does not square with the records of Jesus' life. That we must take account of the history of Jesus Christ, no student of the psychology of religion would deny; but it is exceedingly doubtful if the problems of the Person of Christ get their setting from a study of the Gospels; certainly the problems cannot find their solution in the study of the Gospels alone. It is a problem of what Selfhood involves; and that, as Laird has pointed out, is both a

[1] *The Case for Evangelical Modernism.*

problem for metaphysics and psychology. Psychology shows "that both the unity and continuity of the self are subject to apparent anomalies when carefully examined in the light of the available evidence. The continuity is oddly interrupted; the unity, if not entirely dissociable is, at any rate, a thing of degree."[1] It is not too much to say that the "Two Nature" theory could receive real grounds of support from the light being thrown on the nature of self-hood by recent studies on the psychology of personality. Two natures—shall we say persons or quasi-persons—may exist; and we have evidence that they have existed in one self. On the surface they seem independent of each other, are wholly different in moral outlook and in practically all the characteristic traits associated with the idea of personality even to the point of a different content to consciousness; they may be unconscious of 'each' other. The integration of the self has been broken even to the point of self-consciousness, for one 'self' may disown the other.

It is true that the 'two natures' in these split personalities are as a rule contradictory; but the point is that they have two natures in one self. It is true also that the 'split' personality is abnormal; but 'abnormal' denotes nothing more than 'out of the usual', and abnormality is a thing of degree; and if Jesus had both a human and a divine nature in His one Person—and all theories except those which ascribe to Him no more than a human nature agree on this point, He was 'out of the usual'. No serious student will think for a moment that we are contending that the Person of our Lord is to be explained by the study of abnormal or 'dissociated' personalities; that is not our point. Our point is that the study of the 'Two Nature' theory, which is still the recognised creedal position of the Church, may be approached in the light thrown upon the nature of self-hood by psychological study.

There we must leave the question. All we are concerned with here is the fact that the idea of Jesus as the Incarnation of God

[1] *The Idea of the Soul*, p. 105.

had its birth in the experience of the 'Living Christ', the 'Christ in me' of Christian believers. The problems of Christianity are problems of thought; they rise in the attempt to reconcile the fact that the record of the Gospels gives us a Man; the religious experience gives us something more; and the impression left in the mind of any reader of the New Testament is that of more than a man; or if that is too strong a statement, the impression left on the mind of an intelligent reader of the New Testament is that those who recorded the history of Jesus felt He was something more than a man. As Dr. Headlam has said in his Preface to Dr. Relton's *A Study in Christology:* "The religious consciousness of mankind has never been able to stop there (with his manhood). We turn to the record again and we find that, while it is always that of a man, it is always that of one more than a man. And this conception is clinched by the Resurrection. He dies as man but He rises again as other than man. And the testimony of the record has been added to by the testimony of experience. Christ in religious thought has always been associated in both intellectual conception and in religious experience as in a unique way the source of human redemption and atonement—a redemption which would not be possible unless He were God. So the religious consciousness has equally held that Christ is God."

Evangelical Experience and the Doctrine of the Holy Spirit

The necessity for the warning of Dr. Talbot against the tendency of making theology Christo-centric instead of Theocentric is seen clearly in the neglect of theologians of the past to deal adequately with the doctrine of the Holy Spirit, and the place of the Holy Spirit in Christian experience. That the work of the Holy Spirit could only be fully realised with the departure of Christ seems to be the implication of the last chapters of the fourth Gospel. His work, as *Holy* Spirit, was to be a work in relation to the mediation of the living presence of Christ to the individual soul, and to society.

Perhaps it was natural, as Canon Raven has pointed out, that the early Patristic Fathers should busy themselves mostly with the doctrine of the Person and Work of Christ; for it was Christ that had to be presented to the Græco-Roman world. It was through Christ their own religious experience had come; it was He, they believed, who had "united them" with "the Master-spring of the universe"; and it was to be expected that much of their efforts should be occupied with the "reconciling of their belief in the divinity of Jesus Christ with their conviction of the essential unity of the Godhead". Theologians of today are making good the defect of their predecessors, and some of the best theological writers of our time are concerned with the doctrine of the Holy Spirit; while men like Berdyaev are rehabilitating the status of spirit in philosophical thought.

It would not be untrue to say, that the truly evangelical experience broke into full flower at Pentecost. We are accustomed to date the origin of the Christian Church from the influx of insight and power experienced in that upper room where 'the disciples were gathered with one accord'. It is true that the roots of their evangelical experience lay in their companionship with Jesus during the days of His flesh; but who will deny that it was in and through the Pentecost experience that the roots were quickened; that the full meaning of Christ was intuited; their convictions were clarified; and the 'Jesus of History' became the 'Christ of Experience'? Whatever doubts they had regarding His Messiahship were swept away in that soul-stirring experience.

But if evangelical experience dates from Pentecost, and if the Church was born in that experience, it is just as true to say that the renewal of the Church's influence today, the revival of faith among the masses, the deepening of the personal relationship to God in the individual, and the realisation of the Kingdom of God upon earth, must come from the same source—the experience of the Holy Spirit.

From the very beginning of the Church's history the Holy Spirit has been associated with the personal realisation of God and the progressive experience of God in Christ. Jesus, Himself, received the Spirit at Baptism; and it was the Spirit which drove Him into the wilderness; He appropriates the words of the prophet to describe His Mission, *The Spirit of the Lord is upon me for he hath sent me to preach the Gospel;* to Nicodemus' question how a man could be born again, He answered he must be *born of the Spirit;* He returned to Galilee *in the power of the Spirit.*

It has been said that the Spirit "is not a primary conception with Jesus"; that He was silent on the topic because He distrusted the popular excesses and reacted against the attitude of John the Baptist in that respect. But if we have anything like a true reflection of the mind of Christ in John's Gospel, then undoubtedly the Spirit was more than a subordinate conception with Him. It may be true, as Bishop Gore contends, that it was Paul who formulated the doctrine of the Spirit; but not even Paul goes beyond John in the delineation of the *function* of the Spirit. In the closing chapters of John's Gospel we find the outline of what is every believer's experience of the Spirit. The main function of the Spirit in relation to Christ is summed up in words ascribed to Jesus: "He shall glorify me, for He shall take of mine and shall declare it unto you". To manifest Christ to the world, that is the religious function of the Holy Spirit in relation to Christ.

That the work of the Spirit is far more comprehensive than this has been well argued by Canon Raven and Berdyaev. Our interest, however, lies in the purely religious function of the Spirit in mediating the living presence of Christ to the believer, and bringing about evangelical experience.

The Spirit was to be the teacher and Witness of Christ; He was to elicit the conviction of sin; to operate in the conscience creating the obligation to righteousness; to initiate repentance through which the soul was to be reconciled to God; to guide into all truth; and be a comforter, or paraclete.

Although Paul seems to move away from the direct intuitions of John regarding the Spirit to a more theological expression of the work of the Spirit, there is no radical difference between the two. Paul makes explicit what is implicit in John. To Paul, however, we must look for the Spirit's work in relation to the growth of evangelical experience in the heart of the believer. The Spirit was the power of God; the indwelling means of life in Christ; the indwelling life of Christ in Paul. Through the Spirit he died unto sin and shared in the resurrection of Jesus. It was the Spirit of the Life in Christ Jesus that made him free from the law of sin and death; his conscience was verified by the Spirit; he was sanctified by the Spirit. When he appeals to his converts to discard their sins, it is on the ground that their bodies are the temple of the Holy Spirit. He exhorts his readers to abound in the Spirit; to pray in the Spirit. The Spirit is the Spirit of liberty; He strengthens the inner man, and through Him Christ dwells richly in their hearts. He charged them neither to quench the Spirit nor grieve Him.

In Paul's experience the Holy Spirit and the indwelling Christ seem interchangeable terms; *the Spirit is the Spirit of the Lord.* And, doubtless, in evangelical experience it is difficult to differentiate them; the experience of the 'living Christ' is often identified with the experience of the Spirit. E. F. Scott argues that in the mystical experience of Paul "the historical Christ becomes a universal presence, dwelling in the hearts of men; while the Spirit ceases to be a vague supernatural principle, and is one, in the last resort, with Christ".[1] What we understand Professor Scott to mean is that in Christ the universal principle becomes incarnate, and through Him becomes active in the Christian experience. Dr. Denney comes near to saying the same thing when he writes: "We can think of no presence of the Spirit except the spiritual presence of Christ".

It is doubtful, however, if Paul meant to equate Christ and the Spirit. In his own experience he must have found that the function of the one was different from that of the other; even though there are experiences of 'indwelling' which might be ascribed to Christ or the Spirit, both in experience and thought they are different.

[1] *The Holy Spirit in the New Testament.*

Whatever theological implications Paul's teaching may have, there can be no question of the implication of the doctrine of the Spirit for evangelical experience. He is the source of the faith through which we accept and act upon the religious intuitions; He is the power through which we grow up 'into the stature of a man in Jesus Christ'; He is the medium of the evangelical mysticism whereby the Living Presence of Christ becomes the background and the atmosphere of our conscious Christian life even when we are not engaged in specific religious exercises; He is the source of all that the Evangelical means by spiritual life. Only by waiting upon the Spirit, he believes, can a revival of true religion come; and only by living in the Spirit—'Walking in the Spirit'—can his own spiritual life grow richer and deeper. He is the operating activity of God in the soul, hiding the believer in Christ, shaping the spirit of the Christian until Christ shines through every mood, manifesting Himself in every decision, embodying Himself in every act. The spiritual life is exhibited in the 'fruits of the Spirit'; and these 'fruits' are not ethical accretions laboriously added to one's ethical life, but the natural end of a soul rooted and fed by the indwelling Spirit.

Not the least work of the Spirit is the making of the soul free from the 'law of sin and death'. It is in this freedom that the true liberty of the Christian soul is found. The experience of the believer is that sin is not only cancelled but its power is broken. That liberty is, psychologically, both a freedom from the compulsion of sin, and a freedom before the law. It is not a freedom from the law but a freedom before the law. The conscience is now a direction instead of a prohibition; it allows our behaviour-tendencies to become incorporated into our personality, and they are modified by the total personality; whereas previously they were held in leash lest they should act contrary to the law, they are now swept into the service of the Christian personality. In terms of modern psychology this would mean that the Spirit is the source of *sublimation;* the behaviour-tendencies receive new 'end-motives' to use a good distinction by Dr. Hadfield; that is to say the natural biological and personality motives are not eradicated but their end purposes are changed; their energy is spontaneously re-directed. And it is not merely a matter of re-direction, but there is *a change of mind or of heart, readjustment in the unconscious as well as in the* conscious. The re-direction of energy is due to a *re-direction of love.* That is the silent unconscious work of the Spirit in the soul. Sublimation, like repression, is an unconscious process, but through it we are 'changed from glory to glory'. Sin not only loses its attraction, but the whole attitude towards it is changed.

In like manner the whole attitude to the Law is changed. It is not now a system of prohibitions, or compulsions lying over against our behaviour-tendencies with which they must be made to comply; the spirit of the hired servant is changed for the spirit of the son; the scrupulosity of the conscience disappears; the letter of the Law is changed for the spirit. We remember an article in the *Hibbert Journal*, of some years ago, in which a writer expressed the opinion that the Gospels were inferior to the Old Testament and the *Koran* because they had no details of law by which the individual could guide his behaviour. But this is really the glory of the Gospel. It is true there is no law as to what is our duty to our neighbour; but that is because there is something deeper: 'Thou shalt love thy neighbour as thyself'; there are no detailed rules as to how we shall worship God; there is the profounder imperative: 'Thou shalt worship the Lord thy God in spirit and in truth'. The slavery to the detailed law is displaced by the spirit in which all behaviour towards our neighbour should be inspired. Whatever form of worship any individual prefers the spirit in which he engages in it should be the same. Hence we have freedom before the law but not from it.

The process of sanctification, then, inspired and guided by the Holy Spirit is not a matter of giving up sinful tendencies; it is a positive change of interests, of the values which the behaviour-tendencies seek in their objects. To be free from the 'law of sin and death' is to be free from the law of sinful habit, sinful disposition, sinful attitude of mind; free not because the mind has been emptied of its instinctive tendencies or capacity for acquired desire, but because these have found new end-motives in harmony with the mind of Christ. The behaviour-tendencies become linked with the spiritual ends of the soul, or the spiritual personality. The soul has its own ends; indwelt by the spirit it seeks these ends; and these ends are identical with Christ's! That is why Paul could pray for his converts that they might have the same mind that was in Christ.

We shall have opportunity to touch again on the work of the Holy Spirit when dealing briefly with Sanctification; our main object at the moment is to link the experience of the Spirit with doctrine. All doctrine is rooted in experience. The permanent element in the Gospel, in the 'faith once delivered to the saints' is not in dogma (there is no revelation of dogma) but abides in the evangelical experience, seen first in the Apostles but repeated by generations of Evangelicals, of reconciliation with God, the forgiveness of sins, the liberation from the 'law of sin and death', fellowship with and knowledge of God in Christ through the co-operation of the Holy Spirit, the experience of the Living Christ mediated through the Holy Spirit. Indeed the Holy Spirit initiates, sustains, and continues our experience of God through Christ.

Psychology and the Personality of the Holy Spirit

The Holy Spirit to the Evangelical is not only the source of his experience of Christ, but is also a dogma essential to his conception of God: He is the third Person of the Trinity.

It might be thought that where metaphysicians fear to tread, psychologists are wise not to venture too far. Nevertheless, though psychology cannot penetrate into the jungle of problems raised by the Trinitarian conception of God, it may help to point or suggest a way through the jungle by its increasing understanding of the psychological nature of personality. That is all we hope to do here; and we do it with no dogmatic air of finality, but with the humble feeling that we may be raising more questions than our tentative suggestions are designed to answer.

Whatever contribution psychology can make to the problem of the personality of God as interpreted by evangelical doctrine, it can be no more than some inferences that *may* be drawn from the psychological analysis of personality. We have already seen that the 'ego' which is the subject of analysis by the psychotherapist, i.e. the 'ego' of Freudian psychology, is subject to dissociation. Its unity seems to be a matter of degree; it can be 'split'. It is impossible to equate this ego with the metaphysical concept of personality, which implies both continuity and unity. In a *fugue*[1] the continuity of the ego is broken in a far more serious way than in sleep. Our dreams do show that the normal waking ego is continuous with the mind active in sleep. In a fugue, however, the ego active in the abnormal condition may be wholly different from the ego as known before the 'split' took place. This creates a really difficult problem for the metaphysician.

So far psychologists have fought shy of the metaphysical implications of their subject-matter. Most of them feel that if their science is to remain autonomous, and not slip back into abstract metaphysics, where it was sterile, they must resist the temptation to accept responsibility for the explanation of the Psyche. Dr. Wm. Brown, who has the philosophical equipment to deal with the metaphysical implications of psychology, contends that "the self, the mind that psychology deals with, is not the same as the soul. . . . Psychology is not the science of the soul, psychology is the science of the mind —of mental processes in time. But corresponding with the mental process in time, and as a complement of it, you have the experiencing ego, and that ego has its own reality and its own unity. This is the idea of the pure ego as distinguished from the empirical ego". If we read Dr. Brown aright, then the 'empirical ego' is simply mental process conscious of itself;

[1] Used in Psychopathology for a state of dissociated mental activity over which the subject has no control and of which the subject is, as a rule, unaware.

the science of the soul, of the Subject, the 'pure ego' must be left to metaphysics.

The same position in regard to the study of the nature of the psyche, considered as more than the psychologically-ill ego that the patient presents to the psychotherapist, is taken by Dr. Jung. He recognises that the rational explanation of mental processes is the work of science; but when the study of these throws the student back upon the more ultimate question: "Whence does this consciousness come?", he answers that "At this point science ends".[1]

It is doubtful whether the psychologist is entitled to leave the question there. He is compelled to ask the question, even in the treatment of the psychologically-ill ego, whether the source of consciousness of which Jung speaks or the 'pure ego' of which Dr. Brown speaks has any influence upon the 'empirical ego', or the mental processes which are the subject matter of psychological science. Neither Dr. Jung nor Dr. Brown would, we believe, assert that the 'pure ego' is without influence on conscious process as experienced by the 'empirical ego'. Is there a correlation? Or are we to be thrown back on a theory of Parallelism analogous to the theory held by some in regard to the relation between bodily and mental process?

We cannot but think, after twenty years of psychotherapeutic work, to say nothing of years of previous study, that the soul or 'pure ego' is not without influence upon mental process; or that it plays a part in the causation of mental illness, or may become a therapeutic agent. Professor Laird,[2] rightly in our opinion, refuses to believe that the 'split personality' really involves a break in the continuity of the Self. From observation we should say that it does not. The 'split personality' is conscious that something is wrong; the Dr. Jekyll knows the Mr. Hyde; even the famous Sally Beauchamp was not altogether unconscious of her 'other selves'; and it is agreed that personality 'B' knew personality 'A' and could leave

[1] *Modern Man in Search of a Soul*, p. 279.
[2] *The Idea of the Soul*, chaps. iv and v.

messages for her. Does not this imply that there is something deeper than the 'partial selves' of which she was conscious, or which appeared? When a man weeps because he cannot repent; when a woman is ashamed because she cannot feel ashamed at her own shameful conduct, must we not assume a self deeper than mental process which is in contact with a self that can weep for the unrepentant ego, and be ashamed at the ego's lack of shame? These are not paradoxes. They are commonplaces to the pscyhotherapist, and they provide him with the task, if he is to cure his patient, of eliciting this repentance or shame, or to use purely psychological terms, change his psychological attitude to his behaviour- and emotional-tendencies. Their moral consciousness passes an unqualified judgment upon themselves which they accept as true; whence comes the moral judgment? They cannot experience what they know they ought to experience. Whence the 'ought'?

Is it too far-fetched a speculation to say that the true Subject, the Soul, the self-conscious essence of our being, is other than the mental processes or behaviour-tendencies on which it passes judgment? That it must stand aloof, as it were, until the ego to which the behaviour-tendencies and mental processes belong, 'comes to itself'? Is it not more reasonable to infer that the empirical ego can resist the permeating unifying principles which are the self-conscious essence, as we have already implied in our doctrine of conversion. It seems to us, that a true *cure* comes about when the 'pure ego' gains control of the mental processes and shapes them to its own spiritual ends.

Modern psychology, it seems to us, has laid bare problems of the self which metaphysics dare not ignore; but it has also uncovered facts about experience which will need the help of metaphysics if they are to be understood. Although we can truly say: "My impulses are mine, but not I", we still feel responsible for them.

We have been led into these speculations by the experiential basis of the doctrine of the Holy Spirit. When a man is *born again* he is conscious of something within him coming into being which is not to be identified with his mental processes, his behaviour-tendencies, or the sum-total, named the 'empirical ego'. He is conscious of being a 'new man in a new world'; he is born of the Spirit and he *knows* that his spirit has been *born*.

A word of speculation may be allowed on the bearing of this on the doctrine of the concept of God. God is experienced by the Evangelical as 'Father, Son and Holy Spirit'.

In the analysis of the personality we find more than one centre of consciousness. What is called the 'unconscious' is purposive and dynamic as we have seen. To enter consciousness in thought or phantasy the products of the unconscious have often to clothe themselves in symbols as in dreams or as in rationalisation, or projections in waking life. Must we not assume some element of consciousness below the threshold of the conscious ego, intelligent as well as purposive? In other words, intelligent awareness of mental process is not confined to the conscious ego. If unwanted thought or phantasy must worm itself into consciousness by subtle forms of symbol, etc., something must be aware of the necessity for this. The ego, as all admit, is liable to self-deception. But is it really self-deception? Or is the self deceived by some element of our personality which is really a centre of consciousness? There can be no question, for the psychotherapist, at least, that the unconscious is intelligent, and highly intelligent from the point of view of its own activity and expression. The term 'unconscious' expresses the relation of the conscious ego to it, but not the relation of itself to awareness. The whole self is aware of much more than the conscious ego. In other words, the conscious ego may be unaware of the unconscious ego, but is the latter unaware of itself? It would seem to be aware not only of its own purposes but also of the ego. Post hypnotic suggestion would seem to show this. A patient given under deep hypnosis a suggestion to come again at a time which has been given in minutes and seconds, will apparently unconsciously do the sum in his unconscious; and although he has no knowledge that he has been told to keep the appointment at that time, he turns up. When a man enters a fugue there is a reason for it; he is escaping from something of which he is unconsciously aware, and yet consciously is ignorant of. Hence we are not speculating without grounds when we say that we have two centres of consciousness—that of the Conscious ego, and that of the Unconscious ego.

Can we go further? We have already seen that we do not think ideas, we think with them. They are instruments of thought, i.e. of reflective thought. When I think that John Smith is like John Jones the association takes place in the subconscious; and I simply become aware of the likeness, which I may then scrutinise and even reject. It is the comparison of ideas, their implications, their meaning with which reflection deals, and we believe this has a tremendous effect on behaviour and the shaping of the ego.

But finally, the 'pure ego' is the source of the continuity which we all experience. Whether it is itself a 'variant,' as Professor Laird seems to believe, we need not discuss for the moment. But the sense of continuity, of something which is not to be identified with the procession of thoughts, feelings, emotions, etc., is no figment of the imagination. Were the pure ego part of the procession it is difficult to see how it could know of the procession at all. Are we not then compelled to postulate or infer a third centre of consciousness in the Self considered as the whole? Each may be independent and yet part of the unity of Self-hood? Leave out the unconscious of abnormal psychology and we are still left with the fact that ideas are generated in some part of the self other than the conscious ego; then we have the fact of the conscious ego; then the experience of being a conscious Subject, a Soul deeper than all our behaviour-processes, deeper than any mental process considered as 'mine'; and which can only be described by the term 'I'.

Here, then, we seem to have three centres of consciousness; they are independent in the sense that they can work apparently as though they were dissociated from one another; nevertheless, they act and react on each other; they influence each other. As Mr. Smuts says in his volume on *Holism*,[1] the unconscious may not be heard but it has a vote, and often a very decisive one. In other words, it acts upon the conscious ego. On the other hand, it is the attitude of the ego to what is generated in the unconscious that determines to a large extent what will be repressed; what form the unconscious motives will take when their activities enter consciousness.

The more difficult problem for the psychologist as for the metaphysician is the influence of the 'pure ego' on the ego. "Talent",[2] says Dr. Brown, "belongs to the mind; genius to the Soul." The implication of that is, that every step forward in true thought or progress of any kind is dependent upon the extent to which the 'pure ego' can influence the ego.

There can be no doubt, however, that self-consciousness seems to belong to the 'pure ego' or subject. It is this Subject that experiences shame, repentance; it is the empirical ego that experiences guilt. The moral consciousness of which we see little or no sign in the lower animals is only possible to that inner conscious ego which 'feels' free. We would suggest that moral freedom belongs wholly here. The empirical ego, as we saw in a previous chapter, has no power to determine what will come into the mind; to the degree that the pure ego is interacting with and influencing the empirical ego, to that degrce our reactions are free; and as we saw it is the reaction that matters.

In spite of the fact that we seem to have three centres of consciousness in our persons, there is but one self. It is as Laird has said, a continuant and a variant. The principle of continuity lies, we think, in the 'pure ego'; the principle of variancy in the empirical ego. Nevertheless, we must be careful not to fall into the fallacy of three selves. Perhaps we should speak of selfhood rather than a Self or Subject. What if these three centres of consciousness are the conditions of self-hood? The philosophical idea that the pure ego is the pre-supposition of the empirical ego may be an inadequate explanation of the facts.

[1] *Holism and Evolution*, p. 254.

[2] *Science and Personality*.

Self-hood is not the 'pure ego', but the three centres of consciousness. They are the conditions of self-hood; and the relations within the one Subject.

Naturally the psychologist must move warily when he comes to metaphysics; but is there not a suggestion here for theological writers on the metaphysical questions which the doctrine of the Trinity and personality of the Spirit raises? The psychologist would not identify the Godhead with either Father, Son or Spirit; these are not *modes* of God; they are the conditions of Godhead and relations within the Godhead. There are the three centres of consciousness, like the three centres in ourselves, apparently independent of each other; yet constituting the unity of the personality. The 'modes' apply to man's experience of God; not to aspects of God.

Our speculations have been carried far enough; many may think too far. But they have risen out of the necessity of finding a psychological explanation of Christian or evangelical experience. The Evangelical's experience of God is an experience of Father, Son and Holy Spirit; yet he is conscious of the unity of God; he is not conscious of tritheism, though his expressions of the Trinity may imply tritheism. He knows in his heart that he has been reconciled to the Father, through the Son by the Spirit. He has experience of all three and that experience must find some explanation. The Trinity was no mere outcome of the love for spinning metaphysical abstractions; but arose as all doctrine has arisen, in the experience of the soul forgiven and in fellowship, and deriving all from God. His life is hid with Christ in God. He has "access to the Father, through the Son, by the Spirit". There was no time when the Son was not; from the beginning the Spirit has been operative in creation and creative activity; His function is wider than the religious one of eliciting the intuition of the Gracious God revealed in the Son; or indwelling the soul growing up into the Stature of a man in Christ Jesus. That creative activity, however, in Goodness, Beauty and Truth, in Nature is the study of philosophy rather than either psychology of religious experience or evangelical doctrine.

Psychology and the Authority of the Bible

Before closing this chapter on experience and doctrine we must examine what psychology can say in relation to the authority of Scripture. That evangelical experience is closely linked with Scripture and its interpretation by the Holy Spirit we have already seen in the chapter dealing with the theological emphasis of Evangelicalism. Every revival of evangelical religion has been accompanied by a re-emphasis upon, and a re-acceptance of the authority of the Bible as the record of the Revelation of God, and as revealing the way of life. The Barthian revival in theology is rooted in The Word as that which speaks to the conscience, without qualification, of the righteousness of God.

Naturally the psychologist cannot pass any judgment upon the objective authority of Scripture; he cannot give objective grounds for Brunner's distinction between *general* and *special* revelation. He can endorse, however, Brunner's contention that only the personal can reveal the personal; and he can likewise say, that as a matter of fact, the Scriptures, as revealing the Word of God, elicit an intuition regarding the Righteousness of God and the Grace of God that no other literature does elicit. Not only so, but the intuition elicited has for the individual an authority for the moral and spiritual consciousness stronger than any other intuition.

If, as we have contended, experience is prior to theology, then the task of theology in relation to the Scriptures would seem to be to validate the authority first felt as an intuition.

Let us illustrate what we mean by saying that the Scriptures elicit an intuition that equates them with the Word of God. As far back as 1904 a volume was published anonymously called *The Diary of a Churchgoer*. The writer has been classed as a sceptic and an agnostic as far as the central truths of evangelical faith are concerned. Nevertheless, we have this remarkable passage relative to the effect the Gospel story has often had upon him:

"The story is quite familiar to us. We supply the sentences

beforehand as the reader proceeds. Yet it has happened—one knows not how—it will doubtless happen again—one cannot tell when—that, as the verses follow one another, suddenly out of the well-known story there comes a strange thrilling sense of heights and depths never before scaled or plumbed. Something in the air, something in ourselves, something it may be, in the voice of the reader, in sunny mornings, in country churches, when the scents and sounds of summer come through open windows, in the equable atmosphere of some vast minster, when the words spoken at the lectern are encompassed with stillness—under all varying circumstances, defying calculation and explanation—the new comes out of the old, the passion out of the commonplace, and we say within ourselves, 'This thing is of God'."

That is what we mean when we say that the Scriptures elicit an intuition that they are of God. 'Deep calleth unto deep.' Unless there was that in the soul of man to which the Scriptures could appeal, there could be no such response as we have quoted. The religious consciousness always implies a double response—a response from God's side and one from man's side. We could not attend to God's appeal unless there was something within us with which we could respond; and our capacity to respond implies something in the Scriptures to which we can respond. The Scriptures elicit an intuition, not a dogma. "A dogma", as Whitehead has pointed out, "is the expression of a fact as it appears within a certain sphere of thought"; it can only be understood in relation to a system of thought. With the dogmatic authority of Scripture the psychologist cannot deal; nevertheless he cannot but take account of the fact that the Scriptures elicit a direct intuition of the central facts of evangelical experience.

The Scriptures themselves are the expression of direct intuitions; they express what men have directly intuited as an experience of God as well as their response to these direct intuitions. According to Whitehead, "Expression is the one fundamental sacrament. It is the outward and visible sign of an inward and spiritual grace." If this is true, then there are deeper than dogmatic grounds for the evangelical position that preaching is "The Sacrament of The Word". However that may be, the Scriptures are creative of the evangelical experience; and they conform to Whitehead's doctrine of the relation of expression to intuition. From that point of view, the psychologist cannot do better than apply Whitehead's words to Scriptural authority: ". . . the expressive sign is more than interpretable. It is creative. It elicits the intuition which interprets it. It cannot elicit what is not there. A note on a tuning-fork can elicit a response from a piano. But the piano has already in it the string tuned to the same note. In the same way the expressive sign elicits the existent intuition which would not otherwise emerge into individual distinctiveness. Again in theological language, the sign works *ex opere operato*, but only within the limitation that the recipient be patient of the creative action."

What Whitehead says here about the 'expressive sign' in general can be applied to the Scriptures in particular as the expressive sign of men's experience of God.

There is another point in Whitehead's doctrine of the relation of expression to intuition that applies even more to the Scriptures and to Him in the Epistle to the Hebrews who is spoken of as "the very image of God's substance", than to the examples from literature which Whitehead uses. He says truly: "The history of culture shows that originality is not a process of continuous development. There are antecedent periods of slow evolution. Finally, as if touched by a spark, a very few persons, one, two or three, in some particular province of experience, express completely novel intuitions. Such intuitions can be responded to, analysed, in terms of their relationships to other ideas, fused with other forms of experience, but as individual primary intuitions within their own province of experience they are not surpassed.

"The world will not repeat Dante, Shakespeare, Socrates, or the Greek tragedians. These men, in connection with the tiny groups forming their immediate environments of associates and successors and perhaps of equals, add something once and for all. We develop in connection with them, but not beyond them, in respect to those definite intuitions which they flashed upon the world. Those examples are taken from literature merely for the sake of easy intelligibility." [1]

It seems strange that Whitehead should have failed to include Jesus of Nazareth and the great prophets of Israel or Paul amongst his illustrations. It cannot be doubted that they are the finest examples of the doctrine he is propounding.

Psychologically, then, the authority of the Scriptures lies in the direct intuition they elicit and interpret. As we shall see that intuition leads to Faith, and the Faith leads in turn to new intuitions. It is true that the theologian must find a dogmatic formula for the direct intuition of the authority of the Bible; nevertheless, it is the intuition to which every theologian must come back if he is to rehabilitate the authority of the Scriptures.

[1] *Religion in the Making.*

CHAPTER VIII

The Spiritual Life of the Evangelical

THE spiritual life of the Evangelical has for its aim a life 'hid with Christ in God'. From its beginning the Evangelical is conscious of definite experiences which are denoted by the terms, *Grace*, *Faith*, *Assurance*, *Prayer*, and *Sanctification*, sometimes called *Perfection*. Whatever doctrines have gathered round these terms, they denoted in the first place experiences; and those experiences are continued in the spiritual life of believers now.

FAITH AND GRACE

The experiences of Faith and Grace are intimately linked together in the heart of the believer. It is by Faith that he intuits the Grace of God; and at the same time it is by Grace that he is enabled to intuit God's graciousness; in other words his Faith is the outcome of Grace. God may reckon unto him his Faith as righteousness, but he does not himself so reckon it. As Dr. Moffatt puts it: "When the Apostle sought to transmit 'the light of the knowledge of the glory of God in the face of Jesus Christ' which had dawned upon himself outside Damascus, his good news may be described as a message of proclamation announcing that 'All is of Grace and Grace for all'."[1]

MEANING OF GRACE IN EVANGELICAL EXPERIENCE

The Grace of God is the first intuition of Faith. It is the intuition of the believer that whatever standing he has before God, the forgiveness he has received, the initiative that brought him to God, the continuance of fellowship with God, are all

[1] *Grace in the New Testament*, p. 131.

due to Grace, due to God's free favour; he believes that the Faith that justifies him is *all of Grace*. Theologically, then, Grace is relative to the believer's standing before God. Psychologically, the Grace of God can mean nothing other than the Graciousness of God, and the vision of the writer of the Fourth Gospel of the only begotten Son as full of Grace, was the vision of His graciousness. In other words, the believer experiences the Grace of God as a relationship to himself.

It is not difficult to understand how the experience of God's Grace has come to be confused with the notion of Grace as a 'substance', "a continuous stream," as a 'gift' or even as a 'power'. One writer speaks of "the coming of the Holy Ghost" as a 'double gift', first of all the "gift of the Third Person of the Blessed Trinity Himself, and then of the Grace, infused virtues and gifts which He brings with Him".[1] Again, "The fruit of the divine indwelling is *Habitual* or Sanctifying Grace. . . . Grace is essentially the principle of life."

Psychologically Grace is not an entity; 'infused virtues' seem to the psychologist a contradiction of terms. Grace is the Graciousness of God as experienced in the heart of the believer. Every gift flows from the Graciousness of God, the Graciousness of His love towards us; and to turn Grace into something other than the Gracious love of God is to materialise it. The Grace is not the power or strength we receive in the hour of temptation; it is not the comfort we receive in sorrow; it is not an *entity* that *abounds more than sin*. Nevertheless, there is no contradiction. The power is the gift of Grace, the comfort is the sense of that Gracious presence with the believer in his sorrow; the Grace of God abounds more than sin, in the sense that the latter cannot alter God's Gracious relationship to the sinner. Grace is 'essentially the principle of life' if we mean by 'principle' a relationship between God and the soul. *Habitual* Grace and *Actual Grace* are experiences of the believer, not quantitative or temporal differences in Grace itself.

An illustration from the psychology of the sentiments may help us here. A sentiment of love is a permanent structure of

[1] Harton, *The Elements of the Spiritual Life*, pp. 13-14.

the mind. There is an organisation of impulse and emotion round *the idea of an object*. A man 'habitually' loves his wife, in the sense that in virtue of his love sentiment his relationship to her is permanent. That love sentiment is habitually influencing his life, not simply in relation to her, but to many things. His ambitions may be rooted in that relationship; the control of his appetites will be spontaneously and unconsciously determined by that sentiment, 'for her sake' he may do many things and refrain from doing other things; yet she will not necessarily be present to his consciousness at every moment, not even when he is being definitely influenced by his love of her. A part of that sentiment is the knowledge of and gratitude for her love for him. There will be many times in his life when the sentiment will be acutely active and conscious. There will be times when he will be conscious that it is her love for him and his love for her that make him strong, that sustain him in some experience of contradiction at the hands of life. At such a time she will seem nearer and her love dearer.

In such a way we could conceive 'Habitual Grace' and 'Actual Grace'. God's relationship to the believer is a permanent relationship influencing his life spontaneously and unconsciously at every moment. Just as a man's love sentiment for his wife may be activated spontaneously and consciously by some association or by recollection, so God's Grace may be activated spontaneously or consciously by the believer. On the other hand, there will be times when he will be consciously and acutely aware of his need to realise that Grace; as, for example, when he needs every holy association in his being to help him to resist some temptation. The realisation of that Grace, that gracious permanent love-relationship of God to him will be the channel along which God's power will come to him in his hour of temptation. That is 'Actual Grace'.

Again, when he has sinned, and now realises that he has 'let God down', outraged 'Habitual Grace', and yet is conscious that Grace is abounding more than his sin, he experiences in a very definite way the Grace or graciousness of God. That is 'Actual Grace' at work.

There is a term used by the Reformers, namely, 'Irresistible Grace', which has often seemed to be inconsistent with the freedom of the will. Without entering into the theological or philosophical problems which the term is supposed to raise in the minds of some thinkers, we would suggest that as an experience the term need evoke little or no sense of contradiction between Grace and will. The irresistibleness of the Grace of God is an experience in the sinner's response to God. It is analogous to the irresistibleness of a self-evident proposition, and not to some force acting in a quasi-physical manner on some object. No one experiences any sense of some external power being exercised upon him to accept the self-evident proposition; the irresistibleness of the self-evidence lies in the response not in the proposition. We cannot help seeing the truth of the proposition.

From the experiential point of view 'Irresistible Grace' cannot mean that the Grace of God is saving us whether we will or not; it simply means that we cannot do other than respond to it; we are in a sense overwhelmed by the intuition of that Grace; we cannot resist the response to it; but it is the will that responds and by responding shows that it is not coerced. It is like the irresistible love of a mother that breaks down the self-will of the child. It is like the patience of a loving wife with a drunken husband, which breaks the power the drink exercises over him; the patience and love are not to be resisted; they win the response, and are causal factors in his reformation.

Grace always acts upon the moral consciousness. It gives both direction and content to the will. When the evangelist speaks of 'cold morality', he is not belittling the place of morality in the Christian life; nor does he mean to assert that morality has ceased to be an imperative in that life; he is thinking of the sinner's and the Christian's standing before God. No morality can merit that standing; no faith in one's own moral capacity is a guarantee of moral performance. That is what is implicit in Paul's words, "By Grace are ye saved"; "By the Grace of God I am what I am".

That is a truly deep and real experience of the evangelical believer, however crudely it may have been expressed in evangelical hymns of a revival type. It is a theological dogma of the sinner's standing before God; and yet it is a gracious invitation to the sinner to trust God's Grace for forgiveness. It is well expressed in the familiar hymn:

Just as I am—Thou wilt receive,
Wilt welcome, pardon, cleanse, relieve;
Because Thy promise I believe,
O Lamb of God, I come.

Just as I am—Thy love unknown
Has broken every barrier down;
Now to be Thine, yea, Thine alone,
O Lamb of God, I come.

To sum up, from the Apostle Paul, to whom, as Moffatt says, any study of Grace inevitably leads, to the simple convert at a Salvation Army meeting, the Evangelical believes that "All is of Grace". Everything the believer has, from the original Faith through which he first intuited the Grace that was drawing him to God through Jesus Christ, the forgiveness of sins in which he was reconciled to God, the change of heart and will, the experience of his new regenerated life, to the simple assurance:

I know not where His islands lift
Their fronded palms in air;
I only know I cannot drift
Beyond His love and care

"All is of Grace". The realisation of this Grace becomes more vivid with the believer's wider and deeper experiences of life. The Grace of God sustains him in every experience. It was his first evangelical intuition; it is the content of his Faith at the last, when he feels the gentle pressure of death—"All is of Grace".

Psychology of Faith

Closely linked, as we have seen, is the experience of Faith. On the believer's side, Faith is the condition of his spiritual life and of the fuller knowledge of God which grows with the deepening of his fellowship with God.

No state of mind, however, is more difficult to analyse, because it has such intimate relations with so much in our intellectual, emotional and conational life. 'Belief', 'trust', 'confidence' and love are all involved in the Faith-state. Nevertheless, it is not to be confused with any of these. The Faith-state, as far as we can analyse it by introspection, or infer it from the study of its manifestations in others, always exhibits two characteristic elements, one positive and one negative. From the positive side, it is a set or active attitude of the mind which one may designate 'incipient action'; there is a readiness to act; the necessary energy can be generated instantaneously. On the negative side, it involves the absence of inhibiting or conflicting tendencies. The mind is integrated in relation to the object of Faith. That is why Dr. Wm. Brown can write: "Faith is the completest integration of the mind".[1] Although it involves intellectual factors, it is predominantly a practical attitude. The lack of inhibiting tendencies would mean that the physiological factors involved in the generating of energy are ready to function when overt action is necessary; the lack of conflicting tendencies would mean that psychologically there is an absence of fear, doubt and hesitation, any or all of which would tend to impede action.

Religiously, this means that the thing hoped for is already a possession. "This is the victory that overcometh the world, even our faith." Faith is not a means to victory, it *is* the victory. Dean Inge quotes approvingly from Dr. Du Bose the following which brings out the religious aspect most truly: ". . . In the divine and absolute religion of Jesus Christ, Faith and Fact are treated as having been made one, as being now identical. Faith is not only assurance; it is present possession, the very substance and reality of its object. Assurance is substance, Faith is fact, promise is fulfilment, hope is possession and fruition—all not so much through any inexplicable virtue in Faith itself, as because Faith is the laying hold of and uniting

[1] *Psychology and Psychotherapy*, p. 126.

itself with that Word of God which is at once the substance of all reality and light of all truths."[1]

From the psychological point of view, then, the Faith-state is one in which there is perfect *rapport* between the individual and the object of his Faith; there is complete harmony; there is an absence of inhibiting and conflicting tendencies so that action is harmonious and unimpeded.

It is this unimpeded flow of energy, resulting from the integration of the mind, that gives rise to the emotions of Faith. Trust and confidence are the two fundamental emotions involved, the one objective and the other subjective. If the function of feeling is to initiate and reinforce action we can see why *trust* and *confidence* are often used as synonyms for Faith, and why Dr. Du Bose includes *assurance* as an element in Faith. Wherever there is Faith, the subjective state is one of calm strong confidence, as for example, in obedience to conscience when the moral conviction involves a supreme sacrifice, or action that is likely to arouse hostile public opinion. Trust and confidence are the emotional relations between a patient and the physician, in whom he has Faith; the mutual Faith between business men involves the same relations; neither has the fear that the other will let him down.

Trust is the objective side of the Faith-state emotion; it goes out and has its reference to the object. It involves, as we shall see, love to some degree.

Faith and Belief

All mental process involves cognition, affect and conation; and Faith is no exception. We find that Faith is not independent of belief although never identical with it. That is brought out in the classical chapter on Faith in the Epistle to the Hebrews, the eleventh chapter, a chapter which, as Dean Inge[2] has remarked, does for Faith what Paul did for love in the thirteenth chapter of 1 Corinthians. All sides of Faith are

[1] *Faith and Its Psychology*, pp. 15-16.
[2] *Ibid.*

exhibited in this chapter. Faith and knowledge, Faith and belief, and Faith and action are all linked together. Relevant to our present purpose is the verse: "Without Faith it is impossible to please Him; for he that cometh to God must believe that He is, and that He is the rewarder of them that diligently seek Him". In all Faith there is implicit or explicit belief. This is true of the Faith-state in everyday life. When we enter an elevator we *believe* it will carry us without mishap; when we put our money in the bank we believe in its solvency.

Belief, however, does not always involve Faith. F. C. S. Schiller has argued that belief is always 'activist', and he defines belief as "a spiritual attitude of welcome which we assume towards what we take to be a truth".[1] Unless, however, belief is an element in a Faith-state, it is psychologically no more than assent to a proposition. We *welcome* a belief if it tends to fill up some gap in our thought; but belief depends on the absence of contradiction more than one sometimes realises, although it must not be assumed that absence of contradiction is a criterion of its truth. Belief as an element in a Faith-state is always activist; but the activist element seems to come from the Faith-state itself rather than from any element in the belief. Belief scatters the doubts that would lead to hesitation of action; it clears the way for that state of 'incipient action' so characteristic of the Faith-state.

We may believe in an object without having Faith in it. We may believe in the solvency of a bank without having the necessary Faith to trust our money to it; we may believe in the skill of a physician without having Faith in him.

Faith in God and belief in God are not identical and cannot be interchanged. Faith involves more than belief although it is never found without belief. Professor Conklin has brought this out in his *Psychology of Religious Adjustment*. He writes: "Faith in God presupposes belief in God. Thus Faith must be looked upon as an attitude which includes belief as a part of it. A Faith attitude can be thought of, then, as composed of

[1] *Problems of Belief*, p. 14.

a belief supplemented by a large pattern of action tendencies, which when completed are revealed to be harmonious."[1]

Faith and Love

In Evangelical Faith it will be found that Love is always an element. It is this, it seems to us, that makes trust and confidence such vivid emotional experiences. Trust in a person will be Faith in loving action; confidence is the subjective side of trust, as we have seen, although both are involved in any act of Faith.

It is Faith, then, that initiates action and always involves incipient action. Some element of love is always present in the Faith relation between persons; it may range from simple respect or appreciation of some quality or qualities of the person's character, to the love that exists between husband and wife, and the love between the saint and his God. Professor Grensted goes as far as to say that 'Faith lies in the field of personal relationships';[2] but this would leave out much action in human life which involves more than belief.

It is certainly true that in personal relationships in which Faith is an element love is always found. That is well illustrated in the relation between psychotherapist and patient. The first thing the psychotherapist has to do is to elicit from his patient Faith in himself and not merely in his skill; trust and confidence are always involved; and that implies what is known technically as the 'transference', i.e. a 'love' relationship between physician and patient. Dr. Ian Suttie contends that the task of the psychotherapist is to *love the patient better;*[3] because he believes that neurosis has its origin in the patient's love having been at some time refused. However that may be, the relationship of Faith between patient and psychotherapist must have an element of love.

That Faith, except between persons, does not always involve love, would seem to be the inference to draw from the fact

[1] *Psychology of Religious Adjustment*, p. 243.
[2] *Psychology and God*, p. 78.
[3] *The Origins of Love and Hate*, see chaps. x–xii and chap. xiv.

that we have Faith in other things than persons. It is possible, as Dr. Conklin[1] points out, that we might deepen our knowledge of the Faith-state were we to examine and compare other forms of Faith than the religious. Much of our action from day to day seems to lie within the sphere of Faith and to depend on it. The common element in all Faith seems to be that it can induce action.

It would be a pity to narrow the term to a relation between persons; although one must admit that it is in the personal relationships that we best see Faith at work. It is, e.g., "the child's Faith in the parents, rather than any 'primitive credulity' that accounts for the suggestibility which induces children to accept from the parent their beliefs about God and the many other beliefs necessary for the child's welfare."[2] In all suggestion the element of Faith is involved.

The Ground of Faith

Dean Inge gives a whole chapter in his little volume, *Faith and its Psychology*,[3] to the question of the seat or ground of Faith. Unfortunately, the full discussion of this question is beyond the space we can allow; but the question is really fundamental in many ways.

Such a question has two aspects. We must be careful to distinguish between objective grounds for the object of Faith, that is for the beliefs we have about the object; and the subjective grounds which are nothing else than the Faith-state itself. Although the two are intimately related, they should be kept apart in any discussion on the grounds of Faith. Faith always implies existence:—the existence of the objects of its beliefs as other than our subjective beliefs. We may speak of the grounds of our Faith when we really mean the grounds of the beliefs which our Faith asserts of the object. When we say, e.g., that the ground of our Faith is Revelation, the Church, the Bible, we are not speaking

[1] *Psychology of Religious Adjustment*, p. 241.

[2] *Psychology and God*, pp. 79–80.

[3] *Faith and its Psychology*, p. 42.

of the Faith-state, but of the grounds of the beliefs which are integral to the Faith-state. On the other hand, when we say that Faith is grounded in feeling, we are speaking of the subjective grounds for believing in or trusting the object whatever it is.

It is the subjective or *primary ground of Faith* Dean Inge is anxious to elucidate. This primary ground, he argues, lies in the "deep-seated religious instinct or impulse".[1] He thinks this innate instinct or impulse arises in the psychological necessity which obliges us to assign *values* to our experience: "It is our nature to pass judgments, to call some things good, others bad, to acquit and condemn, accept or reject. We arrange our world according to what we consider the worth of its ingredients to be."[2] "The *values*", he instances, "are the usual values of Truth, Goodness, and Beauty"; and he asserts that "Faith has usually connected these values with the name of God. God—whether the God of theism, pantheism, agnostic monism or deism—is the self-existence *summum genus* in Whom we believe our highest ideals are realised."[3]

Dr. Inge's volume was written in 1909; and it may be quite probable that he would approach the problem from a different angle today. The psychologists of religion have been unable to accept the assumption of a religious instinct, deep-seated or otherwise. Theologians sometimes forget that when they root religion in an instinct they are giving it merely a biological foundation; somehow the roots of religion must be found in the fact of self-consciousness. Be that as it may, there can be no doubt that we do pass moral judgments from an early age; we do discern a true comparison between ideas, and between object and idea of the object; early also we experience some kind of æsthetic emotions. It is doubtful, however, if we could find the primary ground of Faith in the capacity to attach *values* either to experiences or objects.

James Ward, in one of the last articles[4] he wrote, contended

[1] *Faith and its Psychology*, p. 42.
[2] *Ibid.*, p. 43. [3] *Ibid.*, p. 44.
[4] *Hibbert Journal*, January, 1925.

that "First and foremost, Faith is not regarded as cognitive; but rather primarily as just conation and essentially volitional. . . . Life from beginning to end is a striving for self-conservation and betterment. At first there is only the venture of primitive trustfulness in trying open possibilities—a characteristic of developing life in all its stages, and instinct which precedes knowledge and is the chief means of acquiring and increasing it. Such is faith at the very outset of life. But gradually, as knowledge advances this instinctive trustfulness is supplemented by intelligent prevision till at length when the 'age of reason' is reached, definite ideals become ends, not peradventure, but through deliberate resolve."

This 'primitive trustfulness', mainly conative, is, we believe, more a biological necessity than the basis of religious Faith. The fundamental need for moral and rational unity is characteristic of those who, if we may so express it, have become conscious of being Subjects. Conscious of conflicts within themselves, and of the need to resolve them, they seek after God, if haply they might find Him. True religious Faith is rooted in our nature as self-conscious beings, and although it has analogies with instinct in animals, it must not be confused with it. The 'primitive trustfulness' of children, rooted as it is in personal relations with the parents and teachers, may, if one cares to do so, be taken as the original disposition to the Faith-state. If we interpret Dr. Ward's "striving for self-conservation and betterment" in the moral sense, as a striving for the integrity of the moral and rational personality, as the outcome of what Dr. Beatrice Hinkle called 'the prospective aim of personality', then the conflicts between incompatible motives, or the conflict between early accepted beliefs and the experience of life, can be conceived as setting up a tension which has to be overcome; and the need to resolve the tension creates the condition when the more deliberate Faith-state can arise. It seems to us, that the fundamental need of self-conscious beings for moral and rational unity, combined with the 'prospective aim of personality'—a personality only found without—is the true origin of the Faith-state as contrasted with Dr. Ward's 'primitive trustfulness'. In the true Faith-state there is more than the volitional element; there are also the cognitive and emotional elements. There is an implicit belief in an object; there is the outgoing trust in the object; and there is the inner confidence generated by the object. To seek the 'primary ground' of the Faith-state in any of the above processes is to court failure. We believe that the subjective authority which the content of our Faith exercises over us will be found in the capacity of the object to resolve our conflicts or to satisfy the need for moral and rational unity and the prospective, spiritual aim of personality.

These are questions, however, on which we cannot linger. Our interest lies in the life of Faith. "Nobody", as Professor Grensted has remarked, "who considers the matter at all really believes that the climax of Faith consists in an assent to any series of theological propositions."[1] We may assent to every one of the statements of the creeds and yet be far from the life of Faith. "One may believe", writes Dr. Conklin, "in the doctrine of the Trinity; but Faith in God implies living, doing, in addition to one's belief in the nature of God."[2]

The conscious Faith of the Evangelical, beginning in an intuition of the Grace of God, moves him towards reconciliation with God through Christ. By Faith he is able to resolve the contradictions he meets at the hands of life, or those he experiences within his own soul. "I live by Faith of the Son of God who loved me and gave Himself for me." The Object of Paul's Faith resolved his conflicts, and thus generated his strong confidence. By Faith the Evangelical lives; he trusts God; his Faith gives him the assurance that "We can do nothing against the truth but only for the truth", and in that assurance there is born his belief in the overruling providence of God. The conational or volitional aspect of his Faith generates the energy and the enthusiasm with which he attempts to build up his spiritual life in thought, feeling and act. It was in virtue of the energy generated by their Faith that the heroes

[1] *Psychology and God*, Lecture III.
[2] *Psychology of Religious Adjustment*, p. 243.

of the eleventh chapter of the Epistle to the Hebrews fulfilled their tasks.

The purely subjective side of Faith is the calm confidence which always characterises the true Evangelical's life. His mind is stayed upon God, and therefore it is in perfect peace. For him "All things work together for good to them that love God". Believing through Faith that God sent His Son into the world to save the world, he cannot doubt that God will "keep that which (he) has committed unto Him against that day". The belief in God, the trust and confidence of Faith are all implicit in the eighth chapter of the Epistle to the Romans, where Paul almost seems to shout: "If God be for us, who can be against us. . . . We are more than conquerors through Him that loved us. For I am persuaded that neither death, nor life, nor angels, nor principalities, nor powers, nor things present, nor things to come . . . shall be able to separate us from the love of God which is in Christ Jesus our Lord."

The evangelical hymns, perhaps more than any other kind of religious literature, express this utter trust and confidence which are the emotions of the Faith-state, though never the ground of Faith. These emotions give that sense of subjective certitude so characteristic of all religious experience. Professor James did not exaggerate when he said: "How can it possibly fail to cool the fever, appease the fret and steady the nerves when one is sensibly conscious of the fact that one's life, not as a part but as a whole, is in the keeping of One whom one can absolutely trust?"

It is this characteristic evangelical Faith-state that accounts for the confidence with which the Evangelical meets his own sinful behaviour-tendencies. We have seen that Faith integrates the mind; that means that the conscious and the unconscious are open to each other. Repressions are thus lifted; the soul is not afraid to see its own motivations—because courage is the virtue Faith generates; it is a quality of the Faith-state.

Here again, Evangelicalism links up with psychotherapy. Dr. MacCurdy has said that one of the far-reaching principles in psychotherapy is the knowledge of our own motivations and the courage to face them: "If a man has courage, he can overcome any mental disturbance with a little psychological knowledge. Otherwise his environment has to be changed to meet his circumstances."[1]

From the behaviour and personality points of view, we believe this is the greatest contribution of Evangelicalism, and the Faith-state characteristic of it, to the individual's life. With little confidence in himself, but complete confidence in God, he is able to face with courage the psychological knowledge of himself which the conviction of sin reveals. It is the conviction of sin which breaks the barrier between the conscious and the unconscious and thus allows the lusts, the ego-centricity, the vacillations of the will, the appeal of the 'fleshpots of Egypt', the sloth, pride and vanity active in his psyche to become conscious. It is this experience the psycho-neurotic is unable to endure and therefore resorts to repression, and thus fails to achieve personality. Unless Faith can be elicited simultaneously with the revelation of the unconscious, the last state of the individual may be worse than the first. The courage which Faith generates is not the momentary courage of an impulsive act, but a quality of the Faith-state itself. It is needed in our moral and spiritual warfare not once, but all through life. The Evangelical's knowledge of his own heart may often arouse fear; but it is the fear implicit in courage, not the morbid fear that leads to repression. Courage is the virtue with which we meet the situations of life, within or without, in spite of fear. Fear in the Evangelical is the healthy fear of an adult conscience, not the guilt of the 'super-ego':

Many have thought that evangelical hymns tend to be morbid in their references to sin. The contrary is true. The Christian poet puts into words what the true Evangelical never forgets, namely, that he *is* a sinner 'saved by Grace'.

If the Evangelical seems to be more conscious of the baser elements in his soul than most men of other types of religious experience, he is at the same time more conscious through his Faith of the 'power of God unto salvation'. The Faith that makes

[1] *Psychology of Emotion*, p. 441.

it possible for him to receive the revelation of himself is the same Faith by which he appropriates the power to meet his temptations with courage and confidence. His Faith and confidence are in his God. His confidence is not that spurious virtue, 'self-confidence'; but confidence in the Object of his Faith. Hid with Christ in God he believes that nothing can pluck him from God's gracious hand. His prayer is the 'prayer of Faith'; he knows not what temptations he will meet, but because he has Faith and prays in Faith, he is ready for whatever temptations he may encounter.

Our contention is that Evangelical religion gives both the psychological knowledge and the courage to see, meet and triumph over whatever the unconscious can generate in the conscious mind. We may take as illustration any of the great Evangelicals of the past—St. Paul, St. Augustine, Luther, Bunyan, Wesley, Whitefield, Moody—and every one of them would show an intimate self-knowledge of sin and its ways; and there is not one of them who does not exhibit the fact that their evangelical experience gave them Faith with its consequent courage to meet the 'principalities and powers' which, because they are within man's soul, can disturb his whole mental, moral and spiritual life.

The dynamic nature of Faith is not only seen in the manner in which the Evangelical meets the contradictions within his soul; but also in his political and social activities. This is clearly seen in the heroes of Faith recorded in the Epistle to the Hebrews. Evangelical Faith, allied to a political or social ideal, has been one of the greatest influences in history. Wilberforce in his fight against slavery, Livingstone in his love for Africa, drew their strength and courage from their Faith. Cromwell, from all accounts, linked his political activities with his religious Faith. The great missionary societies of all the Churches sprang up in Faith and are sustained by Faith. Evangelicalism is always evangelist by nature. When the Evangelical Faith is linked up with sympathy for the 'lost' and erring, all sorts of institutions spring up to succour and save; when it is linked with sympathy for suffering, it builds our hospitals, children's orphanges, and the hosts of almshouses scattered over our country, and other philanthropic agencies. There can be no question of the power of Evangelical Faith to inspire and sustain good works.

Sanctification

Probably no evangelical word is less frequently spoken or written by present-day evangelical leaders than that which heads this paragraph. Even psychologists like James seem to prefer other terms. James, himself, uses the word 'Saintliness' where we might have expected the more evangelical term Sanctification. More astonishing, however, is the fact, that Dr. Flew, Methodist as he is, in his volume dealing with the history of the subject, prefers the title "The Idea of Perfection in Christian Theology" to "The Idea of Sanctification in the History of Theology".

There is doubtless justification for the use of the wider term in both the latter writers, because they take into account types of Holiness which differ somewhat from the Evangelical's 'ideal for the present life'.

We must confess that the term 'Sanctification' conveys to many the idea of 'sanctimoniousness'; and is heard most frequently in the less educated and narrower sects of Evangelicalism. But on the whole, 'Sanctification' has more New Testament authority for its use than either 'Saintliness' or 'Perfection'. "Called to be saints" is assuredly Pauline, as also 'the perfecting of the saints'. Nevertheless, 'Sanctification', 'Sanctified' and 'Sanctify' are undoubtedly the more frequently used terms, especially when the writers of the Epistles are speaking of the "Christian Ideal for the Present Life".

Sanctification is truly the evangelical term, although all ideas of the Christian Ideal originate in the words of Jesus: "Be ye perfect even as your Father which is in Heaven is perfect".

The evangelical ideal for the present life, then, is Sanctification. It is analogous in Evangelicalism to Monasticism and

Asceticism in other types of Christian experience, although both these may be considered as means rather than ends in themselves. Sanctification is the end of which the decision to follow Christ is the beginning. Wesley calls Sanctification "The Great Salvation" and is careful to distinguish it from conversion. "We do not know", he writes, " of a single witness, in any place, of a person receiving, in one and the same moment, remission of sins, the abiding witness of the Spirit, and a new, clean heart." Religious literature, as well as psychological descriptions of religious experience, can give us instances of sudden freedom from some particular 'besetting sin'; and often this is mistaken for complete salvation. Wesley had too intimate a knowledge of himself to confuse this sudden freedom from a particular sin with 'The Great Salvation'.

The question has often been raised as to whether Sanctification involves sinlessness. Dr. Flew, in his admirable volume, draws attention to the fact that in his own pages "the idea of perfection is not regarded as synonymous with sinlessness". He believes that "freedom from sin must be an element in the ideal"; but he is anxious that the idea of perfection should be positive rather than negative; and we believe he is following the New Testament doctrine when he insists that, "the primary and determinative description is to be sought in the teaching of our Lord about the Kingdom of God as recorded in the Synoptic Gospels".

Sanctification is the Protestant and Evangelical conception of spirituality. It is a spirituality that is not to be identified with the mystics' idea of oneness with God, or with any ascetic ideal. It is a spirituality exercised in relation to our life among our fellow men, and amid the social and political conditions in which we live. It is ethical in its direction and striving; yet spiritual in its motive and end. It is a matter of 'holy living' amid the conditions of everyday life. In the perfectly sanctified life, sanctity and morality would be perfectly fused.

There can be no doubt that the preaching of the Gospel lacks power when anything less than Sanctification is preached. "The work of God", said Wesley, "does not prosper where perfect love is not preached."[1] We ourselves have often observed in large conferences, as for example in annual denominational gatherings, that any speaker who laid emphasis on the sanctifying power of Christ, or on the necessity for Sanctification never failed to 'grip' his congregation. If it is true, as the psychologist avers, that we can only attend to anything if we have something to *attend with*, that is, we select what we attend to, or what attracts us, in virtue of dynamic elements within our psychic make-up, then it would seem that the 'urge to completeness', the 'prospective aim of personality' on its spiritual side responds spontaneously whenever the ideal of completeness or perfection is presented to consciousness by one in whose own life Sanctification is a present possession. To the psychologist, at least, the response to the religious appeal of Sanctification, or exhortation to realise perfection ideals, is rooted in the nature of self-conscious beings, able not merely to evaluate ideals, but also to experience the deep-seated religious motivations.

The psychologist also finds that not a few of the Schisms which have wrought such havoc in the unity of the Church, can be traced to psychological rather than theological causes. Doubtless, the great controversies of the first four centuries of our Christian era were almost wholly due to difficulties of theological statement, and the desire to stamp out heresy. That cannot be said of Montanism, however. In spite of the fact that heresies came to be associated with the movement, it was first and foremost a recall to the Church for a deeper spirit-filled life; a protest against the tendency already at work to harden Christian doctrine. If we penetrate to the roots of the Reformation we find them in Luther's inward struggle against sin and for personal Sanctification. The response of the masses to the Reformation, if not as clearly spiritual as Luther's originating motive, will be found to be deeply coloured by it. Quietism, Pietism, Quakerism, Congregationalism and Methodism all arose in the need of "full salvation", and

[1] Quoted by Dr. Flew. The whole of Dr. Flew's Introductory chapter should be read.

the conviction on the part of many that it was not being preached.

That many of these movements showed extravagances, as many of the 'Holiness' movements of our own times, will not be denied. The tendency to make extravagent claims is not peculiar to religious movements; every advance in science, religious as well as secular, has shown the same tendency. What extravagant claims and applications were made on behalf of Darwin's theory of Evolution! What extravagant inferences were drawn from the science of Comparative Religion, The Higher Criticism and The New Psychology! These extravagances are natural though they are to be deprecated. We cannot use them to condemn the truth of which they are an over-expression.

There is something in the spiritual nature of man that cannot but respond to the appeal of Perfection or Sanctification, something that demands that his religion will 'save' him, body, soul and spirit; and whenever the Church neglects this and offers something less than a 'full salvation' for both individual and society, her numbers dwindle, and her influence among the masses declines. It is when the Church loses her hold among the masses that she becomes weak; and the revival of the Church, like the origin of the Church herself, can always be traced to an uprising of the Spirit in the hearts of the lower classes. Perhaps an exception may have to be made in regard to Christian Science, and the Oxford Group Movement of our own day. Even these movements, however, have their roots in the same spiritual needs as those mentioned above. Whatever we may think of the metaphysical implications of Christian Science, there can be no question that it has responded to the demand for an unconditioned Faith, a 'full salvation'; and the need for Sanctification. The Oxford Group Movement, with its emphasis upon absolute honesty, unselfishness, purity and love, and the claim that we can be wholly 'guided' by God's Spirit, has appealed to a large class of people already within the Church. Although the Movement has over-simplified the necessary psychological conditions of acquiring these 'absolutes', and of discerning the Will of God, and tended "to encourage a form of spiritual exhibitionism",[1] this does not alter the fact that its appeal finds its response in those who feel the need to make a fuller surrender to Christ than the Church has demanded.

The "New Thought" movement in America with its corresponding "Practical Psychology" movement in England appeals to the same need; so also does the tremendous flow of books on psychology from the press. It is the half-awakened Christian, seeking deep in his soul for a full Christian life, to whom schismatic movements appeal. The 'urge to completeness', the 'prospective aim of personality', if once awakened, cannot rest in anything less than their true spiritual end-Perfection or Sanctification.

It would be unfair to imply that the Church, even today, is not cognisant of the strength of the appeal of Sanctification. The 'Retreats' of Anglican and Roman Churches, the Keswick Convention in which ministers and clergy of all denominations take part, the various movements whose aim is the deepening of the spiritual life, all witness to the fact that within the Church herself, there are many who have not forgotten the exhortation to be wholly sanctified. Perhaps it is not too much to say, that the next powerful movement towards revival will arise in the spiritual need for Sanctification within the Church, rather than in any Evangelistic Mission to those outside.

Be that as it may, the emphasis upon the realisation of the Christian ideal in this present life both in the individual and in Society by the Evangelical Churches is a necessity they will neglect at their peril. They cannot afford to offer to the world an "undated millennium"; they must not mumble something about "the Mills of God grind slowly", while the totalitarian states are changing the face of the world in a few years. It is the Church's mission to make totalitarian demands upon the world; and she must be able to accompany those demands with totalitarian promises. The same applies to her appeal to the individual; she demands more than any other institution;

[1] Dr. Wm. Brown, *Psychology and Psychotherapy*, pp. 149 f.

she has more to offer; a truncated salvation can have little appeal. "A vast evangelistic advance can only be sustained if the Christian ideal for this life is steadily set forth in all its beauty and fullness as being by the grace of God something not impossible of attainment. If this principle be vital, it is likely that the ignoring of it will bring impoverishment and arrest" (Dr. Flew).

Meaning of Sanctification

It is impossible and unnecessary to outline, even briefly, the various ideals of Perfection or Sanctification which have been held from the New Testament period to our own day. In an earlier chapter we saw that Jesus laid down no rules for the ethical or spiritual life of His followers. His intuitive insight pierced to principles which are valid in all circumstances. His function was not that of the legislator in this connection; He was prophet more than legislator. The two commandments which He emphasised in answer to the rich young ruler's question regarding eternal life, lay the obligation upon motive and not act: "Thou *shalt love* the Lord thy God with all thy heart, and all thy soul, and all thy mind". Thou *shalt love thy neighbour as thyself*. God was to be *utterly* loved. There is an obligation upon the Christian to love his neighbour, and the love must be whole-hearted and intelligent.

It might seem that the imperative, "Seek first the Kingdom of God and all these things shall be added unto you", says nothing about love. This, however, would be to mistake the meaning of the Kingdom. It is the realm of love, the realm where God Who is love rules. From the psychological point of view the Kingdom must be interpreted in terms of motive and end, and not in terms of social or political structure. To say that the Kingdom of God is synonymous with the rule of God is to say that Love rules over all.

The Beatitudes emphasise the same point. Every one of the qualities called 'blessed' are the qualities of love; they are the ruling motives in a community of brethren.

"The new commandment" which He gave to His disciples was illustrated in diverse ways. What has been called the 'sweet second mile' is just the expression of the fact that Love knows no stint in its service.

No word of Jesus better illustrates his attitude to the complacent righteousness of His day, and the demand of the 'new commandment' than His parable of the Son and the Hired Servant. The whole spirit of His ethic is contained in that parable. The son measures not his service to his father; his motive is different from that of the hired servant. The latter gives no more than his master can claim; but there is no limit to the moral obligations of those who call themselves the servants of God. "When ye have done all the things that have been commanded of you, say: we are unprofitable servants; we have done what we ought have done." The demand is for nothing less than perfect love as a motive.

Turning to Paul we find that when he had to deal with the question of the best gifts to cultivate in the Church's service, he turns aside from the different utilitarian values of the gifts offered to the motive. "Covet earnestly the best gifts; yet show I unto you a more excellent way. . . . Follow after love." Between these two sentences lies the thirteenth chapter of 1 Corinthians. That chapter is so complete in itself that it is often overlooked that it is really part of Paul's argument about the value of the diverse gifts which we may offer to the Church. It is the best commentary on the parable of Jesus we have been discussing. Every obligation may be meticulously fulfilled, apparent generosity may be exercised, and yet if there is no Love there is no profit. Only the heart seeking to be filled and motivated by Love can have uninterrupted communion with God. Christ's demand is, "Ye then shall be perfect as your Father in heaven, for He uplifts His sun over evil and good alike". (The translation is that of Dr. Cadoux.)

What we have said in a previous chapter must be the starting-point of our interpretation of Sanctification. Sin, we saw, is Ego-centricity. The opposite of Ego-centricity is Object-centricity, and in this connection the self would be *enlisted* in the service of God. Only to the degree in which we love can we be motivated by the object—only to the degree in which we love can the needs of the object loved generate and direct our thought. Every Beatitude deals with an object-centred quality of Christian character.

When we apply the same principle to the concept of the Kingdom of God, we can see that, whatever eschatological implications the Kingdom of God had for Jesus and His disciples, the motive and end of the Kingdom will be the same whether it is to come catastrophically, or by a slow and gradual process, whether it is to be realised here or hereafter. The motive will be object-centred. The citizen of the Kingdom will 'seek the things that gain by being shared';[1] the end of the Kingdom will be a community in which all the members are sharing in "the things that gain by being shared". These implications of the meaning of the Kingdom seem to be involved in the teaching of Jesus regarding the Kingdom. We have set them forth in psychological and not in religious terms; but we feel sure that no one can study the teaching of Jesus regarding the Kingdom without coming to the conclusion that it was to be object-centred in both motive and end.

Evangelicalism and the Social Gospel

There can be little question that Sanctification both by Jesus and Paul is conceived of as a manner of living in this world. This inevitably implies a Social Gospel; the community was to be redeemed as well as individuals. In other words, the system of social relationships within which the Christian citizen must live must be such as to make it possible for him to identify himself both with the motive and end of the Kingdom. The system itself, if redeemed, will be a system in which it will become less and less possible for anyone to seek the things which can only be gained at the expense of the poverty, vice or suffering of others. Even the redeemed community cannot compel its citizens to 'seek the things that gain by being shared';

[1] We owe the phrase to Mrs. Bosanquet.

but it can be such as to make Love, to which that motive and end belong, more easily elicited in all its members.

The community cannot, however, be an end in itself; its value lies in its association with God. It is God's Kingdom; our neighbour is God's child. There must be no other motive for seeking first the Kingdom of God or of loving one's neighbour, or of forgiving one's brother except Love. We must seek the Kingdom of God for no other reason than the fact that it is God's Kingdom; we must love our neighbour for no other reason than that he is God's child; we must forgive our brother for no other reason than that God has forgiven him. The motive of evangelical morality or Sanctification must be object-centred. God's love as shown in the miracle of forgiveness evokes our love and gratitude; and these alone inspire to Sanctification and good works. Love always involves gratitude to the loved one for the love given whether it is the love of God or the love of a human being. To the psychologist whose work is to help many to become adjusted to social reality, and to elicit social motives for the hitherto ego-centric motives, there can be no question but that the Gospel must be a social Gospel as well as an individual Gospel. Although his work compels him to deal with individuals, nevertheless, he is in closest contact with society. Many of his patients owe their neurosis to social conditions, unprogressive moral ideals, economic conditions in which love emotions have to be repressed or held strongly in leash; and in recent months not a few have broken down because the fear of war (1938–1939) has added to already existing conflicts within their minds. If the psychotherapist is to adjust his patients to social reality, the society which symbolises social reality must be one in which personality can enlarge, become object-centred, and grow up into adult-hood. The community should be such as to become to its members an object of service, and whole-hearted devotion. No community can enlist its members in whole-hearted devotion unless it is providing them with the means of their moral life and making possible the 'good life'.

The evangelical ideal of Sanctification would thus seem to

involve Love and Loyalty to the 'beloved community'. It will be a Sanctification that takes place not *in our vocation* but *through our vocation*. That was the great contribution of Luther to the idea of Perfection, as both Karl Heim and Dr. Flew have pointed out. Here are Luther's own words: "A cobbler, a smith, a peasant, whatever he may be, a man has the labour and occupation of his craft, and yet all men alike are consecrated bishops and priests. A poor servant girl may say: 'I cook the meals, I make up the beds, I dust the rooms. Who has bidden me do it? My Master and Mistress have bidden me do it. Who has given them the right to command me? God has given it to them. So it is true that I am serving God in Heaven as well as them. How happy can I feel now! It is as if I were in Heaven, doing my work for God.' "[1]

True, as it is, that we serve God through our vocation, there must be something more if we are to be wholly sanctified; and realise the ideal implicit in the parable of the 'unthanked slave'. The 'beloved community' cannot grow unless something more than faithful, and even loving attention is given to our vocation. The community needs service for its own ends, which although they are the ends of the individuals composing it, are also social ends demanding service beyond the individual's vocation, and beyond the reach of paid servants. Public opinion has to be informed and intelligent; charitable and philanthropic institutions are needs of every community; political, social, moral and spiritual ideals can only be generated by men and women who love the community as the sphere in which the Kingdom of God is to be realised. There are many services which a community needs and which can be rendered only by members who have realised that the moral and spiritual heritage is not appropriated by the community like other social products, such as accumulated knowledge, or scientific invention, but must be assimilated by each generation anew. The very motive to seek the things that gain by being shared cannot be biologically or mechanically transmitted; it can only be passed on as the citizens themselves by the example of their

[1] Quoted by Karl Heim in *Spirit and Truth*, p. 171.

own service to the community elicit the motive in the young. In this service we get Sanctification through love for God's community.

Not a little of that service will be given by the believer to the community through service to the Church. Although the Church can never be the mind of the community, it must never fail to be its conscience. It is the Church that transmits the Word of God from generation to generation, not the individual; it is the Church that conserves Christian experience and sustains it. No religion could survive that had not some kind of organisation through which it conserves, transmits and sustains its experience of God, and makes its collective impact upon society.

In a recent article in *The Modern Churchman*,[1] Dr. Major has argued that the best description of the Church is found in the term "Spirit-bearing". He thinks that is a better way to describe the Church than to say that she is Apostolic and Catholic. It certainly comes nearer to defining her essence. She is Spirit-bearing; and she can only bear the Spirit of God to the world through her individual members. Hence the voluntary services which the Church needs in order to be a Spirit-bearing Church must always have the first claim upon her members.

Evangelicalism is bound up with no particular Church polity. The central truths of Evangelicalism are common to all the Churches; Protestant and Catholic. Differences there may be among the Evangelical Churches themselves regarding the Sacraments as 'Means of Grace'; but all have the Cross at their centre; all gather round the Word of God; all trust to Faith and Grace alone for their standing before God. "Concerning the administration of Church affairs", says the Augsburg Confession, "which is not of divine but human origin, it is sufficient to hold to those things which can be held without sin, and do serve the peace and right ordering of the Church."

The polity of the Church, then, is not of her essence, but of her well-being. Her members are those redeemed by

[1] May, 1939.

Grace, who are reconciled to God, whose salvation is of Faith. She exists to establish God's children in the Faith, to proclaim Christ as the Word of God, "the light that lighteth every man that cometh into the world". She is the 'salt of the earth' preserving life from corruption through her experience of the Word of God contained in Holy Writ. Wherever her children gather in Christ's name, there is the Spirit-bearing Church.

Although the polity of the Church is not of divine origin, it must not be regarded as a matter of indifference. If she is the conscience of the community, the means of sanctifying Grace, her organisation and administration must be such as to give her full opportunity to fulfil her function. We are not born into the Church as we are born into the State; we cannot join her membership on our own terms; only those who 'know God otherwise than by hearsay', who have a 'first-hand acquaintance with God' are fitted to occupy her chief offices. Her doctrine must be kept pure, which is not the same thing as keeping it static; her discipline must be courageous; her spoken word must be a "Thus saith the Lord". Perhaps more important than any of these is her maintenance of the "Crown rights of the Redeemer"; her spiritual freedom must be preserved against any encroachments of the State, not only for her own sake, but also for the State's; because history shows that when the Church is weak in herself or fettered by the State, the latter tends to demand from the individual that which should be given only to God. The State becomes arrogant and aggressive in nationalistic demands and denies the implications of the Kingdom of God. Hence the need for efficiency in the organisation and administration of the Church; and for the spiritual purity and loyalty of her leaders.

We seem to have digressed from the experience of Sanctification. This is not, however, the case. *Extra ecclesiam nulla salus.* Just as the State and community give the individual the means of his economic and moral life, so the Church must give him the means of a sanctified life. Outside the Church there is no "Great Salvation". When the Church is weak in moral influence, internally divided, or spiritually lifeless, the children of God are impoverished; and the prospective aim of spiritual personality, the urge to spiritual completeness, which is the dynamic of Sanctification, drives them to dissociate themselves from the particular ecclesiastical organisation, although they remain within the Church as spiritually conceived. If the "sheep look up and are not fed", they cannot but seek new pastures; and the Church herself becomes more impoverished. Hence both the essence and the well-being of the Church are of the most important relevance to Sanctification. The life of prayer, the fruits of Christian fellowship and service, the Sacrament of the preached Word of God, the sanctifying service of and through the Church, the opportunity to widen and deepen the object-centred Love-all should be enriched by life within the Church. The Church should be the 'Family of God' in which the children are 'brought up' and grow up into the 'Stature of a man in Christ Jesus'; in which the fathers in Christ, and the mothers in Israel not only tend the children, but are to them the embodiment of the highest spiritual ideals. Dr. McDougall has argued that for the development of character in the young generation, the embodiment of the moral tradition in the personalities of members of the community is crucial.

Although we have denied ourselves the opportunity of discussing the various controversies which the doctrine of Perfection or Sanctification have aroused in the course of Church history, there is one controversy which we feel should not be altogether passed over. The sacerdotal Churches have tended to create what to the Evangelical seems a needless and false dualism[1] in their doctrine that there are those "who have a special vocation to follow the 'counsels of perfection', and the average run of humanity". "Poverty and celibacy" are amongst the "counsels of perfection" singled out as suited only for the few with special vocation. Those who can undertake to obey these counsels are supposed to reach a greater

[1] See article in *Hibbert Journal*, by C. J. Cadoux, January, 1923.

degree of Perfection or Sanctification. All controversies of this kind, we believe, will be found to revolve round the concepts of Sin and Virtue. If we are right in our contention that sin as distinguished from sins lies in ego-centricity, and that sinful acts are motivated by ego-centricity, whereas virtue is a quality of object-centred sentiments, then we can see that neither poverty nor celibacy is a virtue in itself, even when self-imposed. John Dewey has argued that self-sacrifice is never a virtue *per se;* and we agree with him. It may be a necessity, a necessary duty, but that is not the same thing as a virtue. Self-sacrifice is always a sign that there is disharmony somewhere; it always involves some kind of self-maiming. When Jesus said, "If thine eye offend thee, pluck it out", by implication He deplored the necessity; the self would remain maimed although the offence had been done away with. To be perfect as God is perfect, to be wholly sanctified will mean object-centricity in the highest degree; and the object on which the soul will be centred will be nothing less than God Himself. Such object-centricity is a demand upon all believers: "Seek first the Kingdom of God". The Kingdom comes through the doing of the Will of God, and though some may have the 'vocation' for this or that particular service, that vocation, or their capacity to undertake it, cannot give grounds for discrimination between them and the ordinary run of humanity.

St. Paul had an analogous problem to deal with in the Church at Corinth. There were those, apparently, who insisted that there were degrees of spiritual value in the diverse gifts brought to the service of the Church. Paul admits that one gift may have a greater utilitarian value than another; that is as far as he will go. The diverse gifts are like the different organs of the body; they have need of each other. To clinch the matter Paul leaves the logic of reason for the logic of Faith: "Granted", he seems to say, "that there is a good, better and best amongst your gifts, then you must cultivate the best". That is the logic of reason. "Covet earnestly the best gifts, yet show I unto you a more excellent way. . . . Follow after love." That is the logic of Faith. There is a better than the best, and the thirteenth chapter of 1 Corinthians was written to prove it. Paul's point is that it is not a question as to whether they were exercising their gifts *within* the Church, but *for* the Church. Was their use Ego-centric or Object-centred? Sanctification on this reading to Paul would imply Object-centricity.

This position would seem to clarify another difficulty which often has cropped up in controversies over Sanctification, namely, whether Sanctification involves sinlessness. As long as any branch of the Church holds a derogative estimate of the human organism and its appetites, sin will inevitably tend to be interpreted in biological terms. Anyone who holds this view of bodily appetite will almost certainly be inclined to repress them. The tendencies, in that case, will remain Ego-centric in the unconscious, and will exercise a compulsive influence upon thought and feeling. Obsessive 'impure thoughts' will tend to enter consciousness; depression in which God will seem to have withdrawn His Grace will inevitably attack the individual; and the 'holiness' with which this false view of human nature allies itself, will be an unhappy holiness. Luther did not think we could ever be without sin; but his view of human nature was ascetic and monastic to the end. We cannot exist without our bodies, and if the body be thought to be evil then it follows that we can never be without sin. On the other hand, if we root sin in ego-centricity, in what we have called the 'empirical ego' as distinguished from the soul or Subject, then there seems no reason why we should not, like Paul, press on towards "the mark of our high calling". The sphere of each one's calling will be different, but Holiness will be within the reach of all. That is the evangelical view; and there is nothing in psychology that would give us grounds for saying that the "ideal for the present life" is unattainable. The sphere of sainthood to the Evangelical lies in the common life and daily tasks; and the Saints of Evangelicalism have always been men and women who found their vocation amidst mundane affairs. It is the object-centred love of St. Francis of Assisi that makes its appeal to the Evangelical, not his self-embraced poverty and celibacy; it is the sanctified love of Brother Lawrence, exercised amidst the rush and bustle of his monastery kitchen, that makes "the Practice of the Presence of God" so welcome to the busy Evangelical.

We may fitly conclude this chapter with a quotation from Dr. C. J. Cadoux's article already mentioned: "The Protestant conception of the meaning and worth of our common human life far outstretches the Catholic conception of life. It has no derogatory estimate of the physical and spiritual universe in which we live and offers no apology for our being denizens of it. Its heroes are not the recluses who flee the world to escape its taint, but the men of affairs who plunge into the world to bring to fulfilment in it the Kingdom of God. Its saints are not the begowned and beaded ascetics who bear on their exterior and in their minds the marks of an exclusive 'holiness', but its ideal life is that lived by the housewife and mother, by the husband and father whose hands are hard because of the daily struggle to make material reality a servant of human good, by the economist, the statesman, and the teacher, whose minds endure the constant strain of 'worldly care'—by all, indeed, who seek by means of common duties of the common earthly life to fulfil the purpose of that life divine which is revealed in Christ Jesus."[1]

[1] G. Cross in *Journal of Religion*, March, 1922, quoted by Cadoux.

CHAPTER IX

Some General Applications of Psychological Principles to Church Work

MANY years ago, at a Swanwick Conference, we heard a Canon (now a Bishop) say that all new thought had to pass through three stages before it was finally given the status of accepted knowledge. At first, it was violently attacked; then it was mildly tolerated; and lastly people said, "Oh, we knew that long ago".

The "New" psychology has certainly passed through the first stage. Those of us who pioneered its application to the problems of moral and spiritual conflict are no longer held in suspicion in regard to the character of our motives, or attacked for reducing human life to the level of the animal. There are still a few in the Church and in the medical profession who are in the mildly tolerant stage; but they are harmless; the great majority of thoughtful people now take psychology as a matter of fact, albeit in the spirit, "We knew it all long ago".

Indeed, we must confess that modern psychology and psychotherapy tell us no more about the incompatible motives that tear the human soul asunder than was already in the Scriptures for all to read; but we lacked the perceiving eye and the understanding mind and the believing heart. Modern psychology has elucidated how human motives work, how they become perverted, how they 'split' our personality into flesh warring against the spirit and spirit against the flesh. It has added no knowledge of new motives; albeit it has helped us tremendously to realise how motives in the unconscious may work their havoc in our spiritual life. "Every extension of self-consciousness", said some one, "is a mark of progress." If that is true, the extension of self-knowledge given to us through modern psychology is no short step in progress.

Sublimation and *integration* were not unknown to Scripture writers although they were not called by these names. "Unite my heart to fear Thy name," says the Psalmist; there we have spiritual integration. "Be not overcome of evil, but overcome evil with good"; there we have sublimation. The Scriptures are still an unworked mine of knowledge of human nature, its motives, its moral and spiritual potentialities, its end. If the "Higher Criticism" tended to undermine the authority of the Scriptures in regard to some matters, that cannot be said of the application of modern psychology to the interpretation of the Word of God. On the contrary, modern psychology can bring Holy Writ into its own again, and restore the moral and spiritual authority of its teaching.

Today there are few, either in the Church or in the medical profession, who would question the need of candidates for the ministry or priesthood, or of undergraduates in medicine for a thorough knowledge of the mental processes that lie behind human behaviour. As far back as 1920, the Lambeth Conference reported that there was a growing need that candidates for the priesthood "should be equipped by training in psychology, and be given some acquaintance with the methods and principles of healing. Only so will the clergy be enabled rightly to direct the thought of their people on the subject and discriminate between truth and error." Since then, a committee, composed of members of the medical profession and the clergy, has gone into the question of the possible co-operation between the two vocations in cases of psychoneurotic illness. The Church of Scotland is considering in its Assembly at the present time a report of one of its own committees on the advisability of training her candidates for the ministry in psychological healing. The Guild of Pastoral Psychology in England, composed of both doctors, clergy, and ministers of the Evangelical Churches, has been formed in order to facilitate co-operation between them. The United States of America is far in advance of England in the matter of psychological training of its candidates for the ministry, and also in the co-operation between doctors and ministers in dealing with psycho-neurotic illness.

There can be no doubt in the minds of those who have treated and studied the psycho-neuroses, that all who have anything to do with the upbringing of children, the moral and spiritual welfare of the young, should be thoroughly equipped in the science of psychology. As we saw in the quotation from Dr. Rivers in an earlier chapter, the conditions which predispose the adolescent or adult to neurotic conflicts and serious mental illness in later life are created in childhood. How many parents understand or take account of the conflicts aroused in the mind of their first-born when a second child comes into the home and monopolises the mother? And that is but one of the simpler situations which may lead to maladjustment. The authoritative father and not less the 'very good' father, and the possessive mother, can do irreparable damage to a growing child.

If most parents are ignorant of the psychological conditions and processes of the growth of character and personality, how does it fare with the great majority of teachers in England? These teachers have the children in their care from childhood, through puberty, and in many cases at the adolescent stage. Are they much better equipped to deal with the conflicts which rage during all this period and on the resolution of which, as Rivers said, the future of the child depends? It is very doubtful. They get a certain amount of child-psychology with their educational theory, but little or nothing is taught in our training colleges of the psychological, moral and spiritual conflicts through which the child has to pass.

Nothing would add to the value of the teacher's training more than a special course in their curriculum taken by a skilled psychotherapist, medical or lay, on the Nature and Resolution of Psychological Conflicts. Such a course would help the teacher to discern early signs of neurotic conflict and, perhaps, to prevent early repressions. At least, the teacher could report to the school medical officer the neurotic signs in a child, and perhaps save much misery to child and parents in later years.

The medical profession is now doing much to remedy its defective curriculum in respect to training in the principles of psychological medicine. Nevertheless, no one knows better than the young doctor in his first practice how inadequately he is equipped in his ordinary degree course for dealing with functional nervous disease. Lord Horder, in the opening address to a medical school, is reported to have given the case of a woman who had been sent to him for examination relating to certain symptoms. After giving her a thorough examination he found no sign of organic disease. He said to the woman, "Madam, you are suffering from a wrong attitude to life". There is nothing in Materia Medica that could help a woman in that state. In all probability she had been taking medicine for years.

It is computed by those who should know that in no less than forty per cent. of those who consult the general practitioner for one complaint or another, the trouble is due to psychological causes. That these are not always sexual may be seen from the following illustration.

A doctor asked us to see a patient who had been under his care for some months. There was no organic disease, nor serious depression, but a good deal of tremor and fatigue. The woman had always been of a 'nervous disposition', but had enjoyed healthy interests. Without any deep analysis we found that a month before the symptoms commenced she had been promoted to the head of her department, which entailed responsibility both for the work of the department and for the girls under her care. During the first month she worried a great deal about the work and responsibility; and then the worry disappeared, but with its disappearance her symptoms began. What had happened? Apparently she had repressed her inferiority feelings regarding her fitness. Instead of time increasing her confidence, apparently it tended to increase her feeling of unfitness for the job until it became unbearable; with the consequent result of repression and the appearance of her symptoms. The mere mention on our part as to how she would be able to deal with a girl who needed to be reprimanded caused the tremor to appear. The woman's psychological make-up was simply unable to undertake the kind of responsibility involved in the position to which she had been promoted. She will live happily in a position that gives outlet to the qualities she does possess. The doctor suspected that the job had something to do with the trouble, but he had had no training which would have helped him to find just exactly what it was in the job to which his patient was unable to face up.

It is a tragedy when the parent or teachers bring a neurotic child to the doctor only to find that he is as little able to deal with the trouble as they are themselves. A doctor ought to receive as much training in the anatomy of the soul as he does in the anatomy of the body; and indeed he would probably find that a knowledge of the former would be more fruitful in his practice of healing.

One would naturally think that clergy and ministers would be well equipped to deal with the moral and spiritual conflicts of the soul. Alas! the great majority are as little equipped to deal with them as those of whom we have already spoken. There is a quickening sense of responsibility on the part of those who have the task of training candidates for the priesthood or ministry in the Evangelical Churches; and there is a deep sense of need on the part of many ministers and clergy themselves for the knowledge that psychology and psychotherapy can provide.

One need not belittle the work which good evangelists have done in the Church in order to show that the evangelist probably needs greater knowledge of psychology than any other preacher. An unintelligent Evangelism must have done enormous damage to countless tender souls. Any psychotherapist's consulting room will show heart-breaking evidence of the tragedy that an ignorant or aggressive type of evangelist can do to certain types of harassed and anxious souls. On the other hand, a sane, tender, sympathetic and understanding Evangelism must always be an integral part of the Church's work. There have been men like D. L. Moody in America, and Henry Drummond in Scotland, who had the intuitive gift of the psychotherapist of understanding the conflicts, hesitations, rebellions, vacillations of the human soul. These evangelists needed no academic training in psychology to do their great work—just as some of our greatest teachers of children succeed without much knowledge of educational or psychological theory. In the case of evangelists and teachers alike, however, their success was due not to the absence of psychological knowledge, but to the intuitive gift of the psychotherapist which enabled them to understand spontaneously psychological principles. One must always recognise that psychotherapy, spiritual direction, and Evangelism are arts, not sciences in the true sense of the term. They are an application of science, but not themselves true sciences. Personal factors enter into all work of character—and personality—building or healing which no text-books or lectures can provide. It would be fatal, however, to draw the inference that, because such 'princes of the pulpit' as C. H. Spurgeon, Joseph Parker, or Campbell Morgan had no theological training, that theological colleges are unnecessary; we might as well argue that because men like Sir Herbert Barker and others outside the medical profession have done great work in healing, we could dispense with medical schools, and the theory and practice of medicine. In the same way it would be a fallacy to contend that, because the great evangelists, Moody and Drummond, to say nothing of others, lived before the days of the "New Psychology", modern Evangelism can get on quite well without it. Both these men would have been the first to acknowledge that psychology, as we understand it today, throws light upon the people they were *unable* to help as well as upon those they were able to bring to a fruitful decision. Was not one of Drummond's papers to the Theological Society of Edinburgh entitled, "The Science of Spiritual Diagnosis"? That essay still repays study.

Psychology, however, is not only concerned with conflicts and their resolution; the whole sphere of experience and behaviour is its subject-matter. Like all religious experience, evangelical experience must be validated; it must be presented to each generation in terms of that generation's cultural level and environmental conditions. In Britain we have men like Dr. D. S. Cairns whose apologetic writings have been of untold benefit to those in doubt, and to those who desired to keep their scientific and philosophical outlook on life without sacrificing anything of their religious experience.

Apologetics today, however, must meet the challenge of a materialistic psychology which is not altogether connected with either Behaviourism or Psycho-analysis. Such a psychology, with its inevitable consequence of a pagan morality, a God who is no more than a *projection*, and creeds which are said to be *rationalisations*, is a more deadly opponent of religious experience than rationalistic science or philosophy. It strikes most strongly at Christian morality. The authority of reason has been displaced by the rights of instinct and emotion, while the authority of conscience is made out to be no more than the 'introjected' voice of the dominating father or the overpowering authority of the Herd, which is regarded as a sort of 'super-ego', active in the unconscious.

It is of little use attempting to meet this challenge to religious experience on the part of some psychologists and psychologies with theological arguments. No peace can be had on that basis, and religion cannot live on a truce. Religious faith demands the reality of its Object; religious experience cannot but seek validation; and we think that it can be shown that the psychology of religious experience can give as good grounds for belief in the reality of its Object and its experiences as ordinary psychology can give for belief that the world of sense experience has its Object in the external world. When psychology has had its say, and all its conclusions are examined, it is doubtful whether it actually does raise new problems for the theological apologist; but the problems it does raise should be met on psychological grounds. The metaphysical question remains the same: Are we in direct contact with an external world or only with sense experience? Is 'externality' part of our immediate experience or is it an inference from sense experience? If it is contended that psychology can give us aid in answering these metaphysical questions, then it can give us the same aid when we ask the question: Does my Faith-state bring me into direct contact with God? Do my appetites involve the existence of their object of satisfaction?

Psychologically man has never been able to do without religion, and Freud, along with many others of all schools, admits that were there no religion we should have to invent one if man's heart is to be satisfied. Have we not in this, as Bernard Bosanquet believed, or rather suggested, a possibly new form of the Ontological argument? There is not a single argument produced by the psychologist against theism or the validity of the religious object which cannot be met on psychological grounds.

In relation to the immediate subject-matter of these pages one vital question arises or rather is proposed by the subject-matter itself, namely, does psychotherapy demand an ultimate moral order to which its patients should become adjusted if they are to be wholly cured? Does it necessitate the assumption of an objective moral law to account for the psychological effects which its violation or neglect of moral principle undoubtedly exhibits? It is true that everybody does not break down who ignores or violates the moral order; but it is obvious that such violation or neglect precludes them from realising personality in the true sense of the term. It would seem that just as the organism must reach a certain degree of integration of the nervous system before rational intelligence arises, so a certain degree of moral integration is needed before personality is possible.

We grant that when psychology has had its say, there will still remain problems of validation which only philosophy and theology can deal with; but there are definite theological, to say nothing of moral and philosophical problems to which approach must be psychological; they are problems of experience and what experience involves.

Psychology and Worship

Psychology may come to the help of Evangelicalism not only in relation to the validation of its religious experience, but also in making its worship a more effective means of enriching religious experience. It can also be of invaluable help in devising ways of deepening spiritual life apart from public worship; or in formulating methods of Evangelism that will be effective in bringing the young to a definite decision for Christ; or in making its appeal to those who have 'wandered' far, and become 'lost' in the world.

Psychologically, religious experience is dependent on the religious sentiment. That sentiment is a permanent structure, an acquired modification of consciousness or mind itself. The religious experiences of childhood may be thought of as the original nucleus, or shall we say the original movement of the mind in the formation of the sentiment; they are not sufficient, however, to make religion a permanent habit of behaviour or experience. The content of any sentiment is relative, because the object of the sentiment is continually changing with our increasing experience. It is never the object which is the actual basis of a sentiment but the *idea of the object.*

A man's love-sentiment for his wife, for example, if it is to remain permanently active and to function congruously with her needs and his own, will be continually varying in content. It would be better if we thought of a sentiment as Laird has taught us to think of the Self—a continuant and yet a variant. Such a concept helps us to realise that an individual's sentiment for his wife will be continually changing, especially during the first few years of married life, as new aspects of his wife's personality become revealed to him. His idea of her will change as she changes from the young bride to the mother of his first child, and then the mother of a family; then the comparatively different woman of middle age will demand another change of idea. Each of these new situations means change in the idea of his wife which forms the basis of his sentiment for her. The man whose ideas of his wife refuse to change is likely to be bitterly disappointed.

It is not otherwise with the religious sentiment. The strain upon it is very different in young adolescence and later life. This is because the religious sentiment is the means of our orientation to the world as well as to God. "A full religious sentiment", as Dr. Conklin remarks, "results in a new adjustment, a new orientation, the achievement of an at-peace-with-the-world state of mind."[1] Continuous adjustment has to be made as life brings us new problems, new responsibilities, sorrows, disappointments, perhaps new temptations and even relapses. To meet life religiously, with a faith that never wavers, a joy that does not pass away, with an insight that discerns the Eternal and Infinite amid the temporal flux and the finite actualities, the religious sentiment has to be kept in cultivation. Effort and discipline have to be exercised; the religious emotions have to be generated; and if the will is to be continually reinforced, and the idea of God, which is the basis of the sentiment, is to develop and grow, then reflection must be stimulated.

Hence the need for public worship, and the explanation of the psychological effect of such worship. Our sentiment is reinforced by contact with others who are praying to the same Object, facing the same temptations, feeding on the same Word of God. Doubtless, it is the case that some truly evangelical souls can feed their religious sentiment without sharing in public worship; but it is very probable that they lose much that is valuable in religious experience. One thing is certain, namely, the community loses much by their self-imposed isolation; for public worship is not only designed to help the individual to renew his religious experiences by which the religious sentiment is strengthened and kept growing, but also to witness to the need of community for the Church as the symbol and guarantee of Society's own basis and end in the Kingdom of God. The presence of the Church in the world is the symbol of God's presence in the community; and the worshipper is implicitly witnessing to the spiritual needs of Society as well as receiving himself of the 'unsearchable riches

[1] *Psychology of Religious Adjustment.*

of Christ'. They are wrong who think the world could do without a Church.

All this necessitates that the ordering of worship should be such that the physical relaxation necessary for calm to fill the soul should be secured, that the attention should be spontaneously held by the music, hymns, prayers, and that the mind should become concentrated on the Sacrament of the preached Word. Here psychology should be brought to our aid. Worship should elicit the æsthetic, moral, intellectual and religious emotions. Attention depends on whether the religious sentiment has been stirred to activity; if it is stirred into a pleasant activity the religious experiences are renewed, and the sentiment deepened. Church decoration and church lighting may distract the attention and consciously or unconsciously irritate the worshipper; irrelevant movement on the part of those leading the worship will have the same effect. In every service of public worship faith has to be strengthened, God's presence has to be realised; the will has to be reinforced; fears calmed; joys hallowed; the Grace of God in forgiveness of sins has to be renewed; the spirit of intercession has to be evoked; and, above all, gratitude should be made conscious. Only in so far as gratitude is elicited are the truly deep religious experiences renewed in public worship.

The success of public worship from the point of the individual depends on the degree in which he has been an *active participant;* and the efficacy of any service or form of service may be judged by its capacity to make the worshippers into active participants. Unless the preacher or leader in prayer or the choirmaster is making the worshipper actively participate in his thought, his thanksgivings, intercessions and confessions, or the praise, he is failing in his task.

Gratitude, perhaps more than any other emotion, can stir the religious emotions into very great activity and thus make the worshipper an active participant in the whole service. Principal Jacks has brought this out in one of his essays: "Gratitude", he writes, "means that memory has come to the aid of purpose, and that praise is reinforcing prayer. Gratitude links the past with the future, the debt incurred with the duty to be performed, the service received with the service to be rendered."[1] When religious gratitude is evoked the religious sentiment becomes active at once, and participation in the service follows naturally.

It may be said that we have left out of account the operation of the Holy Spirit. Such an inference would be false and would be based upon an inadequate conception of what the psychologist claims that his science can do for public worship. The form of ordering our worship is the channel along which the Holy Spirit comes. There is not one item in public worship that is not meant to be a channel of God's Grace; the praise, prayer and meditation, the calm and peace of the sanctuary, these are the channels along which the Spirit comes and there are no others in the service of public worship. Psychology tries to make these channels more effective mediums of the Spirit's work; it does not displace Him. It condemns "stunts" to increase numbers, not because they are wrong but because such "stunts" cannot by their very nature evoke gratitude, or stir the religious sentiment into activity. However successful the "stunt" may be in increasing the attendance at public worship it defeats the religious purpose of worship. The soul grows upon what it feeds on and immediately the people who are attracted by "stunts" find that "stunts" are no more than a stimulation of curiosity they quickly fall off and their state is worse than before.

Instead, then, of the psychologist leaving out the Holy Spirit in his study of public worship, he is really emphasising the necessity to order worship along the lines in which the religious sentiment is truly activated; psychological principles can be applied here as in relation to any other sentiment. Why should we call in the aid of psychology to stimulate the 'will to buy our goods' and hesitate to bring to our aid known psychological principles to stimulate the will to worship? The psychology of worship shows us that those who conduct worship should see that the Spirit of God is not hampered in

[1] From the *Human End*, p. 195.

His work of Grace by careless, slovenly, irreverent or thoughtless ordering of the services; for on that worship the great majority have to depend for the renewal of their religious experiences and the deepening and strengthening of the religious sentiment. Many have little time or inclination or opportunity for other ways of keeping their religious sentiment active and healthy.

The psychology of worship, however, is a theme in itself; and Evangelicals perhaps more than the sacerdotal types of worshippers need to study it. Evangelical worship tends to be almost wholly subjective and thus is far more difficult than the more objective types of worship. So much depends for the success of public worship on the individual who conducts the service that no aid to worship should be neglected by him.

It will not be out of place, however, to draw inferences from what we have said about the development and cultivation of the religious sentiment, in regard to a practice which seems to be on the increase on both sides of the Atlantic, namely, the dropping of what used to be called the 'week-night service'. This is really a tragedy from the psychological point of view. If we may draw an illustration from our own experience, then we can say that the regular attendance at the week-night service is now seen to have been the main factor in the deepening and making permanent of our own religious sentiment. It was a weekly "Retreat", a resting-place amid the temptations and intellectual conflicts of adolescence, where strength was gained to renew the battle, and teaching designed for the believer was given. It was at that week-night service that we were established in the faith, and a real love for the Church was born and nurtured.

The Evangelical Churches today seem to have discarded the week-night service; but we are convinced they cannot long do without it without imperilling the spiritual life of their members, to say nothing of the peril to Evangelicalism as a whole.

The religious sentiment needs more than public worship

for its healthy cultivation. Private devotions, the 'Quiet time', the 'Daily portion' are all means of quickening the sentiment. Psychologically, the demand that must be fulfilled here is the same as in public worship. The individual must not be passive, but active. Passivity, if it is not to be dangerous, must be a 'wise passiveness'; and a wise passiveness means an active expectancy, an expectant waiting upon God, a readiness to experience the movement of the Spirit either in the 'Quiet time', during the meditation upon the Word, or while the heart is uplifted in Faith. All the exercises, in addition to being a fellowship with God, are a means of "adjusting the will to the intention of God"; or in psychological terms, a means of continuous re-orientation of the religious sentiment to the changing conditions of life.

The forms of private religious exercise have been worked out with true psychological insight in the Roman Catholic Church; and although these forms are not suited to every Evangelical, the needs they are designed to supply are the needs of all who would deepen and enrich their religious sentiment. Where private devotions are neglected, the appeal of public worship will tend to weaken.

Psychology and Evangelism

The whole aim of Evangelism is what in evangelical circles is called the 'saving of souls'. The evangelistic motive itself arises in the desire to bring to others the richness of the experience of God which religion has brought to those engaged in the work. Unfortunately, much evangelistic work has been left to intensive campaigns. Such campaigns are not to be belittled because they are sometimes accompanied by abnormal phenomena. It is not uncommon for an evangelistic campaign to bring a renewal of religious experiences to already long-standing believers as well as to bring the experience of decision or conversion to those outside the Church.

The ordering of the evangelistic service should be determined by the primary aims of Evangelism. There should be an atmosphere of expectancy; that expectancy should be felt by all who enter the building—an expectancy that decisions will be made, 'souls saved'. Such an atmosphere is full of suggestion to the unconverted; it will tend to create the state of suggestibility, so that many will have the incipient feeling that they are expected to be converted or come to a decision. The attention of the whole audience must be contracted so that the vital aims of salvation are kept at the centre of the audience's consciousness. The conviction of sin has to be elicited, that is crucial. The conviction of sin, however, is not an end in itself; the offer of salvation, the effort to arouse a true repentance should be implicit in the very attempt to evoke the conviction of sin. Hence through the whole of the service, singing, praying, preaching, stress should be laid on the 'joy and peace in believing'. This prevents any tendency for morbid guilt to be aroused, or repression to occur; and if what one may call a happy conversion comes to any individual, his future religious life tends to share in that happiness.

We have already hinted that Evangelism, especially in the form of campaigns, has its dangers. These, however, may be lessened considerably and the efforts made more fruitful by thoughtful preparation, psychological as well as spiritual. Those who are to work in the enquiry rooms should be carefully chosen; they should be men and women of understanding heart to whom confession may be made without fear of their showing to the enquirer any feeling of being 'shocked'. Patient, sympathetic, intelligent handling of a soul in distress is essential. While there must be no condonation of sin confessed, the greatest emphasis should be laid on God's power to forgive and to save.

A danger that is not absent from the narrower Evangelistic Churches, is that the frequency of the campaigns tends to create a type of believer who can respond to no other religious appeal but the 'appeal to sinners'. This is spiritually unhealthy; and in such people the religious sentiment is never deepened, and indeed often fails to permeate their inner life, with the result that there is often a discrepancy between their religion and their morality. As an occasional tonic, participation in campaigns is good for the soul; but a church or an individual that is always in need of evangelistic tonics is not in a good spiritual state. Overflows of emotion should be avoided; although there can be no appeal which does not involve emotion. The danger of eliciting too much emotion is that it defeats its own purpose, especially in young people; often it stimulates the bodily appetites in those who have been recently 'converted' and then trouble results.

Not all clergymen or ministers have the gift of the evangelist as was recognised by Paul in his letter to the Corinthians. As far as possible, however, all should exercise whatever gifts they have in this way, so as to bring the young people to an early decision; and thus the ordering of the weekly public worship should not be bereft of the evangelistic aims.

Psychology and the Evangelical Pastor

Already we have seen that there is a demand on the part of the spiritual director and the evangelical pastor for a knowledge of psychological methods of healing. That demand is being met to some extent by both medical and lay psychologists or psychotherapists. The Tavistock Clinic in London arranged at least one series of lectures designed to help the minister and clergyman to deal with conflicts which involve the loss of religious faith, anxiety, obsessive impulses and loss of spiritual interest.

It is needless here to cover the ground of pastoral psychology. There are some well-informed volumes[1] designed to help the ordinary pastor or spiritual director. Both the clergy and evangelical pastors should avoid the books that oversimplify the psychological and spiritual conflicts, as well as the methods of dealing with them. There is a type of book which gives all the curiosities and morbidities of psychological medicine; but alas, the psychology is left out. This

[1] *Souls in the Making*, by J. G. McKenzie; *Psychotherapy, Scientific and Religious*, by Marcus Gregory; *Introduction to Christian Psychotherapy*, by J. A. C. Murray.

type of book does a great deal of harm, and is more likely to light up complexes in the pastor than help him to deal with his people.

It is very doubtful whether those who make the demand for training in psychological methods of dealing with conflicts realise the nature of the work they are asking to be allowed to undertake. How far is the clergyman or minister able to do the work of the psychotherapist? How far should newly ordained ministers or priests be encouraged to deal with the conflicts themselves? The question is not easy of answer. For one thing, we are anxious not to hinder the introduction into the theological curriculum of lectures on psychotherapy by competent experts. These in themselves will not fit any man or woman to undertake work of the delicate kind needed by a physician of sick souls. There are dangers, both to the patient and the pastor himself, which ought not to be overlooked by those who know what the work entails; and they should be clearly presented to the candidates for the ministry.

In spite of all the objections which can be legitimately argued against the clergyman or minister undertaking to treat psycho-neurotic cases, however, there remains the urgent need that he should be able to understand enough to co-operate with the doctor in incipient cases of disorder, and even with difficult cases. Dr. Wm. Brown, in his *Science and Personality*, has stated the difficulties as well as anyone; and he is wholly sympathetic to co-operation. Personally we have had experience of a few ministers of religion who have done really marvellous work in preventing individuals from falling into serious illness by a wise and timely dealing with their people. These are, however, exceptions. We have seen others who have done great damage by their inadequacy of diagnosis, and whose treatment was ill-informed.

Where there is little or no unconscious motive, but only a mistaken view of human nature as the causative factors in the trouble, the wise clergyman, instructed in the conflicts of the mind and soul, can be of great value to those who are weak in the integration of their mind. And even when the psychotherapist has laid bare the trouble to the patient, the clergyman or minister can be of great benefit to the patient by his message of forgiveness, and by helping the patient to deepen his faith and confidence in God.

The task of the Church, as we see it, is so to teach the young, so to present the Gospel, that neurotic troubles will be prevented. A true Evangelicalism will so present the dangers of sin that they will be faced and not escaped from by a flight into neurotic disease. Sin should never be presented[1] so as to make the individual afraid of it; fear can only repress unless it leads to reflection upon the course of conduct the sin involves. Preachers and teachers should aim at helping the child to acquire a healthy positive conscience, and a comprehensive religious sentiment which will draw all the behaviour-tendencies into its service. It is not enough for the preacher to pronounce judgment upon sin; for as Professor Grensted has wisely remarked, the proclamation of the forgiveness[2] of sin is a very different thing from the pronouncing of judgment upon sin. The true pastor and preacher as well as the spiritual director will woo the will of his people into the service of his Master, where alone they are safe from the curse of repression. He will encourage his people in the practice of confessional prayer, a practice which tends to prevent barriers being erected between the conscious and the unconscious. Complexes or behaviour-tendencies do not in themselves cause neurotic disease; the causative factor is always repression, the resistance of the mind to allow them into consciousness. Knowledge of our complexes, of behaviour-tendencies that are a source of temptation, humbly accepted and never consented to, may lead and does lead to a stronger reliance upon God, a profound gratitude for His saving power and forgiveness, and an ever-growing desire to put on the Lord Jesus Christ as the one true means of sanctification and fellowship with God.

We believe whole-heartedly, that for the minister of

[1] Prof. Grensted, *Psychology and God*. Chapter on Sin.
[2] *Ibid.*

religion to do his work in a truly evangelical way, the knowledge which psychology and psychotherapy can give him is essential. He should have a comprehensive knowledge of the psychology of the growth of character; a specialised knowledge of the psychology of conflicts and their resolution; and a thorough understanding of the unconscious. Such knowledge can only be imparted by those who specialise in some form of psychological healing, and who are in actual practice. It should not be difficult for every theological college to arrange year after year for a special course of lectures by some one with the recognised knowledge and experience.

It has been suggested in some quarters that there should be some centre or centres to which could be sent members of Churches whose symptoms point to definite conflict between the religious sentiment and repressed behaviour-tendencies. We have no doubt that there are in the Church individuals who are qualified to treat such cases; but even then co-operation with the medical profession is necessary. There are often physiological conditions that give rise to behaviour-tendencies which would lead to what is considered by the Church as sin. On the other hand, there are mal-adjustments to marital relations, which such 'physicians of the soul' could treat far better than any medical man; his reassurance, re-inforced by the authority of his office, can allay fears, and prevent repression, in a manner which few medical practitioners can ever hope to effect.